The Psycholog

The Psychology of Action

John L. Smith

First published in Great Britain 2000 by
MACMILLAN PRESS LTD
Houndmills, Basingstoke, Hampshire RG21 6XS and London
Companies and representatives throughout the world

A catalogue record for this book is available from the British Library.

ISBN 0–333–75451–4 hardcover
ISBN 0–333–75452–2 paperback

First published in the United States of America 2000 by
ST. MARTIN'S PRESS, INC.,
Scholarly and Reference Division,
175 Fifth Avenue, New York, N.Y. 10010

ISBN 0–312–23066–4

Library of Congress Cataloging-in-Publication Data
Smith, John L., 1945–
The psychology of action / John L. Smith.
p. cm.
Includes bibliographical references and index.
ISBN 0–312–23066–4 (cloth)
1. Psychology. 2. Human behavior. I. Title

BF121 .S56 2000
150—dc21

99–049206

© John L. Smith 2000

All rights reserved. No reproduction, copy or transmission of this publication may be made without written permission.

No paragraph of this publication may be reproduced, copied or transmitted save with written permission or in accordance with the provisions of the Copyright, Designs and Patents Act 1988, or under the terms of any licence permitting limited copying issued by the Copyright Licensing Agency, 90 Tottenham Court Road, London W1P 0LP.

Any person who does any unauthorized act in relation to this publication may be liable to criminal prosecution and civil claims for damages.

The author has asserted his right to be identified as the author of this work in accordance with the Copyright, Designs and Patents Act 1988.

This book is printed on paper suitable for recycling and made from fully managed and sustained forest sources.

10　9　8　7　6　5　4　3　2　1
09　08　07　06　05　04　03　02　01　00

Printed in Hong Kong

To
Deborah and Natasha
Hugh and my mother

Contents

List of Figures	xi
Preface	xii

1 Introduction   1
  Agency and the definition of psychology   1
    The agent/patient distinction   1
    Action versus behaviour   2
    Behaviourism and experimental psychology   4
  Accounting for action   5
    Reasons and causes   5
    Critical social psychology: the 1970s new paradigm   7
    The negotiation of accounts   8
    From accounts to scripts and models   8
  Plan of the book   10

2 Reinterpreting positivist theories of action   14
  Positivist theories   14
    The theory of reasoned action   14
    The theory of planned behaviour   15
    Self-efficacy theory   15
  Key concepts in the psychology and philosophy
    of action   17
    Willing   17
    Perceived behavioural control   19
    Intention   20
    The intention–behaviour relation   21
    Deliberation and decision   24
    Agency and power   26
    Volition   28
    Interim summary   29

Critical appraisal of the TRA/TPB	30
The operational definition of intention	30
Empirical support for the TRA/TPB	31
A paradigmatic relocation for the TRA/TPB	32
Attitudinal semantics	34
Clusters of accounts	35
The rule for intelligibility	35
Verification of the rule for intelligibility	36
Refinement and extension of the rule for intelligibility	37
Conclusion	40

3 Agency, talk and relativism — 42
The discursive action model (DAM)	42
The discursive critique of the 1970s new paradigm	46
Rhetoric and reflexivity in critical psychology texts	48
Problems with relativism	52
Rorty	52
Death and furniture	53
Language, relativism and discursive psychology	56
Concluding remarks	63

4 The concept of plan in mainstream psychology — 66
Efficacy, expectancy, and value	66
Bandura's social cognitive theory (SCT)	67
Bandura's self-efficacy theory (SET)	69
Rotter and the expectancy-value model	71
Tolman's means–end beliefs in the immediate behaviour space	75
Lewin's topological model	81
Plans	83
Miller, Gallanter and Pribram	83
Schank and Abelson's program for scripts and plans	84
Current work on plans, valence and goals	86

5 Agentic slips and errors — 90
The Freudian slip	90

Cognitive slips	92
Human error and disaster	93
Case studies in the nuclear power industry	94
Reason's generic error-modelling system (GEMS)	97
Transparadigmatic considerations	99
The 4 Rs: rule, role, ritual and routine	99
Critical realist issues	102
Accounting for human error	102
The case study as story	103
Concluding remarks	107

6 Weakness of will — 108
Akrasia — 108
    Definition and preliminary analysis — 108
    Self-regulation failure — 110
    Psychological inertia — 113
    Last-ditch akrasia — 115
Procrastination — 117
    Conceptual analysis — 118
    Procrastination questionnaires — 121
    Paradigmatic triangulation in procrastination research — 123
Concluding discussion — 125

7 Agentic improvement — 127
Time management — 127
    Opening gambits and metaphors — 128
    The right frame of mind — 129
    Strategies for improvement — 130
Counselling — 132
    Rhetoric — 132
    Behaviour modification — 133
    Rational emotive behavioural counselling — 140
Concluding discussion — 145

8 Control: hypnosis and obedience — 147
Hypnosis — 147
    Dissociation theories — 148
    The hypnotic state as a category mistake — 150
    The hypnotic subject as planless agent — 151
    Neodissociation and the dialogic unconscious — 152

	Hypnosis as ritual	155
	Interim summary	157
	Obedience	158
	Milgram's basic experiment	158
	Milgram and the agentic state	159
	Concluding discussion	164
9	**Enigmas: masochism and suicide**	**169**
	Masochism	169
	Masochism as theatre	169
	Masochism as essential identity	171
	Dissociation in masochism	175
	The escape from ordinary identity	178
	Grammatical considerations	180
	Interim summary	181
	Suicide	182
	Rational suicide	184
	Suicide as impulsive escape	185
	Responsibility	186
	Concluding discussion	189
10	**Conclusion**	**193**
	Recapitulation and broader issues	193
	Eclecticism and fusion psychology	203
	A pyramidic framework for agentic analysis	207
	Preliminary orientation	208
	Apex	209
	Upper tier	211
	Lower tier	212
	Base	214
	Concluding remarks	216
Appendix		220
References		222
Name Index		231
Subject Index		235

List of Figures

2.1	The theory of planned behaviour	16
2.2	Semantic mapping for TRA clusters	36
2.3	Conversational test-frame cluster	37
2.4	Extension to the rule for intelligibility	40
4.1	Bandura's (1997) triadic reciprocal causation	67
4.2	A Tolman belief lasso for restaurants	77
4.3	A Tolman belief lasso for menu dishes	78
4.4	Tolman belief lassos from hunger deprivation to gratification	79
4.5	TOTE unit for ironing clothes	84
10.1	Pyramidic framework for agentic analysis	207

Preface

I have been thinking about the psychology of action for a long time and my interest in some aspects of this can be traced back to my undergraduate days at Leicester University. I am particularly grateful for the stimulating discussions I had with my tutors Andrew Colman, James Reason, Robert Thomson and Andrew Mayes and I owe a special debt of thanks to the late Gillmore Lee who, more than anyone, helped to kindle in me what has become a lifelong interest in this topic.

The psychology of action, especially in the context of episodes in everyday life, became the focus of my research when I went to Sheffield University to study for my doctorate. Even though it is such a long time ago, I would like to take this opportunity to thank Peter Warr, my supervisor at the Medical Research Council Unit, for his steadfast support and encouragement at that time. Thanks are also due to my fellow research students and especially to Mary Dalgleish and Gerry Kent.

Turning to the present, I need to acknowledge a debt to many friends and colleagues both within the psychology team at Sunderland University and beyond. Many people have provided me with reference material or have made suggestions for reading. Others have provided supportive conversation. I am reluctant to name names for fear of committing errors of omission but I have decided to take the risk.

I have received specific suggestions for reading in the academic literature from: Glynis Hale (counselling and suicide); Diane Westwood and Sophie Cormack (human error and cognitive slips); Peter Hawkins (hypnosis); Maura Banim (communitarianism and social policy); Paul Sparks, Mark Conner and Tony Manstead (theory of planned behaviour); Tom Buchanan (social learning theory); Mary Talbot (language); Louise Rowe (sports psychology); Leslie Younger (dance notation). I also had a helpful discussion with John Tait (computing and natural language programming). Even though I have not used and followed up all the suggestions and comments that I received, thanks to everybody anyway.

I am particularly grateful to Tom Buchanan for conversations which flowed from our recent research collaboration, even though our empirical work is of no direct relevance to the material I cover in this book. Other, less specific, help has come from Alison Guy, Charles Antaki, Mick Billig and Noel Sheehy, all of whom have been extremely supportive to me over the years. I would also like to thank my other podmates at Sunderland for sporadic but pleasant conversations at the periphery of this endeavour: Brian Ewart, Penny Johnson, Martin Nieland, Jacqui Rodgers, Ros Crawley, Rachel Abbott, Carole Carter and Clive Lewis. And while I'm about it I should also mention my research students: Fay Smith, Cinzia Priola and Magdalene Gougoussi.

Turning now to the production of my manuscript, I would like to start by thanking my friend and colleague David Sanders for his comments on a couple of draft chapters at the stage when I was drawing together the proposal for this book, prior to contacting publishers. Reading through this material was a generous thing for him to do, given that his background is in behaviour genetics and physiological psychology. He was thus able to provide me with comments based upon an outsider's perspective, as it were, but his wider knowledge of philosophical issues in psychology ensured ample points of contact in his engagement with the material.

I am especially grateful to Frances Arnold at the publishers for all her help and encouragement. While she has always provided me with clear and prompt advice on the technical aspects of writing the book, it is the enthusiasm with which she entered into our discussions of the academic content and structure of the book that I have most valued. I think Frances is the perfect antidote to any hint of writer's block.

Turning now to my family, I would like to thank my brother, Hugh, for our weekly telephone conversations, even though they are somewhat tangential to the main academic thrust of this book. As usual, he has been unstinting in his encouragement.

At home I have been helped immensely in all sorts of ways by my partner Deborah Thomas and our daughter Natasha. It is difficult to place a value on all the positive comments Deborah casually dropped into the conversation while we pottered in the kitchen or whatever. I am an early riser and neither of them complained as I clattered about the house to take my window of authorial opportunity with the dawn chorus, especially at weekends. Up with the lark, on with a pot of coffee, rev up the word processor; that's the way to go! I do hope you enjoy the result.

To assist readers with their comprehension and so as not to distract from the continuity of the text, no attention will be drawn to currently unacceptable gender usage in quoted material, although this should not be taken as an acceptance by the author of the use of sexist language.

Acknowledgement

The author and publisher wish to thank Sage Publications Ltd for permission to use copyright material in Chapter 2 which appeared in Smith, J.L. (1999) An agentic psychology model based on the paradigmatic repositioning of the theory of planned behaviour, *Theory and Psychology* **9**(5).

Every effort has been made to trace all the copyright holders but if any have been inadvertently overlooked the publishers will be pleased to make the necessary arrangements at the first opportunity.

Chapter 1

Introduction

Agency and the definition of psychology

If psychology were to be defined as the study of action then this book might simply be entitled *Psychology* in the same way that a book on the chemistry of the elements and compounds would be called *Chemistry* or a book on the biology of living organisms would be called *Biology*. By using the title *The Psychology of Action* I am implying that the term action does not exhaust the definition of psychology. To pursue the analogy with chemistry a little further, a book entitled *Organic Chemistry* might be expected to focus on a different subject matter compared to a book entitled *Inorganic Chemistry*. Setting aside some of the more general concerns of physical chemistry, *organic* and *inorganic* are two complementary categories which, together, might be said to exhaust the subject matter of chemistry. The question then arises as to what might be put in opposition to *action* in order to provide closure for the domain of psychological phenomena. The answer to this question is not straightforward, it goes to the heart of the controversies within psychology, and it goes a long way towards explaining what makes psychology such a fascinating academic discipline.

The agent/patient distinction

An equivalent to the organic/inorganic distinction might be found in a definition of action which contrasts what people do with what happens to them. If what people do is added in to what happens to them then we may arrive at the sum total of the subject matter of psychology. But in order to distinguish what people do from what happens to them, it is necessary to point out that their actions are intentional, that they make plans and do things for a reason, that they may be held responsible for what they do and so forth. If a person engaged in all this activity is referred to as an *agent*, then the person who merely suffers what happens to them may be called a *patient* (not in the medical sense but in the more specialised philosophical sense of the word). The agent/patient distinction falls under the umbrella of *agency*.

Action versus behaviour

Another candidate as an oppositional term for action is behaviour. However, action/behaviour does not really work like organic/inorganic. This is because behaviour can be regarded as a concept in direct competition with that of action for its application to psychological phenomena. Rather than providing a complementary category to that of action, it seeks to usurp it as the primary descriptive category. It is almost impossible to provide equivalent descriptions of phenomena as action, on the one hand, and as behaviour, on the other. For example, consider a hypothetical human being who, for present purposes, may be called Fred:

1. *Behaviour*:
Fred's fingers grip (defined in terms of muscle contraction and so on) the plastic disc and then move it back and forth beneath the pipe through which water at 60ºC is flowing. The water thus cascades over the disc.
2. *Action*:
Fred rinses the plate under the hot tap.

I found it difficult to generate these examples for two reasons. First, it is tempting when providing a behavioural description to attribute causal power to the human beings and thus transform them into agents. So, for example, the verb 'to grip' gave me difficulties because of its active connotations. This is why I felt it necessary to make reference, in parenthesis, to muscle contraction. I am not sure as to how far this succeeds as an attempt to neutralise the word in this regard because the spectre of a person intending to grip the plate still hovers in the background, and would do so even if I had started to move the account down to the level of firing in the neural processes. The words 'tap' and 'plate' are both rich in cultural connotations: the former with urban plumbing arrangements, the latter with conventions relating to food and eating.

The second reason why I found it difficult to provide the above examples of action/behaviour descriptions is because I could not move to a meta-language in which to frame a neutral description against which each of the others could be judged. I think that the behavioural description of washing up or doing the dishes is virtually unintelligible unless the action description comes with it. Moving beyond this specific example of cleaning the plate, if the behavioural description must eschew intentionality and agency, one will be taken down to some rather broad and general phenomena: walking, eating, fighting, smiling and so forth. It is true that walking, if viewed as behaviour, can be described as movements of the limbs, controlled by the muscles. I do not deny that the explanation of walking may be grounded at the level of neurochemistry, as may the explanation of feeding or sexual behaviour, for example. However, it is at this point that we may find that we have left psychology and entered the domain of human physiology. I suggest, as a rough and ready rule of thumb, that phenomena must be capable of being given a description in terms of action or agency in order for them to fall within the domain of psychology. I am reminded of the way de Saussure (1959/1966) distinguishes linguistics from the physiology of sounds:

> The relation is unilateral in the sense that the study of languages exacts clarification from the science of the physiology of sounds but furnishes none in return. (p. 7)

It may be useful to the designers who have to place traffic lights and warning signs on road systems to know something about reaction times and the physiological constraints on translating a visual signal into a foot movement on the brakes, for example, but knowing about the conventions relating to traffic in Britain or France will not help the understanding of human physiology.

Following de Saussure, if I wish to distinguish psychology from the physiology of movements, then a definition of psychology based upon action would do the trick. In order to prise behaviour away from its dependency upon the language of action, I would feel happy to insist that behaviour be spoken of at the level of human movements and sounds. Strictly speaking, on these grounds, I would have been justified in calling this book *Psychology*, rather than *The Psychology of Action*. However, it is by no means the case that psychology would be generally taken to mean the psychology of action and, indeed, it is likely that such an interpretation would be rejected by many psychologists. My choice of title, therefore, is not neutral. I am not so much writing about a sub-category of psychological phenomena as advancing a position.

Behaviourism and experimental psychology

Thomson (1968) places the emergence of modern psychology around about the year 1880, although he acknowledges the importance of philosophers stretching from Locke and Hume, in the seventeenth and eighteenth centuries, back to Aristotle. Boring (1963) sees Wundt as the founder of experimental psychology. He argues that, as a movement, scientific psychology was mainly negative, being directed against philosophy. Thomson (1968), however, suggests that psychology was born of a merger between the dominant philosophy of the early nineteenth century and the contemporary physiology of that period. The adoption of mechanistic scientific methods in psychological enquiries led to problems for some psychologists who felt that subjective mental phenomena did not meet the criterion of being publicly observable. In order not to compromise the scientific status of psychology, its domain of interest was restricted to behaviour which could be observed publicly; mental phenomena were dismissed as being beyond the concerns of psychology. Thomson (1968) summarises the programme put forward by the behaviourist J.B. Watson in 1913 as follows:

> The aim of psychology to be completely objective and scientific is thus to be achieved by reducing psychological studies as far as possible to physiological studies. 'Mental' science must change into 'physical' science. Movements of limbs, secretions of glands, electri-

cal discharges in nerve tissue, verbal utterances, blushing, grimacing, tensing of muscles, are the proper data of behaviour – together with environmental events which may evoke or influence such 'responses'. (p. 165)

The above quotation might almost be regarded as a mission statement for behaviourism.

Accounting for action

In behaviourism the response event, described in physical or physiological terms, is caused by the stimulus event, described in a similarly objective fashion. The two events are linked via the causal law. The response event is not explained by a powerful agent who brings it about. The thing that sets the stimulus–response explanation against an agency account of action is that a human agent is a person, not an event. Without a human agent, there can be no attribution of responsibility and so behaviourist views have striking implications for the notion of human nature (see Skinner, 1988, for example). An agency explanation of action admits that a person may do something for a reason, and that reason may be sufficient for the purposes of explanation; the mechanistic causal account of movements embodied within the action may be otiose. Because explanations in terms of agency very often point forwards to the future to that which the person is trying to achieve, they are classed as teleological and contrasted with the causal explanations which always point backwards in time to the occurrence of a prior event. A fuller discussion of these issues is provided by Harré and Secord (1972).

Reasons and causes

The work of Peters on the place of reason in the explanation of action from a psychological standpoint may be traced back to his doctoral thesis (see Peters, 1949) and this anticipates the so-called new paradigm by at least two decades. Peters (1960) argues that movements *qua* movements can only be regarded as intelligent, efficient, or correct when seen in the context of human action:

> There cannot therefore be a sufficient explanation of actions in causal terms because, as Popper has put it, there is a logical gulf between nature and convention. Statements implying norms and standards cannot be deduced from statements about mere movements which have no such normative implications. (p. 14)

From the above, it can be seen that the inadequacy of behaviourist experiments (which typically deal with responses as movements) to deliver a sufficient explanation of action provides cause for concern, given the marked impact that behaviourism has had on academic psychology over the course of the twentieth century. This is not to say that there is no place at all for causal explanation within the psychology of action. There may be occasions when causal explanations qualify the extent to which a person is deemed responsible for what they do or fail to do. For example, someone with a brain lesion which affects their speech production would not be held responsible for the failure to speak out at a crucial point in an unfolding action. Peters (1960, p. 16) also includes, within this category, the possibility of lapses or breakdowns being caused by unconscious wishes (see Chapter 5 for a fuller discussion of action slips). However, what Peters (1960) does is merely acknowledge that causal explanation may be of some relevance to the understanding of action on some occasions. His primary concern is to provide the antithesis to Watson's behaviourist view of psychology:

> To make explicit the implications of my thesis for psychological theories: If the question is 'Why did Jones walk across the road?' a *sufficient* explanation can only be given in terms of the rule-following purposive model – if this is a case of an action rather than of something happening to him. (p. 15)

At this point I turn to the new paradigm in social psychology (sometimes called ethogenics) which emerged during the 1970s, although I will admit to having some difficulty in knowing how to refer to this paradigm now. Obviously, the paradigm is no longer *new*, and even in the 1970s that epithet was confusing since another, partially related, new paradigm was being developed for humanistic psychology (Reason and Rowan, 1981, state that the London-based humanistic 'New Paradigm Research Group' was formed in 1977, for example). The ethogenic new paradigm emerged, in the 1970s, as a reaction to the doctrine of the objective experiment and may be regarded as a precursor of contemporary critical social psychology (an eclectic movement united by its opposition to positivist psychology). A more general discussion of the roots and heterogeneity of critical social psychology is provided by Spears (1997). I find the ethogenic paradigm to be of particular interest from the perspective of the psychology of action; the concept of agency lies at its heart, and this is not something that can be said of any of the other paradigmatic developments in critical social psychology that have followed in its wake.

Critical social psychology: the 1970s new paradigm

Joynson (1970) published a paper entitled The Breakdown of Modern Psychology, in which he opined that the promise of behaviourism and stimulus–response (S–R) psychology had not been fulfilled. Although the problem of individual differences could be studied physiologically, this would not provide a satisfactory solution since psychology would then be subsumed under physiology. The only way to avoid such a sorry state of affairs would be to allow introspective investigation but that is not something that could happen within the behaviourist perspective. Harré (1971) published a paper entitled Joynson's Dilemma in which he outlined a solution to the problem and this became formalised by Harré and Secord (1972, p. 29). I list what I take to be the main points of their programme as follows:

- Human beings must be treated as agents acting according to rule, and it must be realised that it is unscientific to treat them as anything else.
- Social behaviour must be conceived of as actions mediated by meanings, not responses caused by stimuli.
- The theory of movements, physiology, must be clearly separated from psychology, the theory of actions.

- It must be appreciated that most human social behaviour cannot be made intelligible under the mechanistic, causal paradigm.
- Reasons can be used to explain actions, and not all reasons can be treated as causes in the mechanistic sense, although in some special cases causes may be cited as reasons.

The negotiation of accounts

The central methodology of the new ethogenic paradigm in social psychology became the collection and negotiation of the accounts people give of their actions when asked why they did what they did. In passing, it may be noted that the initial collection of the account (as an answer to the question 'Why did you do that?') is close to what Peters describes as '*his* reason' explanations, while the process of negotiation may be regarded as an attempt to arrive at '*the* reason' or 'the *real* reason' explanations (see Peters, 1960, pp. 3–9). The idea of negotiation is one that has recently come under attack from the discursive psychologists who adopt a relativist stance to such issues. I shall return to this topic in Chapter 3, when I examine the discursive psychologists' critique of the new ethogenic paradigm.

From accounts to scripts and models

Formal episodes such as ceremonies and games were advocated as models for the more informal and enigmatic social episodes occurring naturally in everyday life. This is close to the approach adopted by Berne (1964) in transactional analysis. In transactional analysis, a domestic quarrel between spouses, for example, might be seen as a game for two players. The similarity between ethogenics and transactional analysis ends with the shared interest in games modelling, since transactional analysis is grounded in the psychoanalytic perspective. It is only much later in the development of critical and rhetorical psychology that serious engagement is made with Freudian ideas (see Billig, 1997, for example).

The 1970s ethogenics also incorporated Goffman's (1959) dramaturgical perspective. Researchers tried to discover the 'scripts' which were acting as templates for particular kinds of social episodes. It was thought that these scripts would be revealed through a process of observation coupled with a scrutiny of collected and negotiated accounts. The social episodes under investigation were also analysed for their role–rule structure. In this approach, roles are not unlike the characters in a play and may be defined using an open-ended set of rules covering what is (or is not) expected of the role occupant. Rules, in turn, are defined in terms of prescriptions to put particular plans of action into effect in response to given situations. Rules, in this view, may be used to explain regularities in non-random patterns of social behaviour and are thus loosely analogous to the causal laws of natural science.

In social psychology, the dramaturgical perspective to the analysis of social episodes had its heyday in the 1970s. However, there are some signs that a resurgence of interest may be occurring. For example, Rothenbuhler (1998) provides a treatment of ritual from the standpoint of communication studies and sociology which could easily be incorporated into contemporary critical social psychology. I shall have cause to refer to his work on a number of occasions later in the book.

Harré and Gillet (1994), looking back with hindsight, see the 1970s paradigm as constituting the *first* cognitive revolution, with the *second* cognitive revolution being brought about by the discursive social psychology of the 1980s and 90s. They see the earlier role–rule model of Harré and Secord (1972) as sharing a common interest with other work in the area of artificial intelligence and natural language programming (for example Shank and Abelson, 1977). Thus, in their view, the first cognitive revolution was not confined to ethogenics alone. With regard to the second cognitive revolution, I shall provide a discussion of discursive psychology in Chapter 3.

I have dealt with the 1970s new paradigm at this early stage of the book because it shows how a critical psychology emerged in response to the tensions that surround the distinction between action and behaviour. In the remainder of the book, I shall devote some time to approaches that reside within mainstream psychology which do have a direct relevance for the psychology of action and yet are not especially close to behaviourism. I shall also cover more recent developments in critical social psychology. I outline how I propose to do this in the concluding section of this chapter.

Plan of the book

In Chapter 2, I mingle my discussion of key variables present in three positivist theories with a consideration of concepts relating to the philosophy of action. The positivist models I cover are the theories of reasoned action (Ajzen and Fishbein, 1980), planned behaviour (Ajzen, 1991) and self-efficacy (Bandura, 1977). In their enthusiasm to develop theoretical models for the psychology of action, I think that the positivists have been forced to rifle concepts from across the paradigmatic border, as it were. This is not necessarily a bad thing since much creativity can flow from the bizarre juxtaposition of ideas, although sometimes all that is gained is the oxymoron (in Chapter 10, I talk about eclecticism and the fusion of approaches within the psychology of action in greater detail).

Once assimilated into the positivist paradigm the concepts of agency have to be adapted for quantification and honed for use in the research questionnaires. This is where the positivists earn their spurs, since they must pit their wits against some difficult problems of operational definition. I briefly examine the operational definition of the concept of intention in the context of research based upon the theory of reasoned action.

In the latter part of Chapter 2, I put forward a post-positivist interpretation of the theory of reasoned action as a rule governing the intelligibility of clusters of statements people might make concerning a particular action. This enables me to build a bridge between the positivist approach to action which dominates mainstream social psychology and some of the approaches more closely tied to talk (construed as accounts or discourse) in critical social psychology.

In Chapter 3, I move on to cover both discursive psychology and its critique of the earlier ethogenic paradigm. I conclude that some good concepts and ideas may have been rejected too hastily. I then examine the rhetorical strategies that critical psychologists use in their writing to distance themselves from the formal authoritative style which characterises much of the positivist academic literature (the prototypical example being the experimental lab report). The authors gain this distance by allowing a more personal style to peek through the text using boxes, italics and other typographical devices. This provides them with a frame from within which they can provide a critical commentary on the primary text. In this regard, they have something in common with meta-fictional novelists. I like to think of my analysis of these texts as a deconstruction of their own reflexively deconstructed writing. I must be careful not to claim too much here since I am conscious of the fact that my credibility as a post-modernist is flimsy.

At the end of Chapter 3, I turn my attention to one of the most difficult problems with discursive psychology: relativism. Spears (1997) acknowledges that critical social psychologists are split on this issue and so it's not just me that has difficulties in this regard. The topic goes to the heart of matters concerning language and truth. On balance, I find myself drawn towards critical realism. Even though I consider some of the points made by the discursive psychologists about people like me using death and furniture as the bottom line in our rhetoric against relativism, I still feel inclined to carry on thumping metaphorical tables. This is a big topic, but I shall say no more about the matter at this stage.

In passing, there is one further aspect concerning the material I cover in Chapter 3 which I feel obliged to mention. I think it is safe to say that, as a general rule, critical psychologists (especially discursive psychologists) have a marked preference for qualitative methodology over quantitative techniques. While this is something that I can understand, it is not something that I necessarily endorse. For some, the thought of a computer data sheet, ripe for analysis, can only be displaced by images of walnut treacle tart.

In Chapter 4, I trace the way the concepts of expectancy, value and plan have been used in psychology and attempt to place them in a historical context within the discipline. This brings me to consider Lewin's (1936/1966) concept of the life space and Miller *et al.*'s (1960) work on plans and the structure of behaviour, among other things. With the concept of plan well articulated, it is easier to begin to examine what happens when things go wrong. In this regard I discuss action slips in everyday life, in Chapter 5, mainly from the standpoint of cognitive psychology. This then leads me to Reason's (1990) work on human error in disaster situations. In my discussion of this work I attempt to relate it to perspectives in critical psychology introduced in Chapters 1 and 3.

In Chapter 6, I turn my attention to weakness of will. Weakness of will involves someone acting in a way that goes against their better judgement (a simple example would be a person who eats a cream cake having resolved to eat a low fat diet). I then go on to consider procrastination which I regard as a special case of weakness of will. With procrastination, there exists a perfectly good plan of action yet nothing happens: the essay does not get written; the body does not take itself jogging; the dishes remain dirty.

In Chapter 7, I consider two approaches to agentic improvement. In one, the person works from a manual or self-help book and this may be called the do-it-yourself (DIY) approach. The other involves calling in the professionals and in this case the person undergoes counselling or therapy. With regard to DIY improvement, there is a vast array of self-help books which are readily available from bookshops. Rather than attempt an exhaustive review of this material I examine one text (dealing with time management) in some detail.

Turning to professional counselling, I am unable to cover the full range of techniques available, given the scope of this book. I therefore restrict myself to dealing with those approaches which have close ties with behaviourism. I chose behaviourism because of the tension that exists between the concepts of behaviour and action (see my discussion, above). Behaviourist counselling techniques therefore provide me with a particularly interesting challenge if I am to deal with them from the standpoint of the psychology of action. I provide an alternative interpretation of behaviour modification from an agentic perspective, and then go on to examine rational emotive counselling. In general, I believe that much counselling can be seen as an attempt to deal with problems relating to the person as an agent and difficulties in the execution of plans of action.

In Chapter 8, I consider the issue of agentic control in two distinct but conceptually related situations: hypnosis and obedience to authority. With regard to hypnosis, it is unclear as to whether the hypnotised subjects have relinquished their claims to be autonomous agents or whether they are still, in some sense, in control. Having discussed hypnosis, I go on to review some of the classic social psychological work on obedience to authority. The phenomenon of obedience does have something in common with hypnosis, since control is passed to another (the person in authority).

In Chapter 9, I explore two enigmas in the psychology of action: masochism and suicide. The case of masochism, while involving obedience, introduces further problems for any theories of action grounded in psychological hedonism since the masochist seemingly chooses to suffer pain, bondage or humiliation. I explore the paradox of this in terms of what counts as a rational choice, along with the issue as to whether or not the masochist should really be regarded as displaying symptoms of deep psychological malaise or disturbance. I conclude the chapter with a discussion of suicide from an agentic standpoint; I am particularly interested in this phenomenon as rational action.

In my concluding chapter, I start by drawing together some of the main threads and themes of the book before considering the benefits of taking an eclectic approach to the psychology of action. This leads me to propose that fusion psychology is not necessarily a bad thing in this context. Agentic psychology seems to generate a bewilderingly large array of concepts and eclecticism hardly narrows the field. In order to provide some structure I put forward a conceptual framework for agentic psychology, at the end of the chapter. This is not a predictive model (as might be expected were I to be working within the positivist paradigm); its function is primarily heuristic.

Chapter 2

Reinterpreting positivist theories of action

I shall start with a short description of three theories of action which have been influential within positivist psychology. After this I shall consider some of the key concepts contained within these theories, alongside those drawn more widely from the philosophy of action.

Positivist theories

The theory of reasoned action

Ajzen and Fishbein's (1980) theory of reasoned action (TRA) has been the dominant paradigm for research into the psychology of action over the course of the past two or three decades, with the possible exception of Bandura's (1997) self-efficacy theory (SET). The TRA was originally put forward as a model of intention by Fishbein and Ajzen (1975), with attitude and subjective norm as the two predictor variables. In the attitude component the consequences of putting the intention (for example to smoke cigarettes) into effect are assessed: each of the consequences (for example getting lung cancer, or feeling relaxed in social situations) is rated in terms of a positive/negative evaluation of the ensuing state of affairs and also in terms of the subjective probability of its occurrence. For each consequence these ratings are multiplied together and the products for all the consequences are then summed to produce a total score for the attitude component. It is on the basis of this computational procedure that the model is sometimes described as an *additive-multiplicative expectancy-value* model.

The subjective norm component follows precisely the computational pattern of the attitude component. However, here it is the person's perceptions of the social expectations held by significant social others (for example spouse, parents, work mates) as to what he or she ought to do in terms of the behavioural intention in question. The information for this and the person's motivation to conform to such expectations is normally obtained using a rating scale. For each significant other, the social expectation rating (sometimes called 'normative belief') is multiplied by the rating for the motivation to conform to the social other. These products are then summed to produce the total score for the subjective norm component. This total is then added to the total for the attitude component to provide a prediction of intention.

The theory of planned behaviour

Ajzen (1988, 1991) has extended the TRA to take account of perceived behavioural control and this current version is known as the theory of planned behaviour (TPB). A diagrammatic representation of the TPB is provided in Figure 2.1 and a full description of the algebraic equations which formally define the TRA and TPB are given in the Appendix. Where possible, I shall deal with the more technical aspects of these theories with a light touch and will provide references to the academic journals for those readers with a background in quantitative methods who may wish to explore that side of things in greater depth.

Self-efficacy theory

Turning now to self-efficacy theory (SET), Bandura (1997) defines perceived self-efficacy as referring to 'beliefs in one's capabilities to organise and execute courses of action required to produce given attainments' (p. 3). He also says that 'beliefs of personal efficacy constitute the key factor of human agency' (p. 3). The essence of SET is that the stronger the efficacy beliefs, the better the agent (or the more likely it is that the agents will

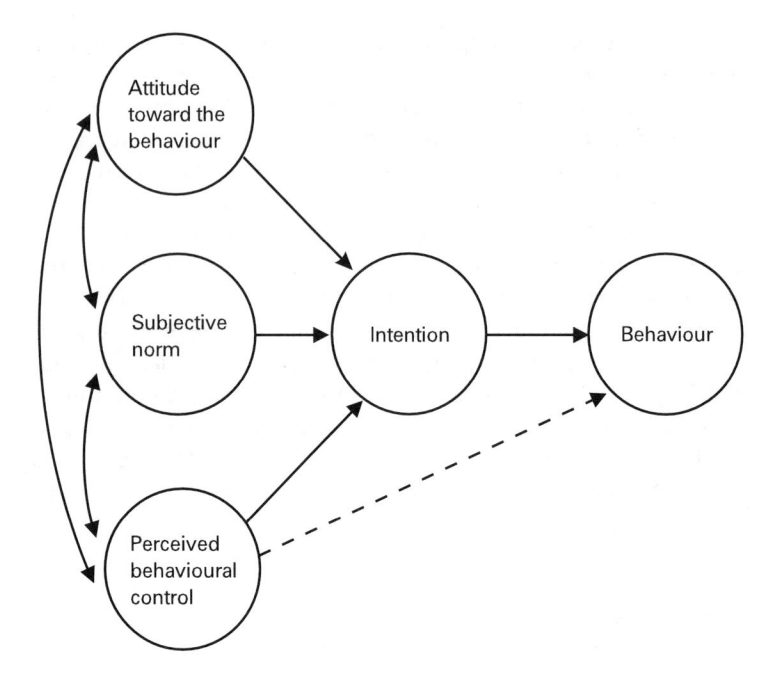

Figure 2.1 The theory of planned behaviour
(Adapted from Ajzen, 1991)

be successful in what they do). On the surface, it may seem as though Bandura's (1997) theory falls comfortably within the ethogenic new paradigm for social psychology which I described in Chapter 1, especially with regard to the talk of agency and so forth. It may seem perverse of me to resist this classification of the theory and to insist that it be firmly regarded as falling on the positivist side of the paradigm divide, but self-efficacy is measured in a similar way to the concepts in the TRA/TPB and treated just the same as a predictor for subsequent behaviour. The research methodology of SET disqualifies the theory as a serious contender for a post-positivist theory of action, despite the fact that it affects to operate within an agentic language game.

I shall return to a fuller discussion of SET in relation to Bandura's (1997) wider research programme in Chapter 4 where I trace the roots of his theoretical ideas back to the work of Rotter. For present purposes, then, I shall pretend that self-efficacy can just about be subsumed under the perceived behavioural control component of the TPB.

My next task is to talk about some of the main concepts contained in the positivist theories from a broader, philosophical standpoint. This will eventually lead me to a more focused consideration of the concept of intention and its operationalisation in TRA/TPB research questionnaires. From there I develop a linguistic interpretation of the TRA, from a new paradigm perspective. In this way I attempt to generate a post-positivist theory of intention which may provide a better integration with the concerns of contemporary critical psychology. And that will lead me, in Chapter 3, to a consideration of discursive and rhetorical psychology.

Key concepts in the psychology and philosophy of action

The language of action contains a number of interrelated concepts and terms which together form what Gauld and Shotter (1977) refer to as a hermeneutic circle. What is meant by this is that it is often difficult to talk about one term in isolation from the others. Thus, in the discussion of my first concept, *willing* (below) I find it helpful to draw attention to the second concept of perceived behavioural control when making the distinction between willing and *wishing*. Yet part of what is meant by perceived behavioural control relates to the ease with which wishing might be converted into willing.

Willing

I shall start by considering the way James (1892/1910) describes voluntary action, since this will lead me to the concept of willing:

> Desire, wish, will, are states of mind which everyone knows, and which no definition can make plainer. We desire to feel, to have, to do, all sorts of things which at the moment are not felt, had or done. If with the desire there goes a sense that attainment is not possible, we simply wish; but if we believe that the end is in our power, we will that the desired feeling, having, or doing shall be real; and real

it presently becomes, either immediately upon the willing or after certain preliminaries have been fulfilled. (p. 415)

James starts with desire and moves to wish or will. The bifurcation occurs with the sense that attainment may (or may not) be possible and this is close to the notion of perceived behavioural control, discussed below. The belief that the end is in our power is, perhaps, closer to the concept of self-efficacy than to perceived behavioural control. That which is desired, the focus of our will, is something that can be conceptually related to a number of other frameworks. With regard to the TRA, the desire will be registered in terms of the evaluation of the consequences of action. Where desires are expressed as goal states to be attained (or where evaluation is negative, to be avoided), they may be accommodated within the concept of plan (see Chapter 4). Although I am here moving away from the behaviourist paradigm, it may be noted that the concept of reinforcement is intimately yoked to the concept of desire whether the behaviourists like it or not.

One potential danger in isolating the concept of willing for special treatment is that it could be construed as a prior event and thus subsumed as the antecedent condition within a strictly causal explanation of action. Wittgenstein (1953), like James, endorses the idea that willing is an integral part of action and not something separate from it:

> 615. 'Willing, if it is not to be a sort of wishing, must be the action itself. It cannot be allowed to stop anywhere short of action.' If it is the action, then it is so in the ordinary sense of the word; so it is speaking, writing, lifting a thing, imagining something. But it is also trying, attempting, making an effort, – to speak, to write, to lift a thing, to imagine something and so on. (p. 160e)

By drawing attention to the fact that action flows seamlessly from willing, I may be guilty of oversimplification. I shall return to consider the concept of volition in greater detail in a later sub-section. Apart from the question of volition, there may be impediments to the flow of action over which the agent has little control.

Perceived behavioural control

For James, the desire leads to the act unless there is some impediment in which case the desire remains at the status of a wish. An intention, if reported, would on this view act as a promissory note or marker that the act was in train. James uses something very much akin to perceived behavioural control (a feature of the TPB) in order to make the distinction between wish and will. I think that, on this basis, it is only possible to hold an intention for something which can in principle be willed. Ajzen (1991) addresses this issue:

> It should be clear, however, that a behavioral intention can find expression in behavior only if the behavior in question is under volitional control, that is if the person can decide at will to perform or not perform the behavior. Although some behaviors may in fact meet this requirement quite well, the performance of most depends at least to some degree on such non-motivational factors as availability of requisite opportunities and resources (for example time, money, skills, co-operation of others). Collectively, these factors represent people's actual control over the behavior. (pp. 181–2)

From the above, it is tempting to regard any mismatch between actual control and perceived control as an error in terms of self-efficacy beliefs. However, I will proceed by regarding perceived behavioural control as a screen or filter at the boundaries between wishes and intentions. It may be obvious that some desires will be condemned to remain as wishes; for someone lost in a desert the desire to drink a pint of beer may be a case in point. On the other hand, some desires will cross with ease into the domain of intentional action; an able-bodied person walking in a garden desiring to go over to a bush in a nearby border in order to smell the roses should encounter no difficulty.

So far, I have emphasised the direct translation of desire to action unless there is some impediment, in which case the desire remains at the level of a wish. I also warned against placing something between the two, such as a volition, which might count as a prior event in a causal explanation of action. I think that this must be borne in mind with regard to the concept of intention. Intention may come into play when people are required to reflect on their situation or to report on what they are doing or trying to do. If a person desires a number of things, to be told which they intend to do and which they do not intend to do is informative. It need not thereby be interpreted as a report of their 'having an intention' (thought of as a mental event causing the action). Rather, the discovery that an action was intended might lead to an exploration for the reasons behind the action and I examine this consideration below.

Intention

Before I link the concept of intention to reasons for action, I shall first elaborate on Fishbein and Ajzen's (1975) approach to the concept of intention, as set out in their model. They start by making the conventional distinction between affect, cognition and conation. They then separate conation into behaviour and behavioural intention. They provide some conceptual analysis of behavioural intention, although they stop short of a formal definition:

> In many respects, intentions may be viewed as a special case of beliefs, in which the object is always the person himself and the attribute is always the behavior. As with a belief, the strength of an intention is indicated by the person's subjective probability that he will perform the behavior in question. It can thus be recommended that the strength of an intention, or more simply, 'intention', be measured by a procedure which places the subject along a subjective-probability dimension involving a relation between himself and some action. (pp. 12–13).

Although Fishbein and Ajzen (1975) make no bones about equating intention with prediction, Anscombe (1963) alerts us to the fact that a distinction may be made between the two. She points out that 'I am going to be sick' is usually a prediction; whereas 'I am going for a walk' is usually an expression of intention (p. 1). This is a level of subtlety not easily dealt with by questionnaire items in the TRA/TPB. To challenge the interpretation of intention as prediction is to tug against the theory's positivist moorings.

In fairness, Ajzen (1988) does state that his prime goal is to understand human behaviour and not merely to predict it.

Anscombe (1963, p. 8) says that much of what a person does will be things done intentionally. She then explores the concept of intention by moving away from causal explanation. Intentional actions, for her, are those actions where the question 'Why?' is given application. The question 'Why?' is refused application by the answer 'I did not know I was doing that' and also when the action was involuntary (this would cover reflex movements, for example). Anscombe, having acknowledged that people often do what they intend to do, then leads us towards a concern with accounts of action. Although Anscombe's analysis is philosophical in nature, there is in principle no problem in moving to the psychology of action from her position. I have already indicated that accounting methodology is a central concern in Harré and Secord's (1972) ethogenic social psychology and it has also featured strongly in Antaki's (1988, 1994) treatment of everyday explanation, for example. The important fact to note is that by moving in the direction signposted by Anscombe one leaves the positivist research paradigm of the TRA/TPB and enters the realm of critical social psychology.

The intention–behaviour relation

The relation between intention and behaviour is researched within the TRA/TPB paradigm but the model can only report the extent to which the one matches the other in a particular study. The theory remains silent on the question of how intention translates into behaviour. James sheds some light on this issue when he considers the gap between our current state and the desired state in an engaging discussion of the problem of getting out of bed on a cold and frosty morning. It is possible that the ubiquitousness of central heating has robbed James' illustration of some of its power, although a faulty boiler in the depths of winter is all that is needed to restore its vividness. His position is that we will do what we intend providing there is an absence of any conflicting notion in the mind. He rejects the idea that we eventually get out of bed because of some inner struggle or moment of decision:

We suddenly find that we have got up. A fortunate lapse of consciousness occurs; we forget both the warmth and the cold; we fall into some reverie connected with the day's life, in the course of which the idea flashes across us, 'Hollo! I must lie here no longer' (James, 1892/1910, pp. 424–5).

James' description is refreshingly vivid and it certainly rings true for me. His account is grounded in a phenomenological description of consciousness. On the one hand, there is the narrowing of attention at the moment prior to leaping out of the covers with the exclusion from consideration of the important factors of warm bed and cold bedroom. On the other hand, there is a switch of agentic mode from vacillation or at best akratic intention to command.

The more contemporary expectancy-value models of intention and decision making (such as the TRA) should have no difficulty in taking into account the person's evaluation of warm bed or cold bedroom and the subjective probability associated with the occurrence of these states. In the TRA this would normally be done with a 7-point paper and pencil rating scale and the scores would be fed into the attitude component of the TRA equation. The problem for contemporary expectancy-value models is that it is not possible for them to give pride of place to the issue of whether such expectancy-value considerations will be present in the person's mind at any particular time. In the TRA, expectancy-value considerations are treated as part of the attitude component and I think that it is relevant that within this tradition of social psychology there is a close conceptual relationship between attitude and personality trait. So the tendency is to regard expectancy-value ratings as relatively stable and as enduring over time.

Stout (1898/1938) also links voluntary action to personality. However, he does so by drawing upon the concept of self in an all-embracing fashion. Speaking of deliberation between two competing alternatives, he says:

> Voluntary action does not follow either of the conflicting tendencies, as such; it follows our preference of the one to the other. It is the conception of the self as agent which makes the difference. The alternative is not 'this?' or 'that?' but 'shall *I* do this?' or 'shall *I* do that?' Each line of action with its results is considered not in isola-

tion but as part of the ideally constructed whole for which the word 'I' stands. The impulse of the present moment belongs to the self of the present moment; but this is only a transient phase of the total self. If the impulse is realized the completed action will take its place as a component part of the life-history of the individual. He may live to regret it. (p. 630)

The interest in relating action to autobiography through the concept of self is a theme taken up by the new paradigm in social psychology (see De Waele and Harré, 1979; Harré, 1983). Stout's concluding comment 'He may live to regret it' cements action to responsibility. His concern with the broader context has a Gestalt feel to it. I think it is something that the discursive psychologists downplay, with their obsessive tendency to make the most of variation (I come to discursive psychology in Chapter 3). They do this partly to avoid any possibility of being associated with the notion of personality trait which they regard as needless reification on the part of the theorist. Given that I like the dramaturgical standpoint, I welcome Stout's viewpoint for the ease with which it abuts to the notion of character.

The tendency in the TRA to regard ratings as stable over time militates against the emphasis being placed upon the somewhat fickle moments of consciousness James describes (see above) where attentional shifts can wipe out whole stacks of expectancy-value data as obsolete or irrelevant at a moment's notice. Yet to me James' description indicates that this is where the research emphasis might best be placed. James brings out not just a shift in attention but also a shift in what might loosely be described as agentic mode.

Obedience to a self-generated order is something that Harré (1983) sees as close to the heart of agency. His view, somewhat surprisingly, is reminiscent of Bandura's (1997) earlier social learning theory, as opposed to the later notion of self-efficacy. Harré (1983) suggests that the development of agency in an individual begins when the child learns to obey orders:

> By being forced to listen to the exhortations of others, I learnt to exhort myself, and by watching others push each other into action, I learn to bestir myself. (p. 193)

Harré sounds like James who, in the quotation given earlier, bestirs himself with the exhortation that he must 'lie there no longer'. I shall return to discuss problems of this nature in Chapter 6 where I discuss akrasia and the weakness of will and in Chapter 8 where I examine obedience to authority. Of course, sometimes action does not ensue because the agent has difficulty on deciding which course of action to pursue when faced with conflicting or competing alternatives, and it is to a consideration of this that I now turn.

Deliberation and decision

The idea that normally we do what we wish unless there is some conflicting notion in our minds underpins James' notion of deliberation and decision. When we have a number of alternatives before us, the one conflicts with the other and hence we experience indecision, since any one act is inhibited. The underlying motives or reasons may wax and wane over time so that we sometimes experience extended periods of vacillation. Eventually, a decision may come 'for good and all', as he puts it.

James distinguishes five types of decision. The reasonable decision involves a rational balancing of the books, free of coercion, and this matches quite closely the contemporary expectancy-value model used in the TRA. James stresses the importance of seeing such decisions as building up case law which will then enable us to identify a future situation as one of a known class and thus to act unhesitatingly in a stereotyped way. This is close to the notion of habit or schema. I also think that a parallel can be made with Ryle's (1949/1963) path-making analogy for theory construction:

> If a farmer has made a path, he is able to saunter easily up and down it. That is what the path was made for. But the work of making the path was not a process of sauntering easily, but one of marking the ground, digging, fetching loads of gravel, rolling, and draining. He dug and rolled where there was yet no path, so that he might in the end have a path on which he could saunter without any digging or rolling. Similarly, a person who has a theory can among other things, expound to himself, or the world, the whole theory or any

part of it. But the work of building the theory was a job of making paths where as yet there were none. (p. 272)

James' period of indecision where alternatives are weighed up and conflicts are explored is rather like the farmer's path-building phase in Ryle's analogy. Ryle's point with regard to theory construction is that once it has been built, the person can be asked questions about it or can explain all the various aspects of it with some fluency, without having to go through the earlier construction phase in halting fashion. In a similar way, a person asked to account for their intentions may well be able to provide an explanation on demand. Part of that account may consist of a summary of the various comparisons of alternatives and the weighing up of the advantages and disadvantages of acting (or refraining from so doing) which were originally considered in the deliberation phase. A criticism that is sometimes made of expectancy-value models, such as the TPB, is that individuals may not go through the extensive computational process implied by the theories. The point that may be taken from a consideration of Ryle's example is that this may well be the case for many intentions, even though a more deliberative process may have occurred previously. One further point regarding the TPB is that there is not normally any way of knowing at which particular phase of the deliberative cycle the respondents are positioned at the precise moment of data collection. Indeed, the act of completing a standard TPB questionnaire may be tantamount to structured path building for some research participants.

In the second and third types, James suggests that the decision occurs before all the evidence is 'in' (James, 1892/1910, p. 431). The alternatives appear equally balanced and we grow tired of endless deliberation. The TRA/TPB would be capable of detecting individual respondents who were equally balanced in any of three ways. First, the positive items in the attitude component could balance the negative items, both having similar total absolute magnitudes. Second, the same thing could occur, only with respect to the subjective norm component. Third, an equal and opposing balance could be struck between the attitude and subjective norm component. In principle, then, the TRA/TPB could detect and explore these decisively awkward situations but it has not typically been used to monitor how individuals move through such vacillatory phases over time.

In the second type of decision James suggests that we let ourselves drift in some direction accidentally determined from without. It may be that an important aspect of indecisive individuals is that they find it difficult to recognise the arbitrariness of some decision situations or, if they do, they are nevertheless unable to throw the mental dice, as it were. In the third type, the force comes from within ourselves as we find ourselves spontaneously moving to one of the horns of our dilemma. In the fourth type, our circumstances change abruptly and we no longer place such importance on some of the previous considerations. This would be like dropping some of the items from a TPB questionnaire. According to James, such change might be brought about by grief or fear, for example. Finally, James introduces a fifth type of decision, set apart from the other four because of the 'slow dead heave of the will that is felt in these instances' (James, 1892/1910, p. 433).

Agency and power

James' position on the will is not that different from Locke's (1690/1964). In describing the modes of thinking Locke says:

> when the mind with great earnestness, and of choice, fixes its view on any idea, considers it on all sides, and will not be called off by the ordinary solicitation of other ideas, it is that we call intention or study. (p. 157)

If the object of Locke's intention is something that we might do, then if there is an absence of Jamesian conflicting notions, the act will occur. Locke pursues the discussion of will in the context of the concept of power:

> Power thus considered is two-fold, viz. as able to make, or able to receive any change. The one may be called active, and the other passive power. (p. 162)

The idea that agency is intimately connected to power is one that Harré and Secord (1972) incorporated into the ethogenic new paradigm (see Chapter 1). At one point they explore the intermediate region between things done to people and things done by them:

> [It] … is really the nexus of three dimensions of difference, that between patient and agent, that between being acted upon and taking action, and that between being the effect of a cause and being the result of a rationally guided action. (pp. 156–7)

At this point I will do no more than make the observation that Harré and Secord (1972) and Locke (1690/1964), above, are concerned with human endeavour in the round. By keeping in mind the fundamental distinction between what people do and what happens to them, Harré and Secord (1972) are drawn to the importance of the concept of intention as pivotal to this distinction and this leads to them to advocate the adoption of the two radically different forms of explanation in these separate realms with causal explanation being normally more appropriate for things that happen to us and teleological explanation for things that we do.

I find it strange that this important distinction has been relegated very much to the background in the TRA literature. The distinction may have been lost because the domain of the TRA is narrowed solely to intentional behaviour. By setting up the attitudinal and subjective norm components as predictor variables for intention, the model locks itself formally into causal explanation for intentional behaviour. This bizarre step escapes attention because the TRA has no need to use the mode of explanation (teleological versus causal) as a device to flag up the distinction between action and behaviour. It is the fact that the TRA never has to talk about behaviour (since it only has to deal with action) that enables this legerdemain to succeed. Paradoxically, it is behaviour that is the real target of TRA predictions and I think that this explains why the concept of intention gets distorted into that of behavioural intention within the TRA/TPB. In this regard I regret that I do feel that the TRA/TPB is a conceptual mess.

Volition

In my earlier discussion of willing, I indicated that both James and Wittgenstein saw nothing coming between desire and its object providing there was no impediment. Here I want to examine, in a more direct fashion than I did before, the idea that a mental act may cause the action to occur, in a mechanistic sense. This is an issue that Wittgenstein addresses:

> 613. In the sense in which I can ever bring anything about (such as stomach-ache through over-eating), I can also bring about an act of willing. In this sense I bring about the act of willing to swim by jumping into the water. Doubtless I was trying to say: I can't will willing; that is, it makes no sense to speak of willing willing. 'Willing' is not the name of an action; and so not the name of any voluntary action either. And my use of a wrong question came from our wanting to think of willing as an immediate non-causal bringing about. A misleading analogy lies at the root of this idea; the causal nexus seems to be established by a mechanism connecting two parts of a machine. The connexion may be broken if the mechanism is disturbed... 614. When I raise my arm 'voluntarily' I do not use any instrument to bring the movement about. My wish is not such an instrument either. (Wittgenstein, 1953, pp. 159e–60e)

This idea of a mechanism is explored also by Ryle (1949/1963). I shall provide a quotation from Ryle at this point since I believe that it will help to expose the mechanistic character of the TRA/TPB:

> Men are not machines, not even ghost-ridden machines. They are men – a tautology which is sometimes worth remembering. People often pose such questions as 'How does my mind get my hand to make the right movements?' and even 'What makes my hand do what my mind tells it to do?' Questions of these patterns are properly asked of certain chain-processes. The question 'What makes the bullet fly out of the barrel?' is properly answered by 'The expansion of gasses in the cartridge'; the question 'What makes the cartridge explode?' is answered by reference to the percussion of the detonator; and the question 'How does my squeezing the trigger make the pin strike the detonator?' is described by the mechanism of springs, levers and catches between the trigger and the pin. So when it is

asked 'How does my mind get my finger to squeeze the trigger?' the form of the question presupposes that a further chain process is involved, embodying still earlier tensions, releases and discharges, although this time 'mental' ones. But whatever is the act or operation adduced as the first step of this postulated chain-process, the performance of it has to be described in just the same way as in ordinary life we describe the squeezing of the trigger by the marksman. Namely, we say simply 'He did it' and not 'He did or underwent something else which caused it'. (Ryle, 1949/1963, p. 79)

The TRA may be guilty of being swept into the chain processes of which Ryle speaks, since it is assumed that the behaviour is caused by the having of an intention, and the intention, in turn, is caused by the state of the mental data described in the attitude and subjective norm components of the theory. I find it difficult to see how the TRA/TPB could escape Ryle's criticism.

Interim summary

In Chapter 1, I started by talking about the definition of psychology and the tension that exists between behaviourist and agentic perspectives on psychological phenomena. It was largely in response to the failure of behaviourism and, more broadly, experimental psychology to deal adequately with agency that the new paradigm for social psychology emerged in the 1970s. Despite their attempts to use the language of agency, I have suggested that the major psychological theories of action (TRA, TPB and SET) are best regarded as being located within the positivist paradigm of the doctrine of the objective experiment. My introductory examination of some of the key concepts in the psychology of action, such as intention or deliberation, has led me towards the ideas of the new paradigm and away from the positivist theories (TRA, TPB and SET). I am convinced that in the latter an attempt is made to use the language appropriate to the discussion of agency but that the research founders due to the lack of an adequate methodological infrastructure. I shall have more to say about the SET in Chapter 4 but in the remainder of this chapter I shall concentrate on the TRA/TPB. I shall start by examining the way the concept of intention has been operationalised within the TRA/TPB.

Critical appraisal of the TRA/TPB

The operational definition of intention

Within the TRA/TPB research paradigm, intention (along with the other components) is typically measured using paper and pencil questionnaire items. The classic source which lays down the principles for the construction of such questionnaires is to be found in the Appendix of Ajzen and Fishbein (1980). I have previously examined a number of questionnaire items which I selected, in a casual if not random fashion, from a number of recent studies (see Smith, 1999).

I will provide just one example to illustrate the way intention may be construed as a prediction of a minimal occurrence of behaviour within the target category. Morrison *et al.* (1996) measured schoolchildren's intentions to drink alcohol using the following item: 'When you are in the next grade, do you think you will drink alcohol?' The response scale had four points meaning definitely, probably, probably not, and definitely not. This item, tapping into a prediction of behaviour, is superficially like Anscombe's (1963) 'I am going to be sick'. However, if it is regarded as being concerned with intention, the item cannot distinguish between the subject who wants to drink, intends not to, but thinks realistically that she or he will cave in to desire or social pressure, on the one hand, and the subject who wants to, intends to, and predicts she or he will do. Similarly, there is no possibility of distinguishing the subject who does not intend to and predicts she or he will not, from the subject who does intend to, doesn't really want to, and predicts she or he will not in the end do so. What is needed to explore the way intention works in these cases is to collect the accounts of those individual subjects who have interesting combinations of responses. The gross statistical techniques of multiple correlation and so forth are impotent to provide any analysis requiring individual focus. A move away from the positivist paradigm would be necessary before the appropriate accounting methodology (as outlined in Chapter 1) could be embraced to further such investigation.

Limitations of space do not permit me to describe the fruits of my analysis in any detail here. However, if I were bent on producing a destructive critique, I might at this point be tempted to jettison the TRA/TPB on two counts: in the previous section the theories did not fair well in terms of the conceptual analysis of some of the key terms; in the present section the theories faired little better in terms of the operational definition of the concept of intention. However, any rejection of the TRA/TPB at this stage would be premature, since I have not yet considered the strength of the empirical support for these models and it is to this that I now turn.

Empirical support for the TRA/TPB

The TRA/TPB have generated a large body of research covering a wide variety of topics. One of the earliest summaries of results in this area was provided by Fishbein and Ajzen (1975) and they reported multiple correlation coefficients for the predictions of intentions to perform various behaviours, drawn from 16 studies, as averaging at $r = 0.746$. In plain English, this means that on the whole people whose attitudes and social expectations are positive will tend to hold a positive intention to do that which is in question (and the reverse pattern for those with a negative intention). Although subsequent empirical support may not always have turned out to be quite as strong as this, it is nevertheless impressive. Sheppard *et al.* (1988) conducted a meta-analysis of 87 separate studies (participants N = 11,566) and they found strong support for the model, with an average correlation of $r = 0.66$. Further meta-analyses and reviews have been carried out by Hausenblas *et al.* (1997) for studies within the domain of exercise behaviour, Godin and Kok (1996) for applications to health-related behaviours, and Blue (1995) for exercise studies. The general findings were broadly supportive of the TRA/TPB.

The empirical status of the TRA/TPB has also been assessed in a series of reviews of attitude and attitude change which have appeared regularly in the *Annual Review of Psychology* (see Eagly and Himmelfarb, 1978; Cialdini *et al.*, 1981; Cooper and Croyle, 1984; Chaiken and Stangor, 1987; Tesser and Shaffer, 1990; Olson and Zanna, 1993; Petty *et al.*, 1997). These reviews have been generally supportive, although reviewers have made several points of criticism. There is, for example, some concern over the use of correlation techniques in the analysis of data and there is some disagreement over the scoring conventions adopted by the model (I have examined these issues in some detail elsewhere; see Smith, 1996). There are proposals that the model should be extended to include further variables, such as habit or prior behaviour. There seems to be some support for the idea that behavioural expectation may operate as a superior predictor of behaviour when compared to intention and this is something that has been confirmed in the meta-analyses, reported above. However, the overriding conclusion is that the empirical support for the model is strong.

This is an interesting situation. On the one hand, I have made a number of critical points against the TRA/TPB and, on the other hand, I have discovered good empirical support for it. It is the empirical support which makes me reluctant to dismiss the theory out of hand, from the standpoint of critical social psychology. My strategy, therefore, will be to provide an alternative interpretation of the TRA/TPB, grounded broadly within critical psychology (although not necessarily discursive psychology). In doing this, I shall indicate how the empirical support for the TRA/TPB might best be interpreted.

A paradigmatic relocation for the TRA/TPB

I will begin my act of reconstruction by asserting an equivalence between talk and questionnaire response, a tactic unlikely to be applauded by discursive psychologists. In order to build my argument, I focus primarily on just one component of the TRA/TPB (the attitude component) and simplify even further by considering the case of the single attribute (just one consequence, such as getting cancer from cigarette smoking), rather than that of multiple attributes in combination (cancer plus social relaxation plus bad breath would provide three attributes for the cigarette smoking example). This simplification is not only helpful for my exposition but is also a legitimate step for me to take on formal theoretical grounds since the model should work for the single attribute.

I then extend my argument to cover the complete set of statements that one would expect to find in the full TRA/TPB model. This would include items relating to the attitudinal component, the subjective norm component, perceived behavioural control and intention. For each of the three 'predictor' components, items could be broken down to include both parts of the multiplicative pairings (thus for an attitude item, statements might cover both expectancy and value). At this point, my journey across the paradigmatic barrier commences as I name the TRA/TPB questionnaire item set a *cluster of accounts*. This is where the fun begins.

As stated above, I do not deny the strength of the empirical evidence supporting the TRA/TPB. At the risk of oversimplifying, I think of this evidence as one big, very big multiple correlation coefficient. Let me call it BIG C (for 'BIG Correlation'). Put like this, BIG C expresses a property of the universal cluster of accounts. Although any particular cluster of accounts for a specific topic (such as cigarette smoking) will have its own particular BIG C, I want to think big; I want to think of universal clusters.

Items entering the universal cluster of accounts may be classified in accordance with the terms mentioned in the TRA equation which is the formal algebraic statement of the theory (see Appendix). I have to take this classification scheme as valid for the universal cluster of accounts because BIG C is so big. The classification, of course, comprises none other than the familiar TRA/TPB components (attitude, subjective norm and so forth). The TRA equation, therefore, provides a rule governing the way particular items may be mixed and matched, on the basis of their classification, in any particular cluster of accounts. In another act of renaming I pull the TRA/TPB further still across the paradigmatic barrier: I now see the TRA equation as a *rule for intelligibility*.

At this point, the interesting research questions become:

- How can the rule for intelligibility be checked out?
- How can the rule for intelligibility be extended or improved?

At first glance, it might seem that I could save myself the trouble of checking out the rule for intelligibility by pointing to BIG C. But by now I've travelled to a new paradigm and BIG C is really the currency of the old paradigm. Using the currency of BIG C is not the only thing that won't work in the new paradigm. I doubt very much whether the TRA/TPB questionnaire could be taken across the border checkpoint, in its present form.

In the new paradigm, new methods and new research techniques will have to be developed not just for checking out the rule for intelligibility but also for extending and improving it. Having set out the thread of my argument, I return to the beginning and to the notion of attitudinal semantics.

Attitudinal semantics

In the TRA/TPB research paradigm the data needed to pinpoint a subject's attitude is typically obtained by the use of paper and pencil questionnaire techniques (see Ajzen and Fishbein, 1980). The discursive psychologists regard such techniques as placing unnatural constraints upon the respondents' linguistic repertoire and, more importantly, as creating a situation which neglects the illocutionary force that such statements might have in everyday contexts (see Edwards and Potter, 1992). While I understand their objection, it does not unduly upset me. To respond to a questionnaire item is to generate an utterance act (see Searle, 1969) and questionnaires are now so commonplace, at least in western culture, that they might almost pass for an extension of what de Saussure calls the ideographic system of writing (de Saussure, 1959/1966, p. 25).

I take questionnaire responses (yoked to the item itself) to be representations of accounts which could in principle be produced in conversation whenever someone enquires as to what the speaker's attitude is on a particular topic or, indeed, asks for some justification of an attitude which the speaker has stated or is assumed to have held. Expectancy-value models of attitude can thus be seen as formal models which, although abstracted away from the world of natural spoken discourse, nonetheless address semantic issues located within that world. To be more specific, the models define how statements concerning expectancy and value may be joined to particular expressions of attitude.

Put another way, the expectancy-value equation may be seen as a rule which defines an intelligible surface across the attitudinal semantic space. When a subject's actual position is triangulated from measured expectancy, value and attitude responses, it is then possible to see whether or not the subject is situated at an allowable location in terms of the attitudinal surface created by the rule (see Smith, 1996, for a fuller and more technical exposition of this idea). If the rule operates routinely within a given socio-linguistic community, ordinary language users of that community should be able to distinguish instances where this rule is transgressed from those where it is not. I define a transgression as an instance where a position triangulated from a given set of expectancy, value and attitude statements or data does not fall upon the attitudinal surface specified by the model in question. If we assume that a particular model is correct, then, other things being equal, ordinary language users will find it easier to identify instances of transgression in those cases where the distance between the actual triangulated and the predicted theoretical positions is greatest and it is these cases which will appear least intelligible to them.

Clusters of accounts

I want to pursue the idea that all questionnaire items of the TRA/TPB, and not just those of the attitude component, can be mapped into a form which could in principle resemble everyday discourse. Of course, sometimes one would have to be very creative and perhaps the questionnaire item taken together with the response should first be seen as a question–answer adjacency pair which in turn can then be rendered into the form of a simple sentence or statement. I see items laundered into this format as forming accounts relating to the action in question and this provides me with a bridge to the new paradigm in social psychology (see Chapter 1). Thus the data in a TRA/TPB questionnaire may be thought of as mapping on to a set or cluster of accounts which are bounded by their relevance to the act in question. Such a cluster might possibly include a statement of the person's intention or behavioural expectation and, in the case of explanatory discourse, a report of their actual behaviour in some circumstances.

The rule for intelligibility

Looked at this way, I interpret the TRA equation as a rule for intelligibility governing discourse clusters whose contents are defined by their concern with particular actions. Insofar as the TRA research studies yield data from non-interacting individuals (that is, the questionnaire respondents) I see these studies as having something to say about *virtual* linguistic communities, rather than actual social interlocutors. Although not designed to be a universal grammar, this approach perhaps leans more towards Chomskian linguistics than to discursive psychology (I discuss discursive psychology in Chapter 3). The magnitude of the multiple correlation coefficients reported (referred to as BIG C in my preamble, above) may therefore be construed as reflecting the strength of the rule for intelligibility as it operates in the particular virtual linguistic community studied. The way I see accounts and clusters mapping on to TRA items and questionnaires, respectively, is illustrated in Figure 2.2.

Verification of the rule for intelligibility

I have previously used clusters of accounts mapped on to the TRA equation as a conversational test-frame for verifying the proposed rule for intelligibility (see Smith, 1982). An example is given in Figure 2.3 where question–answer pairs form accounts which represent the various components in the TRA equation. The basic contents of test-frames comprise a cluster of statements covering the attitude and subjective norm relating to a particular action. To these basic statements may be added a statement of intention either in the positive or negative direction (the open-ended question at the foot of Figure 2.3 may, for the moment, be disregarded). It is possible, therefore, to produce clusters that, when mapped on to the TRA equation, either produce a balanced equation or one that does not balance

CLUSTER (discourse)	⇐ MAP ⇒	TRA QUESTIONNAIRE
ACCOUNT* (sentence)	⇐ MAP ⇒	TRA ITEM + Response
WORD (smallest semantic unit at bottom of the hierarchy)		

*While the term 'account' comes from the 1970s new paradigm social psychology, 'speech act' would be a closer equivalent for 1990s discursive psychology.

Figure 2.2 Semantic mapping for TRA clusters
(Adapted from Smith, 1982)

(the example in Figure 2.3 does not balance). In a previous study (Smith, 1982), I cast such clusters in the guise of interviews between doctors and patients in a psychiatric setting and had subjects rate the conversational clusters in terms of the rationality of the patient protagonist. Those protagonists producing clusters which mapped to balanced TRA equations were rated as less irrational than those where the TRA equation did not balance. In a parallel condition the clusters were set in the guise of oral examinations for English language students. In this condition, the students producing balanced clusters were rated as more linguistically competent than those producing imbalanced equations.

I turn now to the refinement and extension of the rule for intelligibility using a technique which may be regarded as a variation on the conversational cluster test-frame used in the verification study described above.

Refinement and extension of the rule for intelligibility

The test-frame cluster in Figure 2.3 contains a set of statements which map to an imbalanced TRA equation, together with an open-ended request for a further account at the end of the frame. It is assumed that an account given in response to this request would, when added in to the existing set, render the cluster more intelligible. In a previous study (Smith, 1982), I

PERSON A	PERSON B	TRA analysis
'Do you think you'd enjoy the film?'	'Yes, I'm certain I would.'	*Attitude* = positive
'Does your partner want you to go?'	'Yes, she said I ought to go.'	*Subjective norm* = positive
'Do you think she's right?'	'Yes, I agree with her.'	*Motivation to conform* = positive
'So do you intend to go?'	'Well, no I don't actually!'	*Intention* = negative
'Why not?'		Open-ended question

Imbalanced TRA Equation: $A_{(positive)} + SN_{(positive)} \neq I_{(negative)}$

Figure 2.3 Conversational test-frame cluster

collected statements from subjects that they thought might be offered by the protagonist in the test-frame by way of response. These statements I regarded as additional accounts and in the first phase of analysis I scrutinised them to see whether they might be dealt with by the existing rule for intelligibility. Where an account could be easily mapped on to an existing component in the TRA equation, it offered no potential for refinement or extension of the rule for intelligibility. In a test-frame dealing with a possible visit to the cinema, for example, an account referring to the fact that it had started to rain (and therefore the protagonist would get wet travelling to the cinema) points to an additional negatively evaluated outcome which could be accommodated by the existing attitude component in the TRA equation. I was more interested in accounts which seemed to pose difficulties when it came to mapping them on to the existing TRA equation. The accounts which seemed to demand an extension or refinement of the rule comprised three categories and, in dealing with these, I was then prompted to go on to improve the way the plans are represented in the context of the model.

Frustrated enabling conditions

First, some accounts related to frustrated enabling conditions (see Abelson, 1973, 1975). For example, in order to go to the cinema the protagonist might have to arrange for a baby-sitter. This is a condition which must be met before the intention can be put into effect. It did not seem to me to be like a consequence at all. I originally carried out this work prior to Ajzen's extension of the TRA into the TPB. It is possible that these accounts relating to frustrated enabling conditions could now be dealt with by mapping them on to the perceived behavioural control element of the TPB.

Negative gating

Second, some accounts were concerned with negative gating (see Abelson, 1973). A simple example would be that the protagonist had already promised to go to a restaurant with a friend (the execution of the 'restaurant' plan would prevent the 'cinema' plan going ahead, since the pursuit of the former plan would block the latter).

Superordinate moral principles

The third group of accounts invoked superordinate moral principles. An example taken from the cinema data would be where the protagonist was thought not to approve of the high salaries paid to film stars (thus all film-going would be barred on the grounds of this moral principle). The existing TRA equation cannot really deal with hierarchically organised moral expectations since it is an additive model.

Representation of plans

Returning to my previous work on the rule for intelligibility (see Smith, 1982), I decided to retain the TRA equation (or at least a diagrammatic representation of it), but only as an element incorporated in a larger conceptual structure. I found it useful to use Abelson's (1973) molecular approach to the representation of plans which focuses on states and the actions which are required to change them into goal states. This approach enabled me to develop a descriptive model for the representation of accounts of action which is closely tied to considerations of plans and the executive facet of action (see Figure 2.4).

Eagly and Chaiken (1993) indicate the point at which theories of attitude may interface with theories of planning:

> Although theories of planning that emphasize goal setting and feedback control have not been formulated as attitudinal models, the goals these theorists emphasize can be translated into attitudinal terms. Thus, for an attitude theorist, goals are end states or outcomes toward which people hold positive attitudes. (p. 191)

What Eagly and Chaiken (1993) do not do is bring out how theories such as the TRA may be more fully integrated with the sort of approaches to planning put forward by Miller *et al.* (1960). I shall explore this issue further in Chapter 4 where I shall also cover some of the more recent material concerned with goals and self-regulation (see Karoly, 1993; Karniol and Ross, 1996; Palatano and Seifert, 1997).

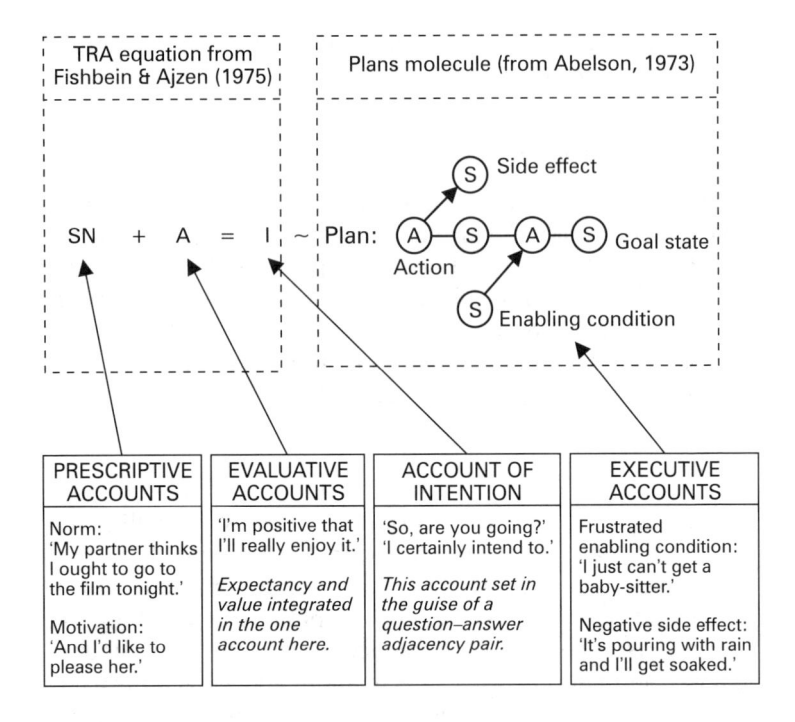

Figure 2.4 Extension to the rule for intelligibility
(Adapted from Smith, 1982)

PRESCRIPTIVE ACCOUNTS	EVALUATIVE ACCOUNTS	ACCOUNT OF INTENTION	EXECUTIVE ACCOUNTS
Norm: 'My partner thinks I ought to go to the film tonight.' Motivation: 'And I'd like to please her.'	'I'm positive that I'll really enjoy it.' *Expectancy and value integrated in the one account here.*	'So, are you going?' 'I certainly intend to.' *This account set in the guise of a question–answer adjacency pair.*	Frustrated enabling condition: 'I just can't get a baby-sitter.' Negative side effect: 'It's pouring with rain and I'll get soaked.'

Conclusion

I started this chapter by considering three major positivist theories of action (TRA, TPB and SET) in a way that drew heavily on the philosophy of action. My examination of key concepts in the psychology of action pulled me towards the post-positivist paradigm I had already introduced in Chapter 1. I argued that the positivist theories are frustrated in their attempt to use the language of agency by their commitment to positivist methodology. The way the concept of intention has been operationalised within the TRA/TPB research reinforced this impression. However, I take seriously the empirical findings of the TRA/TPB. Being unwilling to trap myself within a positivist theory of action, I was forced to place an alternative interpretation upon these findings, from a post-positivist standpoint. This

I did by construing the TRA/TPB equation as a rule governing the intelligibility of clusters of accounts relating to a given action. The notion of attitudinal semantics led me to novel methodological techniques for verifying and extending the rule of intelligibility. Finally, I put forward ideas for linking such a rule more explicitly to the concept of plan and its representation. I shall return to the concept of plan in Chapter 4. Before I do that, I shall consider discursive and rhetorical psychology, along with the problem of relativism which seems to come with the discursive territory.

Chapter 3
Agency, talk and relativism

In Chapter 2, I examined some of the positivist theories of action. I commence this chapter with a consideration of the discursive action model (DAM) put forward by Edwards and Potter (1992). In Chapter 1, I described the reaction away from mainstream experimental psychology by the 1970s new paradigm social psychologists. I also indicated that this movement could be seen as the precursor to the discourse analytic approach developed in the 1980s (by Potter and Wetherell, 1987, for example) which, in turn, led to the DAM and, more broadly, to the discursive psychology of the 1990s (a view that is more or less endorsed in Harré and Gillett, 1994). In writing on the psychology of action, I have to be careful not to take the whole of discursive and critical psychology under my wing. I shall therefore restrict myself as much as possible to matters that are germane to my primary interest in the psychology of action, although there will be some sections in this chapter where I stray a little from this main theme. I start, therefore, with a summary of the DAM.

The discursive action model (DAM)

While the central facet of Edwards and Potter's (1992) DAM is concerned with action, the question of how facts are actively created and how people are held accountable for their actions and their factual assertions is also considered. The DAM is best understood as a model for *discursive* action and I will say a little more about what I mean by this. Edwards and Potter (1992) recast traditional cognitive phenomena, such as memories and attributions, as things that people and groups *do*. It is in this sense that their model is concerned with action. The reason why the DAM is a model for discursive action, and not for action in the wider sense found in the 1970s paradigm of Harré and Secord (1972), for example, is that they are talking about speech acts. Edwards and Potter's (1992) model is developed very much in the spirit of Austin (1962) and Searle (1969).

Speech act theory is concerned with the social function of speech and its origin is usually traced to Austin's 1955 William James lectures at Harvard University (Austin, 1962). Austin's work may be regarded as a reaction away from formal logical systems for representing linguistic statements which could be found to be true or false. Austin pointed out that statements (what he called 'constatives') might be distinguished from 'performatives'. With the former a state of affairs is described, with the latter something is done (a ship is named, a command is issued, a warning is given and so forth). He later modified his position to say that even when statements are made something is done. This goes some way to explain why the DAM sees the making of factual statements as action. Austin also says that even when performatives are uttered an element of stating or describing will be involved. His theory was subsequently elaborated and formalised by his pupil Searle (1969) who distinguished illocutionary acts (stating, questioning, commanding, promising) from propositional acts (referring and predicating) and utterances. It could be argued that discursive psychologists work mainly from transcribed utterances and that their interest in the function of such utterances ties in with Searle's position. According to Searle, talking is performing acts according to rules and a theory of language should be regarded as part of a theory of action.

Potter and Wetherell (1987) embrace more than just face-to-face utterances in their interpretation of discourse:

> We will use 'discourse' in its most open sense… to cover all forms of spoken interaction, formal and informal, and written texts of all kinds. So when we talk of 'discourse analysis' we mean analysis of any of these forms of discourse. (p. 7)

This breadth of interest is then reflected in their commitment to function, as the following quotation from Wetherell and Potter (1988) indicates:

> Discourse analysis can best be understood by introducing the interconnected concepts of function, construction, variation and the analytic unit: the interpretative repertoire... Essentially, discourse analysis involves developing hypotheses about the purposes and consequences of language. (pp. 169–70)

In the 1970s new paradigm the interest in talk was mainly focused on talk about action (and this was translated into the central methodological technique known as the collection and negotiation of accounts). The DAM reaches beyond talk about action to talk in and of itself. It is this aspect of the DAM which is pushing me into areas relating to language that I would rather skirt, if I had the chance. But, as will become increasingly obvious as I progress through this chapter, there is no way I can avoid it.

The DAM is not just concerned with the acts that can be achieved through speech; it is also concerned with the way action is reported. The objective here is to examine the rhetoric people use when reporting material *as factual* when they have something of a dilemma on their hands, owing to their stake or interest in the matter. This is still close to speech act theory and the idea that the making of a statement involves performance. I think that in the 1970s new paradigm, such statements would have been construed as accounts and the investigators would then have felt obliged to check out any which they suspected were tainted by stake. The negotiation of accounts is not a feature of discourse analysis. In order to understand why this is so, it is necessary to consider the fact that speech act theory is not the only foundation for discursive psychology; semiology has also been influential.

Potter and Wetherell (1987), declaring their interest in semiology, point to both de Saussure (1959/1966) and to Barthes (1972) as being of importance in this regard. They are particularly taken by de Saussure's emphasis on the arbitrariness of the linguistic sign. This leads to the acknowledgement that words, rather than simply being used to name objects in an unproblematic fashion, have to be considered in relation to the position they occupy in the rest of the language. The meaning of a term is not decided simply by checking the term against the appropriate object in reality, it is dependent on what other words oppose and inform the sign in question. Language does not provide a window on the world and it should not be seen as a calculus through which the truth of statements may be checked out in the 'real' world. This is why the negotiation of accounts is not to be found within discourse analysis. Although Harré and Secord (1972) were at pains to say that accounts were always revisable in principle, the option of squaring accounts with the 'facts' of the matter was always there in the 1970s new paradigm. It is my understanding of the DAM that while factual reporting should be scrutinised for stake and interest the investigation should involve no more than rhetorical analysis.

The third facet of the DAM is accountability. The point addressed here is that while issues of agency and responsibility will often feature in reported events, these same issues will also be present at the superordinate level of the person doing the reporting. In Chapter 2, I provided a quotation from Stout concerning the relation between a particular action and the individual, seen in the round, as it were. There are many theoretical niches to run to from this position. Harré and Secord (1972) brought out the importance of honour. Goffman (1959), through the possibility of managing the impression we create using our personal fronts, opens up scope for the presentation of honest and trustworthy personae. Once agency and responsibility are admitted at the superordinate level of the person, it is difficult to avoid making judgements and generalities across time and once this is done it is extremely difficult not to stumble into the lair of the trait theorist. I acknowledge that a discursive psychologist would be the last person on earth to become a palindromatic reifier when it comes to personality. I'm getting carried away here; let me take stock.

I have no quarrel with the idea that people do things in talk. This is well covered by the notion of speech acts. However, I do not regard all action as consisting of speech acts. For example, the landing of a plane may involve talk between the pilot and the air traffic controller but this may be only a part of the act of successfully landing the plane. And *that* talk may not be especially interesting from a speech act theoretic point of view. It seems to me that the scope of investigation is narrowed considerably when research is focused exclusively on transcribed speech and text. I am therefore anxious that the rejection of the 1970s new paradigm social psychology may have been premature. Because this has important implications for the way the psychology of action is now developed, I shall set out the reasons as to why I think Potter and Wetherell's (1987) critique of the 1970s paradigm fails.

The discursive critique of the 1970s new paradigm

Potter and Wetherell (1987) focus their critique of ethogenics on Marsh *et al.*'s (1978) study of British soccer aggression. This is an entirely sensible strategy, since this book was at the time *the* major example of empirical ethogenic work to have been published. While I do not want to spend too much time raking over arguments put forward more than a decade ago about an empirical study carried out over two decades ago, I feel the need to re-examine them, briefly, for the reasons I have stated above. I don't want to reject good methods, such as observation and the negotiation of accounts, unless absolutely necessary.

In essence, Potter and Wetherell (1987) argued that Marsh *et al.* (1978) treated the soccer fans' discourse in different ways, depending on how it suited them. Potter and Wetherell (1987) felt that sometimes the researchers saw the accounts as revealing what was really happening on the terraces (a reality involving minimal violence) whereas at other times the researchers interpreted the accounts as supporting the idea that a frisson of excitement and danger abounded (see Potter and Wetherell, 1987, pp. 61-2). They argued that Marsh *et al.* (1978) provided no method or criteria for making the distinction between the genuine (little violence) and the rhetorical (bloody mayhem) accounts.

In dismissing Marsh *et al.*'s (1978) treatment of their interview data, Potter and Wetherell (1987) rejected the central methodological technique in the 1970s new paradigm: the negotiation of accounts. I think this was unnecessarily harsh. Marsh *et al.* (1978), through their footnotes, provide plenty of independent evidence through police and ambulance statistics on arrests and accidents to support the accounts. The evidence indicated that violence was not at a high level in that situation.

Stepping back for one moment, it is obvious that checking the accounts with the facts is not something that will make any sense to a relativist. The facts in question came in the form of footnotes. The only thing open to a discursive psychologist is to examine the rhetorical function of such footnotes. This might be done by exploring the way the footnotes are used to shore up factual claims. Other arguments might focus on the extent to which the footnotes lend an illusion of objectivity and authority to the assertion, in the case of the soccer research, that not much violence had occurred. I'm not happy with this. I take ambulance statistics as an indicator of real blood on real noses and real fingers trapped in real turnstiles. I shall return to this issue later in the chapter when I consider relativism in more detail.

Marsh *et al.* (1978) describe the behaviour of the fans at the matches, especially when they were engaging in conflict with the opposition, on the basis of their video-taped records of the spectators at the ground. I think that Marsh *et al.* (1978) could have made more of this observational data than they did, but that is not too important. Apparently, this material indicated that there seemed to be a reluctance on the part of the pursuers ever to catch up with the group they were chasing. Therefore, the observational data also seemed to support the accounts which asserted that the violence was minimal. It may be noted that observation forms no part of discourse analysis. Once again, if a relativist believes that there is no way the language of accounts can be checked against an objective reality, there is absolutely no sense in bothering with observation in the first place.

Another way in which Marsh *et al.* (1978) checked their accounts was to play the recorded interviews back to participants. This enabled them to query instances where hyperbole was suspected. In other words, the researchers not only collected their accounts but they then negotiated them with the research participants. This caused some of the more outlandish original claims to be revised or changed.

In sum, the reasons why discursive psychologists reject both observation and negotiation, as ways for checking the status of accounts, go beyond any particular empirical study, such as that carried out by Marsh *et al.* (1978). These reasons relate to an endorsement of relativism and a reluctance to admit that language could possibly provide a window onto an external reality (against which the truth of statements could be checked out). I shall return to this topic of relativism a little later in the chapter, since I find the idea of using observation and negotiation in order to triangulate the accuracy of accounts very appealing. Before I do this, there is one further topic I wish to consider from the point of view of the DAM which is concerned with the rhetorical construction of factual knowledge. I want to examine the way critical and discursive psychologists reflexively build deconstructive elements into their own texts.

Rhetoric and reflexivity in critical psychology texts

In psychology, the literary style of the lab report is formal and impersonal. It can be argued that the style itself lends the reporting an authority which it doesn't deserve. The objective style of the scientific discourse fosters the feeling that the findings or the content of the study being reported may provide the reader with a glimpse of reality. Providing the reader is properly trained in the scientific language game, the lab report should allow the secrets of the real world to be yielded up in the telling. Discursive and post-modernist psychologists deconstruct the language of the scientific report in order to show that it could be otherwise. By attacking points of architectural weakness in the text they may, through their acts of demolition, be successful in exposing the suppressed personality, biographical situation or group allegiances of the author. In this way, hidden aspects of the author's stake in the scientific outcome of the reported study may be rendered transparent and the reader's faith in the scientific objectivity of the research thus be shaken. I have already explained that stake in the context of factual reporting is one of the central concerns of the DAM (see above). Deconstruction, however, merely provides the critical social psychologist with the opportunity for critique. A more interesting challenge presents itself to the critical psychologist as author of his or her own academic text. If the critical psychologist's writing is not to be confused with that of psychologists in the scientific mainstream, some way will have to be found to flag this up to the reader.

By applying the concept of frame to a piece of writing, it is possible to express the hierarchical relationship of different parts of the text to one another and, usually, to grasp which part is the figure and which the ground. If we consider the general content of the text of the book which I am currently writing (and you are currently reading) as an anchor, then other frames might be specified in terms of their position relative to this basic level. Let me describe this basic level as writing at *frame one*. I can tell you that, at frame one, I have sometimes had difficulty in choosing appropriate metaphors to aid me in the exposition of my material. The previous sentence thus breaks frame with frame one and we may call this *frame two*. Technically speaking, I could be regarded as moving to *frame three* in this sentence if I were to comment on the way in which frame two text provided comment on frame one. Clearly, it is not difficult to become caught up in what may seem like an infinite arrangement of Russian dolls, given the hierarchical nature of frames. Were this a novel, as opposed to an academic text, moving between frame one and frame two could be seen as a meta-fictional tendency (see Waugh, 1984).

The reflexive deconstruction of positivist writing has been done with some degree of success and examples have now entered the stock of common academic knowledge, especially within the domain of social psychology (see Stringer, 1990; Stainton Rogers *et al.*, 1995). This leaves contemporary authors with something of a rhetorical dilemma. To adopt the scientific style without breaking frame could be interpreted as either a deliberate attempt by the author to hoodwink the reader, or as a damning show of post-modernist naiveté on the part of the writer. I now propose to examine some examples of academic writers who break frame in a self-conscious way in order to shift what Lodge (1992) refers to as the 'authorial voice' from the scientific authority figure to the meta-commentator or self-reflexive critic.

The conventions for writing academic text in *critical* psychology have not yet been fully established. Edwards and Potter (1992) provide an example of successful frame breaking when they express some of their doubts and worries as to how to report their DAM. They do this by the inclusion of what appears to be a transcript of a conversation between themselves and they place it within a box on the printed page (Edwards and Potter, 1992, Box 9, p. 155):

Derek: DAM.

Jonathan: What's the matter?

> *Derek*: No, the discursive action model. People are going to say it's not a proper model. I mean, it doesn't really tell you how things work. It's not very specific.
> *Jonathan*: You mean it's not a psychological process model? That's the point, isn't it?
> *Derek*: Well, yes, but why call it that? It's just going to annoy everybody...

That this is done somewhat self-consciously is borne out by the fact that they comment explicitly on their use of 'boxes' as a device to introduce an element of reflexivity into their writing:

> A number of these boxes address the reflexive questions which inevitably arise when writing a text full of reports, descriptions and explanations which is all about the very status of reports, descriptions, and explanations. That is, we have tried in a small way to face up to the consequences of our theory for our own practice. (Edwards and Potter, 1992, p. 11)

Graphical conventions are thus one way to carry off frame breaking. Further opportunities are provided by shifting the register in which the text is written. Stainton Rogers *et al.* (1995) engage in frame-breaking activities to a far greater extent than Edwards and Potter (1992) but they, too, have to find a way to flag this up. They adopt the device of using an interpolated interlocutor (II) who they refer to by initial as the author of their out-of-frame text. The following extract occurs where the authors introduce II. Like Edwards and Potter (1992), they also set out the frame-breaking text as a transcript of a conversation. The contributions made by II are rendered in italics.

(II) Can I interrupt for a moment?
AUTHORS: What? Who – who are you? What's going on here? We were just getting into the swing of starting our book. Authors don't expect interruptions.
(II) Allow me to introduce myself (as Mick Jagger used to sing). I call myself the 'Interpolated Interlocutor' (II for short – pronounced 'Aye-Aye') and my reason for insinuating myself into your text is to ask some

of the questions your readers may be wanting to ask themselves, but can't... (Stainton Rogers *et al.*, 1995, p. 3)

The use of the formal device of an interpolated interlocutor is an effective way to introduce an element of frame breaking into the text of the book. What I would describe as the frame two text of II has also been given a distinctive typographical code through the use of italics, lest it be confused with the primary text at frame one. But, as if this is not enough, Stainton Rogers *et al.* (1995) also switch register when operating at frame two. The 1960s reference to Mick Jagger is rich with connotations of student unrest, sit-ins, and challenges to academic authority. It has a conversational informality that would not be found in serious scientific report writing.

Armistead (1974) in *Reconstructing Social Psychology* provides a more natural way of distancing himself from the impersonal authority of the scientific author by providing autobiographical material at the start of his book. However, he sets this aside after only four sides of his introduction. I think that he began to feel the strain and acknowledged the fact that there was a limit on the extent to which he could break with the stylistic conventions of academic writing in the social sciences by saying that he had been 'self-indulgent enough as it is' (p. 10). I'm not sure that Armistead's biographical material really succeeds as a tool of deconstruction. By placing the material in a coherent block at the start of the book, it has the feel of a displaced preface; the text of the remainder of the chapter is reasonably well insulated from it.

In sum, a number of techniques have been used by critical social psychologists in order to render their academic text distinguishable from that of positivist reporting. In particular I have considered strategies based upon graphic design, the use of reflexive dialogue, shifts in the textual register and the inclusion of autobiographical material.

These rhetorical techniques serve to foster particular impressions of the author. Critical psychologists use these techniques to enable the reader to see the author as a possibly fallible human being and in this way they hope to subvert any tendency on the reader's part towards forming an impression of an objective and impersonal authority in the authorial voice. The explicit discussion of rhetoric in relation to report writing does not normally appear in positivist writing, although it could be argued that the topic is dealt with implicitly in journal style guides and undergraduate laboratory course textbooks. I believe that it is the relativist standpoint which not only informs decisions about rhetorical style in the production of text in critical psychology but also provides the foundation for many of the critiques which are generated by the discursive psychologists. Any difficulties with relativism can be expected to permeate these critiques, whether the arguments are aimed broadly at positivist psychology or are narrowly focused on particular methodological techniques such as the negotiation of accounts or the use of observation (see my discussion of Marsh *et al.*'s, 1978, research, above). I think it's time to take the bull by the horns, albeit with a deep breath and a slightly heavy heart.

Problems with relativism

I shall use Rorty (1991) in order to define and clarify what is meant by relativism and realism, since his ideas underpin Potter's (see Potter, 1996, for example). Having done this, I will examine Edwards *et al.*'s (1995) Death and Furniture paper in some detail, since this is tantamount to an explicit rebuttal of the realist arguments by the discursive psychologists.

Rorty

Rorty (1991) sees realists as wishing to ground solidarity to objectivity by construing truth as correspondence to reality. Pragmatists, on the other hand, may be distinguished from realists by the fact that they wish to reduce objectivity to solidarity. Rorty (1991) expresses it as follows:

> For pragmatists, the desire for objectivity is not the desire to escape the limitations of one's community, but simply the desire for as much intersubjective agreement as possible, the desire to extend the reference of 'us' as far as we can. (pp. 22–3)

He explains that relativism is the traditional epithet applied to pragmatism by realists even though pragmatists do not hold a positive theory about something being relative to something else. Rather, he sees truth merely as a 'commendatory term for well-justified beliefs' (pp. 23–5). At one point he uses a particularly striking metaphor:

> What we cannot do is to rise above all human communities, actual and possible. We cannot find a skyhook which lifts us out of mere coherence – mere agreement – to something like 'correspondence with reality as it is in itself'. (p. 38)

Having used Rorty (1991) to provide a sketch of realists and what I take to be relativists, I am now in a position to consider Edwards *et al.*'s (1995) Death and Furniture paper.

Death and furniture

Edwards *et al.* (1995) give their aims as follows:

> 'Death' and 'Furniture' are emblems for two very common (predictable, even) objections to relativism. When relativists talk about the social construction of reality, truth, cognition, scientific knowledge, technical capacity, social structure, and so on, their realist opponents sooner or later start hitting the furniture, invoking the Holocaust, talking about rocks, guns, killings, human misery, tables and chairs. The force of these objections is to introduce a bottom line, a bedrock of reality that places limits on what may be treated as epistemologically constructed or deconstructible. There are two related kinds of moves: Furniture (tables, rocks, stones, and so on – the reality that cannot be denied) and Death (misery, genocide, poverty, power – the reality that should not be denied). Our aim is to show how these 'but surely not this' gestures and arguments work, how they trade off one another, and how unconvincing they are, on examination, as refutations of relativism. (p. 26)

I shall sample some of their arguments and subject them to critical scrutiny. I shall start with 'furniture' and then move on to 'death'.

Furniture

Edwards *et al.* (1995) defuse the furniture argument by naming it as a device or a rhetorical construct. They note that the ease with which furniture can be apprehended makes it a relatively hard case for relativist deconstruction. They go on to encapsulate the realist's table-thumping argument in the following way:

> Show us [the challenger and the assumed audience-of-fellow-realists] how we are wrong. Show us the contingent, could-be-otherwise, socially constructed, really-not-real character of this table – if you can. (p. 29)

Edwards *et al.* (1995) accept this challenge, saying that it is surprisingly easy and even reasonable to question the table's given reality:

> It does not take long, in looking closer, at wood grain and molecule, before you are no longer looking at a 'table'. Indeed, physicists might wish to point out that, at a certain level of analysis, there is nothing at all 'solid' there, down at the (most basic?) levels of particles, strings and the contested organisation of sub-atomic space. Its solidity, then, is ineluctably a perceptual category: a matter of what tables seem to be like to us in the scale of human perception and bodily action. (p. 29)

I have to say that I do not find this response very convincing. The point about the table-thumping demonstration is to show that the hand won't go through it. Moving discussion to the molecular level could be interesting but not in the way Edwards *et al.* (1995) do so. If the discussion is to shift to the molecular level, I think the question to be addressed is why the mass of molecules which make up the hand and arm and which are bounded by the molecules of the skin can move through the air, displacing the gas molecules with ease, and yet are brought to a standstill when the system of molecules comprising the hand meets up with the system of molecules comprising the surface of the wooden table. An additional question would be what happens to the air molecules that appear to be trapped between hand and table as the hand approaches the table with speed. Specifically, the additional question might be cast in terms of how wave patterns are caused in the air which result in the auditory perception of the 'Bang' as the hand comes into contact with the table. On a technical point, I think that they have shifted modalities when attempting to make their perceptual argument. They have resorted to conventional or electronic microscopes to make the point that what looks solid may look less solid under extreme magnification. However, the key sense modalities in this demonstration seem to me to be that of proprioception and touch. There is no equivalent to (visual) magnification in these modalities.

Edwards *et al.* (1995) then proceed to attack the demonstration on the grounds that only the piece of the table beneath the hitter's hand is thumped and therefore question the fact that the rest of the table be included as solid and real. Again, I am not convinced by this. First, if the problem really is that we have to find something whose surface area is less than that of the average hand, this should not be hard to do. A fence post or a small tree stump might do but, at the risk of changing the nature of the demonstration slightly, a chicken's egg could be substituted with more spectacular dramatic and rhetorical effect. They then pose the question of how this demonstration, in the 'here and now', is supposed to stand for the table's continuing existence. Taking Edwards *et al.* (1995) at their word, one could set up the demonstration on the hour every hour, for a whole day. Maybe every Monday at noon for a year. They then ask how the demonstration is to stand in for all other tables. I suppose I could imagine the demonstration taking place in a large auction room where, lot after lot, a different table is brought in and the auctioneer/realist taps the table with the gavel. I grant the authors that this sort of demonstration could not go on for ever and that all tables could not be tested in this way.

Death

Edwards *et al.* (1995) also discuss death. One argument they advance against the realist conception of death is in terms of the difficulty of being sure as to whether various borderline states/cases may be unambiguously classified as falling into this category. They refer to the non-simultaneous criteria of brain death, the point when life support might as well be switched off, cryogenic suspension, and the precise moment of death. This reminds me of the arguments about *when is a beard not a beard*. There may well be those indefinable classes of the unshaven, the designer stubble, the closely cropped whiskers, but that does not mean that the clean-shaven face cannot be distinguished from the full and bushy beard. I do have some difficulties with their line of reasoning. For example, if my aunt died ten years ago, I would not expect to see her call round for a visit right now. I certainly do not see this as being related to questions about language and how it is used.

Edwards *et al.* (1995) then move into another line of argument. This time they talk about the social construction of death as murder, manslaughter, capital punishment, killing in war, justifiable homicide, *crime passionnel*, accident and suicide. I cannot follow the reason why this list is paraded as an objection to realism. There seem to be two separate issues: one concerns the realist view of death, as a non-linguistic or supra-linguistic state of affairs, the other how such a death might be construed in society.

In sum, I have not been convinced either by the furniture or the death arguments. I therefore move on to consider some material on language and relativism.

Language, relativism and discursive psychology

In this section I shall consider some material which is basically critical of the linguistic turn in philosophy. I shall then go on to consider the way in which the discursive psychologists distance themselves from Chomskian linguistics.

Norris, de Saussure, Dennett

Norris (1996) is an outspoken critic of relativism, postmodernism and, in general, the linguistic turn in philosophy. He feels that the linguistic turn has taken hold across numerous disciplines and that this has happened in the wake of Saussure's much-vaunted 'revolution' in the field of structural linguistics. He says:

Its chief effect, as I argue, has been to promote an outlook of far gone epistemological scepticism, joined to the cultural-relativist doctrine that questions of truth and falsehood (or right or wrong) are always internal to some specific language-game or localised 'form of life', and must therefore be judged only in accordance with their own immanent criteria. (p. x)

Because semiology is regarded as one of the foundations of contemporary discursive psychology, and because Norris (1996) identifies it as being at the heart of the linguistic turn, I will briefly consider de Saussure's position and then indicate, drawing on Dennett (1996), that the problem might not be as bad as we are led to believe.

De Saussure (1959/1966) stresses the idea that we understand the meaning of a word in language by noting what it is different from ('in language there are only differences', p. 120). He uses the following example to make this point:

> Modern French *mouton* can have the same signification as English *sheep* but not the same value, and this for several reasons, particularly because in speaking of a piece of meat ready to be served on the table, English uses *mutton* and not *sheep*. The difference in value between *sheep* and *mouton* is due to the fact that *sheep* has beside it a second term while the French word does not. (pp. 115–16, emphasis in original)

Of course, the use of 'mutton' to describe the meat on the table has largely been replaced by 'lamb' in post-war Britain. Setting this aside, I think the illustration still makes sense but it is not clear that we should be unduly worried by it. Dennett (1996) acknowledges that whenever an agent acts, the agent does so on the basis of a particular understanding or misunderstanding of the circumstances. But he stresses that all that is required is that we know at least roughly what an agent's beliefs and desires are; he denies that we necessarily need to know exactly how the agent understands the task:

> The intentional stance can usually tolerate a lot of slack, and that's a blessing, since the task of expressing exactly how the agent conceives of his task is misconceived, as pointless an exercise as reading poems in a book through a microscope. (p. 55)

Dennett's (1966) line is to reduce massively the magnitude of the problem of linguistic relativism. He does this partly by putting the difficulties of translation into perspective:

> People often emphasise the difficulty of accurate and reliable translation between human languages. Human cultures, we are told, are too different, too 'incommensurable' to permit the meanings available to one speaker to be perfectly shared with another. No doubt translation always falls short of perfection, but this may not matter in the larger scheme of things. Perfect translation may be impossible, but good translation is achieved every day – routinely, in fact. Good translation can be objectively distinguished from not-so-good translation and from bad translation, and it permits all human beings regardless of race, culture, age, gender, or experience, to unite more closely with one another than individuals of any other species can. (p. 12)

Although Dennett's remarks are addressed to the problems of translating between languages, they may also have some relevance to the difficulties of moving between language games within a given language. The notion of language games leads me directly to Wittgenstein.

Wittgenstein and discursive psychology

Norris (1996) sees Wittgenstein as one of the progenitors of the linguistic turn in philosophy, along with de Saussure. As such he may be expected to be of relevance to discursive psychology. However, his influence is not at all direct. For example, in Potter and Wetherell (1987) there are only two references to Wittgenstein in the index, neither of which involve matters of importance. In the later Edwards and Potter (1992) book, there are only four indexed references to Wittgenstein's work; three of these are passing references dealt with in a single line of text or so. The most substantive reference occurs at a point where they assert that their allegiance lies with the later Wittgenstein of the *Philosophical Investigations* where he is looking for the uses of language for constructing truth inside language games (p. 40). Potter (1996) mentions Wittgenstein in passing half-a-dozen times but without the need to cite any of his works in the bibliography.

Although my consideration of three of the most central books in the development of discursive psychology (Potter and Wetherell, 1987; Edwards and Potter, 1992; Potter, 1996) has revealed only scant influence of Wittgenstein, the link to the notion of 'language game' has been established. I shall therefore provide an assessment of Wittgenstein, drawing on the work of some of his commentators and critics, in order to bring the invocation of Wittgenstein by the discursive psychologists into perspective.

Budd (1989, p. 1) summarises Wittgenstein's understanding as to what the philosophy of psychology might be as the construction of perspicuous representations of everyday psychological concepts (this aim being achieved by the delineation of the grammar of psychological words). Rather than providing an analysis of psychological concepts in terms of bringing to light something hidden, Budd (1989) suggests that Wittgenstein proceeds merely by describing how these psychological words are used.

Grayling's (1996) appraisal of Wittgenstein indicates that if his goal was to be perspicuous, he did not succeed. Speaking of his style, he says:

> It is vatic, oracular; it consists in short remarks intended to remedy, remind, disabuse. This gives the later writings a patchwork appearance. Often the connections between remarks are unclear. There is a superabundance of metaphor and parable; there are hints, rhetorical questions, pregnant hyphenations; there is a great deal of repetition. (pp. 117–18)

I feel that the following extract from Wittgenstein (1953) might count as an example of the sort of thing that Grayling has in mind:

> 309: What is your aim in philosophy? – To shew the fly the way out of the fly-bottle. (p. 103e)

Once an overly reverential attitude towards Wittgenstein is discarded, this remark can be seen as deeply patronising by psychologists. A further example, this time of a slightly gnomic proposition, would be the opening line of the *Tractatus*: 'The world is all that is the case' (Wittgenstein, 1921/1974, p. 5).

Grayling (1996), reflecting on the unusual character of Wittgenstein's writings, finds that:

> when one advances beyond the manner and reflects on the content, the irresistible feeling is this: that the journey through Wittgenstein's circuitous, metaphorical, sometimes opaque negations and suggestions is long; but the distance it takes one is short. (p. 119)

Grayling's remarks, above, provide a deflationary comment on Wittgenstein's style and this may be no bad thing for any psychologist who is made to feel like a failed escapologist. Grayling (1996) also says that one of the reasons so few philosophers agree with Wittgenstein's basic outlook is that he overstates the case that philosophical perplexity arises from linguistic misunderstanding.

This overstatement of linguistic difficulties squares with the views of Dennett, which I discussed earlier in the chapter. This is, perhaps, a slightly different issue to the one of the coherence and correspondence theories of truth which underpin the relativist and realist positions respectively. The relativists argue that we can never escape from language; if we are not operating in one game, we will be in another. Rorty's (1991) metaphor of the skyhook (see earlier in this chapter) is apt here: there is no way that the realist can climb out of language to take a peek at the reality which lies beyond. However, the attempt to provide a theory which applies to all languages comes very close to flying; I turn to Chomsky.

Chomsky

Potter and Wetherell (1987) distance themselves from Chomsky. There are three topics which provide contrast between Chomsky's approach and discourse analysis: the competence/performance distinction, the role of the speakers' intuitions, and the importance of speakers' creativity (Potter and Wetherell, 1987, p. 10).

First, with regard to the competence/performance distinction, the underlying competence to generate grammatical sentences may be distinguished from the actual performance or production of sentences in Chomsky's theory. The rules describing the underlying competence are typically regularised, standardised and decontextualised. Potter and Wetherell (1987) flag up the possibility of circularity since Chomskian researchers typically do not check out their theories against messy ordinary talk in everyday situations.

Second, Chomsky identifies the linguistic performances which are suitable for analysis on the basis of the speaker's intuitions concerning well-formed sentences. I think that the discursive psychologists would be reluctant to take on trust the speaker's intuitions, especially if the speaker happens to be the person who produces the theory.

Third, a further problem concerns the speakers' creativity. Potter and Wetherell's (1987) interpretation of this seems to be that if speakers are so creative in their performance, then there will be massive variation in ordinary talk with many wholly unique utterances. The task of working with performance data will thus be so daunting that there will be a temptation to cut straight to the more manageable level of competence and the set of generative rules.

Putting these three aspects together, Potter and Wetherell (1987) suggest that the idealised sentences used by generative grammarians are far removed from the sort of things that can be seen in the verbatim transcripts of ordinary people in conversation. I reproduce, below, the conversation Potter and Wetherell give when making their point (from Button and Casey, 1984, in Potter and Wetherell, 1987, p. 13; I have simplified the transcription to some extent).

N: Anyway
H: =pk! Anyway
N: So
H: .p=
N: =You'll come about eight. Right?
H: =Yeah
N: =Okay
N: Anything else to report.
H: (.3)
N: Uh m:::
H: Getting my haircut tihmorrow
N: Oh rilly?

I have to admit that I read this transcription from a standpoint which is basically unsympathetic to Potter and Wetherell (1987). I don't find the interaction snippet especially difficult. It seems to me that N asks H to confirm the arrangement (H is coming at 8.00) which H duly does. N then asks H to say if there is anything else to report and H confirms that there is (the haircut plan) and N responds with interest or surprise ('Oh rilly'). I fail to see this sort of transcript material as being particularly messy, from the point of view of the psychology of action.

Chomsky seems to be working on the problem of language from a very general point of view. Writing some years after Potter and Wetherell's (1987) book, Chomsky (1996) states in his introduction to the theory of principles and parameters (written with Howard Lasnik):

> We are concerned, then, with states of the language faculty, which we understand to be some array of cognitive traits and capacities, a particular component of the human mind/brain. The language faculty has an initial state, genetically determined; in the normal course of development it passes through a series of states in early childhood, reaching a relatively stable steady state that undergoes little subsequent change, apart from the lexicon. To a good approximation, the initial state appears to be uniform for the species. Adapting traditional terms to a special usage, we call the theory of the state attained its grammar and the theory of the initial state Universal Grammar (UG)...
>
> Two fundamental problems, then, are to determine, for each individual (say Jones) the properties of the steady state that Jones' language faculty attains, and the properties of the initial state that is a common human endowment. We distinguish between Jones's competence (knowledge and understanding) and his performance (what he does with that knowledge and understanding). The steady state constitutes Jones's mature linguistic competence. (p. 14)

A theory such as Chomsky's, in order to be species specific to the human race, will need to be cast at a deep level if what it has to say is to be applicable to any *actual* language. I can see what Potter and Wetherell (1987) are getting at when they criticise Chomsky for neglecting the close reading of naturally occurring language but it is difficult to see how the minutiae of ethnographic analysis could ever be used to address inter-language theoretical concerns. Chomsky appears to be perfectly alert to the types of thing addressed by speech act theorists in terms of performance. When he says that the steady state permits infinite use of finite means, he has in mind two senses of 'infinite use'. One relates to competence and the specification in a language of an infinite range of structural descriptions (SDs); the other is concerned with performance:

> The second sense of 'infinite use' has to do with Jones's performance as he makes use of his competence to express his thoughts, to refer, to produce signals, to interpret what he hears, and so on. The language faculty is embedded in performance systems, which access the generative procedure. It is in this broader context that questions of realisation and use of SDs arise, questions of articulation, intentionality, interpretation, and the like: How does Jones say X? What is Jones talking about? What does Jones take Smith to be saying or intending to convey? And so on. We might think of the SD as providing instructions to the performance systems that enable Jones to carry out these actions. (p. 15)

Given this awareness of intentionality and attributional issues in performance, there may be some hope that there may be a way to bridge across these two rather different research paradigms at some point in the future.

Concluding remarks

The discursive psychology outlined in Potter and Wetherell (1987), Edwards and Potter (1992) and Potter (1996) embraces the relativist stance and a more direct alignment with this position is provided in Edwards *et al.* (1995). Potter, in particular, draws on the influence of the pragmatist philosopher Richard Rorty in this regard. The opposing realist perspective is consonant with the doctrine of the objective experiment which epitomises mainstream psychology. I have already intimated that the realist experimental approach does not offer a good foundation for a psychology of action and I would endorse the critique which was put forward by Harré and Secord (1972). Potter and the discursive psychologists, however, distanced themselves from the 1970s new paradigm psychology. As far as I can tell from Harré and Gillett's (1994) remarks on the first and second cognitive revolutions in psychology, Harré seems to have followed the discursive psychologists to a large degree in this regard.

The position appears to be that the 1970s new paradigm occupies a position somewhere between the realist philosophy of mainstream experimental psychology and the relativism of discursive psychology. In addressing the critique which Potter and Wetherell (1987) put forward concerning Marsh *et al.*'s (1978) ethogenic work on soccer aggro, I found myself defending the 1970s new paradigm against the discursive attack in a way that appeared to be pulling me towards a form of critical realism. Furthermore, I was not especially convinced by Edwards *et al.*'s (1995) treatment of the realist bottom-line death and furniture arguments.

Norris (1996) sees the widespread trend towards sceptical or relativist philosophies of science as assimilating truth to the shifting currency of in-place consensus belief. However, he points out that such views have their opponents:

> The challenge has come from various quarters, among them the Critical Realist school of thought whose chief proponent is Roy Bhaskar, himself much influenced by the work of Rom Harré. Central to their case is a 'stratified' conception of reality, knowledge and human interests where distinctions may be drawn between, on the one hand, a realm of 'intransitive' objects, processes and events – that is those that must be taken to exist independently of human conceptualisation – and on the other hand a 'transitive' realm of knowledge-constitutive interests which are properly subject to critical assessment in terms of their ethical and socio-political character. (p. 162)

Norris makes the connection between Harré and Bhaskar. Norris also draws on Kant, which is something he shares with the early Harré. The influence of Kant upon Harré is perhaps nowhere more apparent than in his discussion of the relevance of the spatio-temporal matrix for an understanding of personal being (Harré, 1983); in this there seem to be striking parallels with Kant's (1781/1993) treatment of the transcendental aesthetic in the *Critique of Pure Reason*. The similarity between Norris and Harré cannot be pushed too far; Harré also draws positively from Wittgenstein, whereas Norris attacks him for his part in the 'linguistic turn' in philosophy.

Returning to the above quotation, Bhaskar's (1989) critical realist stance would enable me to resolve some of the problems raised by Edwards *et al.*'s (1995) relativist interpretation of death. From the critical realist perspective, the death of someone might be construed as an 'intransitive' event (in terms of blood and guts on the pavement, for example), while leaving open the possibility of understanding their death (in terms of suicide or murder, for example) at the 'transitive' level.

In sum, I move ahead unashamedly retaining much from the 1970s new paradigm in social psychology, having considered and rejected many of the criticisms advanced by the discursive psychologists. I find myself aligned more to a critical realist stance than to the relativism of Rorty or Potter. I am happy for both the negotiation of accounts and for observational techniques to be associated with research into the psychology of action. I have no problem with using creative analogy, dramaturgical or otherwise. I am not averse to modelling or metaphor in the construction of theory. I regard neither speech act theory nor ethnomethodology as the sole province of discursive psychology, and can see much in both these domains that may be of use in the psychology of action. I feel happy to examine social action for its rhetorical aspects as and when the need arises, but I do not feel that rhetorical considerations necessarily exhaust what is interesting about action. On this positive footing I therefore move on, in the next chapter, to examine some more theories of action with close ties to the positivist paradigm. I shall start by revisiting Bandura's (1977) theory of self-efficacy (briefly considered in Chapter 2) before proceeding to a consideration of the concept of plan.

Chapter 4
The concept of plan in mainstream psychology

I shall start by tracing the origins of Bandura's ideas back to his 1960s social learning theory and then on to the work of Rotter in the mid-1950s. It would be a mistake to interpret this as an excursion into the archaeology of knowledge. My approach is conventionally modernist: closer to Sherlock Holmes than to Foucault.

One of the delights about tracing the origins of theoretical ideas is that the roots so often contain surprises. For example, in the previous chapters I have gone to some lengths to indicate the paradigmatic fissures that have opened up over the past two or three decades within social psychology. With Tolman and Lewin, I shall have time-travelled to a period which antedates the so-called crisis in social psychology. It is possible to find, in their work, ideas which fit into both sides of the contemporary paradigmatic divide. In a sense, I am writing this book against the intolerance expressed by the insiders of particular schools of thought towards their paradigmatic outsiders; a phenomenon rife in both camps, I feel (see Chapter 10 for a discussion of eclecticism). Towards the end of the chapter, I shall return to the present by considering some of the review literature covering contemporary research into plans and goal setting.

Efficacy, expectancy, and value

In Chapter 2, I swept Bandura's SET under the carpet by subsuming it within the perceived behavioural control component of Ajzen's TPB. Here, I shall deal with his ideas more directly, starting with a consideration of his social cognitive theory (SCT) before tackling the SET and social learning theory (SLT). This will be my route back to the work of Rotter.

Bandura's social cognitive theory (SCT)

In Bandura's (1997, 1986) SCT human agency is pinned to an interdependent structure involving *triadic reciprocal causation* (see Figure 4.1). Triadic reciprocal causation is one of those terms that roars like a lion but, to slur my metaphor from cat to dog, its bark may be worse than its bite. Bandura uses the term 'causation' to mean functional dependence between events. He lists the three major classes of the determinants as behaviour, internal personal factors (including cognitive, affective and biological events) and the external environment. Not much would appear to be left out by this structure; I find it reminiscent of Lewin's (1936/1966) definition of the life space as being the totality of possible events (I discuss Lewin's work later in this chapter).

However, the question of the clarity of the model must hinge on how the notion of causation is cashed out. I find it useful to draw on the concept of the 'null hypothesis' as an analogy for understanding the SCT. What Bandura (1997) says about causation is tantamount to a description of a null model (in a similar sense to that of a null hypothesis). All the causal links within the triad are regarded as reciprocal. There is no assumption that

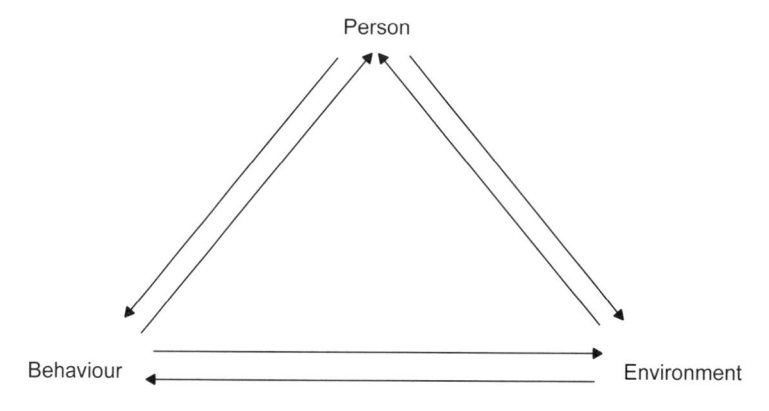

Figure 4.1 Bandura's (1997) triadic reciprocal causation

these reciprocal causal forces are of equal strength. The impression is given that causation may go *any* way, with *any* thing, at *any* time. Under such circumstances it seems to me to stretch things a little too far by insisting there is a causal model in operation. It could be argued that Bandura (1997) has merely provided a rather conventional classification for all the possible phenomena that one might find in a Lewinian life space.

Drawing on the work of Giddens (1984), Bandura (1997) reaches out to a more sociological interpretation of agency than might be expected from a psychologist. Thus he sees people as both producers and products of social systems. He sees social structures in terms of human beings occupying designated roles from which they carry out the authorised social practices of their society. Such individuals interact with others who may seek to change these practices. Endorsing Giddens' (1984) position, he sees this is as a fluid and dynamic system which avoids sharp distinctions between individual and society and resists the dualism between social structure and personal agency. SCT also embraces the view that human agency may be extended to the collective. The way in which Bandura (1997) construes this (as an emergent property of groups) brings him close to a Gestalt perspective, although this is not explicitly stated in his writing. The way he introduces the concept of collective agency resonates with other contemporary writers in this field. With regard to the 1970s new paradigm (see Chapter 1), the issue of collective agency was discussed by Harré (1979), for example. A slightly different perspective, drawing on actor network theory, is brought to bear on collective agency by Fuller (1994) who argues that the more people that have agency within a given collective or group, the less each individual can have of it (in this fashion it is construed as something of a scarce good, in the economic sense).

Bandura (1997) also puts forward some interesting ideas on freedom which he defines positively as 'the exercise of self-influence to bring about desired results' (p. 7). By this he does not merely pass agency to thought. He states that agent causation involves 'the ability to behave differently from what environmental forces dictate rather than inevitably yield to them' (p. 7).

The rhetoric of SCT brings with it mixed messages. On the one hand, the talk of agency belongs to the new paradigm. On the other hand, the talk of reciprocal triadic causation feels closer to positivism. I propose to explore the historical origins of the SCT in the hope that this will remove some of the ambiguity.

Bandura's self-efficacy theory (SET)

Bandura (1977) put forward the SET in the context of therapeutic trials which were being carried out at that time with the aim of improving treatments for people suffering from snake phobias. It was hypothesised that therapeutic success would be a function of the extent to which the level and strength of self-efficacy was altered for the better. The clinical trials were successful and the findings supported the hypothesised relationship between perceived self-efficacy and pertinent behavioural changes.

In the introductory sections of Bandura (1977) it is possible to trace the links back to social learning theory (SLT). He claims that 'because acquisition of response information is a major aspect of learning, much human behaviour is developed through modelling' (p. 192). However, responses learned observationally are then later refined through self-corrective adjustments based on feedback from performance. This is where cognition begins to play a major part, as the effects of one's own behaviour are learned and translated into cognitive representations of the contingencies:

> Reinterpretation of antecedent determinants as predictive cues, rather than as controlling stimuli, has shifted the locus of the regulation of behavior from the stimulus to the individual. (p. 192)

The estimation of the subjective probabilities of the occurrence of the consequences of action provides a direct link between the TRA and SLT. This is not to suggest that the TRA was the inspiration for SLT, or vice versa. Neither are the origins of the SLT present, in any obvious sense, in the classic Bandura *et al.* (1961) bobo doll study, even though this paper did provide a demonstration of the importance of modelling in the learning process. It is in the slightly later text of Bandura and Walters (1963) that a more explicit discussion of the origins of SLT appears:

According to Rotter's social-learning theory (1954/1973), for example, the probability of the occurrence of a given behavior in a particular situation is determined by two variables – the subjectively held probability (expectancy) that the behaviour in question will be reinforced and the value of the reinforcer to the subject. (p. 2)

The contribution of Bandura and Walters (1963) to theoretical development was the insistence that SLT must take into account the role of vicarious reinforcement. In other words, the probability that a particular consequence (positive or negative) will flow from an action may be learned by observing what happens to someone else, and not necessarily by experiencing the consequence directly.

While I acknowledge that a strict reading of Rotter's theoretical equations may give the impression that he takes no formal account of vicarious learning, I feel that Bandura does him something of an injustice on this count. For example, Rotter (1954/1973) discusses the problems facing the psychotherapist when the patient does not himself display the behaviour that the therapist might directly reinforce. He comments on the fact that Luchins (1942) demonstrated that one can draw a person's attention to cues which were previously present, but not attended to, using verbal techniques. In this way, the need for direct experience is obviated. Rotter (1954/1973) goes on to say:

> Similarly, the therapist can direct the patient's attention to the relationship between the behavior of others and the gratifications or subsequent rewards that others obtain. Sometimes that has been accomplished merely by the patient being placed in a situation where he can observe these relationships or have an opportunity to observe that he may not have had before. (p. 340)

Rotter would here appear to be anticipating the design of Bandura et al.'s (1961) study by several years. Rotter acknowledges that expectancies of positive consequences created through therapeutic discourse will not be as high as those where the patient attempts the behaviour in their own life situation and is reinforced by someone important to them. But the importance of the therapeutic discourse lies partly in the way it may act to improve the patient's abilities in creative problem solving. It is at this point that Rotter (1954/1973) may be seen not only to have anticipated Bandura's social learning theory but also Bandura's theory of self-efficacy:

> It is the purpose of therapy not to solve all of the patient's problems, but rather to increase the patient's ability to solve his own problems. (Rotter, 1954/1973, p. 342)

If the patients' problem is that they are afraid of snakes, and the result of therapy is for the patients to have an increased ability to solve this problem, then they presumably have increased their self-efficacy.

I now wish to pursue the link between Rotter's theoretical ideas and the expectancy-value model of action (I have already discussed a contemporary version of this, in the form of the TRA, in Chapter 2). I shall therefore leave Bandura's work to one side.

Rotter and the expectancy-value model

Rotter (1954/1973) presents his social learning theory of personality in formal fashion setting out numbered postulates and corollaries. In passing, it may be noted how different this rhetorical style is to that of the contemporary critical and discursive psychologists I discussed in Chapter 3. It would appear that there was a preference for this formal, almost mathematical style in the 1950s, since a very similar format was adopted in the expression of personal construct theory (see Kelly, 1955; Bannister and Fransella, 1971). The similarity to personal construct theory does not stop at the superficial level of rhetorical strategy; the term 'construct' is also given a formal definition at the start of the exposition of Rotter's (1954/1973) theory:

> A construct is a term that represents an attempt to abstract the nature of an event or events. It is dependent upon the orientation, the point of view, or problem of the observer as well as upon the 'real' nature of the event; and although an adequate construct is a function of the event, it never corresponds exactly to the event. Since there is no way of determining the correspondence of the construct to the event or events it seeks to represent, constructs may be evaluated only in pragmatic terms (that is usefulness in prediction). (p. 85)

Rotter's (1954/1973, p. 85) definition of an event as 'anything that has a locus in space and time' is similar to Harré and Secord's (1972) definition of an episode. The remarks Rotter makes about the difficulty in determining the correspondence of construct to event are very similar to those that Harré and Secord (1972) make concerning the negotiation of accounts. Rotter's (1954/1973) solution is, independently, that advocated by the pragmatist philosopher Richard Rorty and taken up enthusiastically by the discursive psychologist Jonathan Potter. It is interesting that in tracing Bandura's influences back to Rotter I have stumbled upon some conceptual similarities with the ethogenic and discursive psychologists introduced in Chapters 1 and 3.

Returning to Rotter's (1954/1973) theory, I do not intend to go through all the postulates and corollaries; I focus on those that are of most relevance to the psychology of action. In this regard, I start with the seventh and final postulate:

> The occurrence of a behaviour of a person is determined by the nature or importance of goals or reinforcements but also by the person's anticipation or expectancy that these goals will occur. Such expectations are determined by previous experience and can be quantified. (Rotter, 1954/1973, pp. 102–3)

The seventh postulate seems to anticipate the kernel of the TRA. It even anticipates some of the suggestions that have subsequently been made for improvements to the basic model of the TRA, such as those designed to take into account prior behaviour (for example Bentler and Speckart, 1979).

Rotter's third postulate enables me to provide a bridge between Rotter and Harré's middle period. By this I have in mind Harré's work on personal being (Harré, 1983) where he appeared to be moving away from the rather rigid role–rule models of his earlier ethogenic phase, but had not yet moved wholeheartedly into the discursive camp. The link between Rotter (1954/1973) and Harré (1983) may be discerned from the following:

> Behaviour as described by personality constructs takes place in space and time. Although all such events may be described by psychological constructs, it is presumed that they may also be

described by physical constructs as they are in such fields as physics, chemistry and neurology. Any conception that regards the events themselves, rather than the description of the events, as different is rejected as dualistic. (Rotter, (1954/1973, p. 90)

Harré (1983) was also at pains to move away from Cartesian dualism and he achieved this by offering a dualism between persons and selves, as an alternative to mind and body. He spoke of the spatio-temporal matrix as offering the backdrop against which the psychological reality of persons-in-conversation took place. I have always thought of Harré's ideas on autobiographical research (see De Waele and Harré, 1979) as an exercise in revealing the traces left by persons as they traverse the spatio-temporal matrix and in this regard he shares some common ground with Rotter.

Rotter provides a further contemporary edge in his first postulate:

> The unit of investigation for the study of personality is the interaction of the individual and his meaningful environment. (Rotter, 1954/1973, p. 85)

While this establishes Rotter's debt to Lewin's (1936/1966) field theory, it also provides some evidence that Rotter held hermeneutical predilections. Although he would appear to be an operator within the language game of learning theory, his first postulate places him some considerable distance from the position occupied by Watson, for example (whose stance I summarised in Chapter 1). Interestingly, it is much later that hermeneutics is brought to the fore in psychology by Gauld and Shotter (1977). I have already explained that meaning lies at the heart of Harré and Secord's (1972) new paradigm social psychology (see Chapter 1).

Apart from having an expectancy-value-based learning theory, Rotter also developed ideas concerning the internal or external locus of control for one's behaviour. Rotter (1966) defines internal–external locus of control in the following way:

> an event regarded by some persons as a reward or reinforcement may be differently perceived and reacted to by others. One of the determinants of this reaction is the degree to which the individual

perceives that the reward follows from, or is contingent upon, his own behavior or attributes versus the degree to which he feels the reward is controlled by forces outside of himself and may occur independently of his own actions. (p. 1)

The concept of an internal–external locus of control belongs to Rotter only in the sense that he devised a psychometric scale to measure a person's position along the continuum. The concept itself has wider application. In Chapter 1, I spoke of the distinction made in the philosophy of action between agents and patients, between what people do and what happens to them. Within psychology, attribution theorists (see, for example, Jones and Davis, 1965; Kelley, 1967) make the distinction between internal and external causal attributions. The difference between Rotter's theoretical position and that of the attribution theorists is primarily one of perspective. It is the view of the protagonist that is important for locus of control whereas it is the view of the observer which takes precedence in attribution theory.

In many ways, Rotter (1954/1973) comes across as a man ahead of his time. For example, he endorses the view that the reification of concepts results in wasted effort in terms of learning theory research, and in this sense he could almost pass for a 1990s discursive psychologist.

> As psychologists... we can choose to study different aspects of behavior and then use terms, words, or constructs to represent what we perceive. The aspect of the behavior we choose to abstract, however, is not a separate part of the subject's action, nor is it some entity within the individual. The words are distinct and different from the event. The question is not 'does this word truly describe the event,' but 'Is this construct a useful or valuable way to attempt to describe or explain some abstraction from the subject's behavior?' (p. 37)

Rotter's interest in the misuse of words by psychologists in their representation of behaviour is evocative of Wittgenstein; the reluctance to see language as a window on reality is something he has in common with Potter and Rorty.

Two figures cited as positive influences in Rotter's (1954/1973) work are Tolman and Lewin. There are a number of similarities between Tolman and Lewin which make the fact that both influenced Rotter understandable. I shall take Tolman first and then move on to consider Lewin. This will then lead me on to the classic work on plans and the structure of behaviour from Miller *et al.* (1960).

Tolman's means–end beliefs in the immediate behaviour space

In Tolman's (1951) model of action the dependent variable (of behaviour or action) is linked to the independent variables indirectly via the intervening variables. Tolman groups the independent variables into three sets: physiological (heredity, age, sex, drugs, endocrines and so on), conditions of drive arousal or satiation, and the stimulus situation (environmental entities presented to the actor at the given moment). It is the intervening variables that give Tolman's model its distinctive feel.

The immediate behavioural space takes centre stage in Tolman's representation of action; it is a concept closely tied to Lewin's (1936/1966) topological psychology, as can be seen from the fact that behaviour is said to arise from locomotion through this space. The immediate behavioural space takes input from both the stimulus situation and the need system, the latter also being affected by the conditions of drive arousal. However, the picture is a little more complicated than that since both the need system and the stimulus situation provide input to the belief–value matrix which, in turn, also has an input to the immediate behaviour space.

It is Tolman's (1951) belief–value matrix which is particularly germane to the concerns of this book. The idea of a belief–value matrix can be traced through to Rotter's work and on to the theory of reasoned action put forward by Fishbein and Ajzen (1975), discussed in Chapter 2. Tolman demonstrates how the matrix operates using the example of someone going to a restaurant. Interestingly, this particular illustration resurfaces a quarter of a century later in Schank and Abelson's (1977) work on scripts and plans in the context of artificial intelligence programming.

Tolman's (1951) diagrammatic representations of the belief–value matrix are somewhat idiosyncratic and they are visually very 'busy'. Indeed, from the perspective of the 1990s, the diagrams of both Lewin and Tolman might be dismissed at first glance as eccentric blueprints for strange inventions in the Heath Robinson mould. No doubt they were more closely in tune with the academic rhetorical style of the 1930s. I particularly like Tolman's lassos and corkscrews (the nomenclature suggesting that the electronic circuit diagram was not the source of his inspiration). In order to simplify the exposition of Tolman's belief matrix diagrams, I shall build up one of these matrices, adding in one 'belief lasso' at a time. I shall base my example on Tolman's (1951, pp. 291–4) figures, although I have rotated them through 90° for what I believe to be greater ease of viewing.

In Figure 4.2 the fork of the belief lasso covers the location of hunger deprivation in the need system and then loops down to capture a number of possible restaurants. The squares or cells represent abstract images of objects, not actual concrete objects, and they may be given a value. For Tolman, the lassos represent means–end beliefs and, as such, may be regarded as equivalent to the beliefs in the attitude component of the TRA. In Figure 4.3, I have brought in the next level of the matrix and this involves a lasso which covers a range of restaurants and links them to a set of possible foods. The final lasso in Figure 4.4 takes the action from foods to hunger gratification. As one moves through the action, from layer to layer, a particular behaviour is necessary for locomotion through the immediate behaviour space to take place: *searching* (for the chosen restaurant); *spending* (to obtain the ordered food); *eating* (to gratify the hunger and thus reach the goal state). Tolman acknowledges that while his lassos capture the notion of means–end belief, the cells of the matrix need to be tagged with an evaluation. When this is done (using plus and minus signs in Tolman's scheme) the matrix appears to match not only the belief but also the evaluation components in the TRA. The degree of mapping between the two models is, however, rather superficial.

It may be useful to think about where Tolman is going with his model. He sums up by focusing on the definition of a locomotion:

> To summarize, a locomotion is a *selection* from one or more perceived immediately possible behaviors (that is, the region in which the behaving self is initially located) *as the way to* get to such-

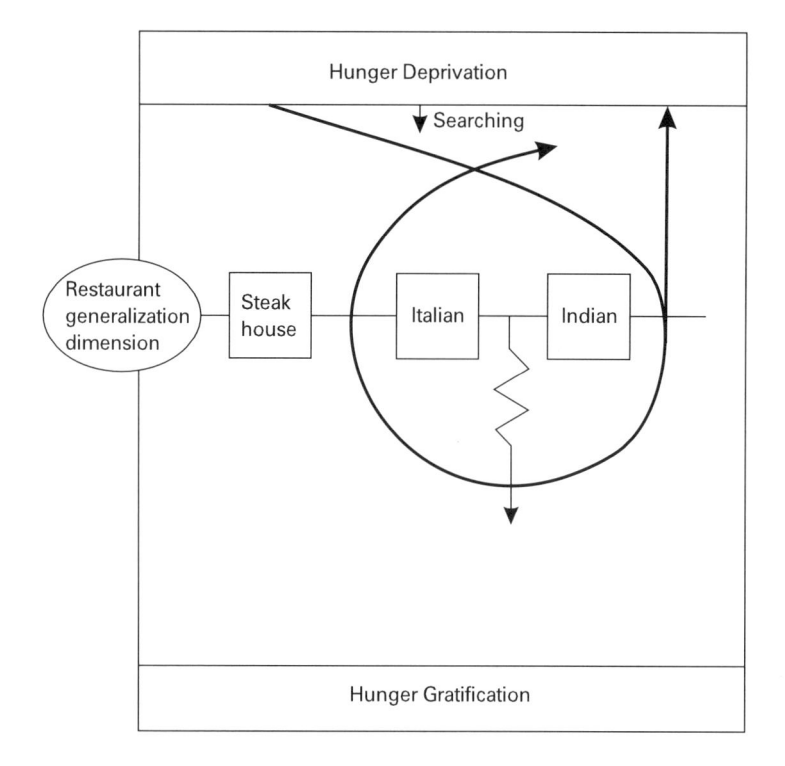

Figure 4.2 A Tolman belief lasso for restaurants

and-such other potentially possible behaviors (the region to which the behaving self is locomoting). A locomotion in the behavior space is thus not a behavior itself but a selection or a series of selections which *result* in a behavior or in behaviors. (p. 300, emphasis in the original)

The above summary suggests two ways in which Tolman's model differs in a matter of emphasis from the TRA/TPB. First, it highlights selection from a range of possible behaviours whereas the TRA is concerned with the formulation of an intention (to act or not to act) with regard to the particular behaviour in question. In terms of the restaurant illustration, the TRA might focus on a trip to the 'Floating Pizza' restaurant and the cost and anticipated gustatory delights of the various foods might be seen as consequences in the TRA equation. Thus the

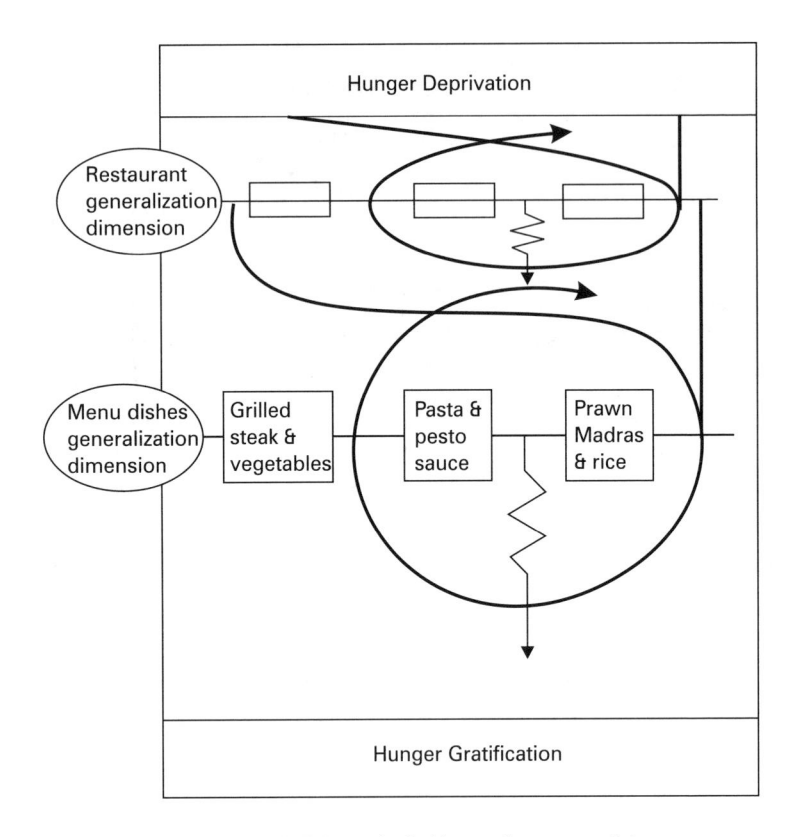

Figure 4.3 A Tolman belief lasso for menu dishes

TRA cannot be seen as identical to Tolman's model in this regard. Second, I feel that Tolman places more emphasis on the means (the way to get from one level in the action plan to another) than happens in the TRA. The extension of the TRA to the TPB appears to bring means–end questions to the fore but does so only in the rather negative sense of ruling out what Tolman would describe as 'locomotions' where the degree of freedom to act is impaired. In my view, the strength of Tolman's model is to highlight the executive facet of action and its relation to the individual's system of beliefs and values. This is something that hovers somewhat in the background in the TRA/TPB.

Tolman does entertain the notion that a set of modal values could obtain for a particular matrix and that this would provide

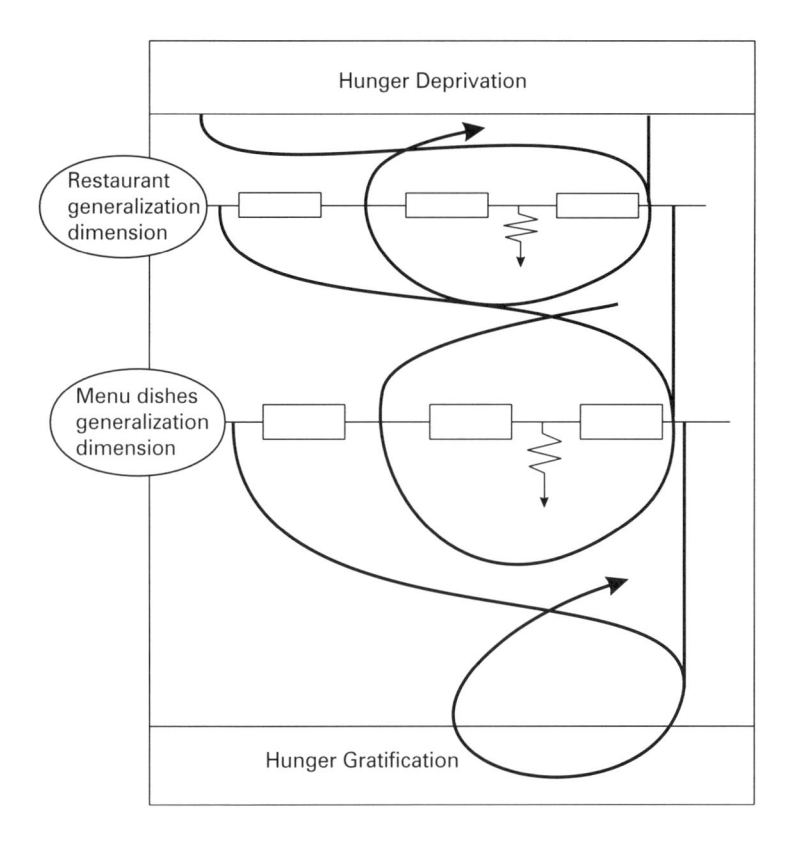

Figure 4.4 Tolman belief lassos from hunger deprivation to gratification

a representation of a culturally and sociologically determined belief–value system as shared by a community of individuals. This begins to sound not too dissimilar from a symbolic interactionist stance (see Denzin, 1995, for an account of the symbolic interactionist tradition in the context of critical social psychology). Of course, the notion of quantifiable modal expectancy-value matrices is not something that is likely to cheer the symbolic interactionist's heart, and I will leave this speculative link dangling.

Tolman talks about obtaining questionnaire data from which a picture of the modal belief–value matrices for particular cultural groups could be obtained. He even gives some examples of the sorts of question that might be asked:

What kinds of food do you like? Name six varieties of food in order of preference. What do you like about each of these six? For each of these six foods what types of restaurant would you go to and in what order? List all the considerations you would take into account in choosing the one kind of restaurant or the other. (p. 295)

While Tolman (1951) might be regarded as anticipating the sorts of things the contemporary market researcher might do in focus groups, this is not something that would be entertained by the discursive psychologists. There is generally an abhorrence of gross generalisation in discursive psychology, which is seen to lack contextual sensitivity. This is not to say that focus groups could not be subjected to discourse analysis; such data fit the method like hand and glove. However, were focus group data to be analysed discursively it is the speech acts contained within the data that would be the target of the analysis; the goal of constructing a modal belief–value matrix would form no part of the discursive agenda.

Returning to Tolman's restaurant example, it is easy to see how his model could be used in the monitoring of changes in cultural taste. A modal matrix for the British gustatory experience could be used to reflect the massive shift away from the ubiquitous 'fish and chip shop' culture of 1950s Britain to the near universal endorsement of Indian, Chinese, Italian and American fast food outlets in the 1990s, for example.

Another very interesting idea that Tolman puts forward is that of the modal matrix for an individual:

It may be drawn, that is, to represent not the actual momentary absolute magnitudes of the values, the beliefs, and the categorizations, but rather their average or modal magnitudes relative to one another. In other words, a matrix may be drawn to represent merely an equation in which specific absolute magnitudes have not yet been substituted. When a matrix is so drawn, the absolute magnitudes on any specific occasion will be arrived at by the substitution in this matrix equation of the then-and-there absolute magnitudes of the attached need or needs and of the specific stimulus situation. (p. 295)

I find the notion of an individual's modal matrix interesting in the context of an objection that is sometimes raised against conventional attitude theory by discursive psychologists. The argument runs along the lines that variation in the expression of values can often be observed to occur within the discourse of particular individuals at different times within a conversation and between different conversations. This should not be the case if attitudes are, like personality traits, stable over time. If Tolman's model is taken on board, then some degree of variation should be not only tolerated but expected and the discursive objection becomes less threatening.

My search for material which may be said to have influenced the contemporary approach to the psychology of action, as embodied by the TRA/TPB and the SET, took me to the work of Rotter and from thence to Tolman. Both Rotter and Tolman take notice of, and would appear to be influenced by, Lewin's topological psychology and I now move on to consider his work.

Lewin's topological model

Lewin (1936/1966) starts from the position that one can 'hope to understand the forces that govern behavior only if one includes in the representation the whole psychological situation' (p. 12). The approach to representation adopted by Lewin is to use topological diagrams. He makes the point that in general the methods of psychology have encouraged classification and descriptive summaries using statistical methods, and that only in clinical case studies does one usually find a more concrete description of the psychological environment. He goes on to suggest that the case study approach has much in common with a literary approach and holds up writers such as Dostoevski as providing descriptions of how the different facets of an individual's environment are related to one another and to the persons themselves. Lewin argues that 'if psychology is to make predictions about behavior, it must try to accomplish this same task by conceptual means' (p. 13). In other words, Lewin is not advocating that psychologists become novelists, but that they share some of the novelist's orientation to the treatment of individuals within the life space as a whole, using an abstract conceptual scheme which must be developed or adapted for the purpose. In this, Lewin's ideas can be seen to anticipate some of those in the critical social psychology of the 1990s. For example, Murray

(1995) describes 'narrative psychology' as a new field of research which extends the narratological study of how stories work into extra-literary domains. Murray (1995) points to Frye's (1957) schemes for the analysis of western literature as providing useful tools of analysis (schemes based on the four *mythoi* of romance, comedy, tragedy and satire, for example). Apart from Murray's work, approximately one third of Shotter and Gergen's (1989) *Texts of Identity* is devoted to a consideration of drama and narrative in the construction of identities. It would therefore be a mistake to think that Lewin's work was only of relevance to the expectancy-value models when considering contemporary approaches to the psychology of action.

Towards the end of his exposition of topological psychology, Lewin (1936/1966) discusses the problem he faces in distinguishing degrees of reality or, as he puts it in the opposite direction, degrees of irreality:

> A daydream, a vague hope, has in general less reality than an action; an action sometimes has more reality than speech; a perception more than an image; a faraway 'ideal goal' is less real than a 'real goal' that determines one's immediate action. (p. 196)

I indicated in Chapter 3 that Potter and Rorty argue that it is impossible for language to provide a window on reality. This is not Lewin's concern. He uses not language but topology as his model for reality. His position does involve an acceptance of objective physical reality but he then wants to move away from this through shades of grey, as it were, into the realm of fantasy. He represents these degrees of irreality in the third dimension of his models; two-dimensional depictions of the life space are thus stacked like pancakes with the bottom one firmly planted in the real world and the top in the land of make-believe.

The daydreams and vague hopes to which Lewin refers (in the above quotation) may come to nothing unless sharpened into closer alignment with tangible, achievable goals in mundane reality; the concept of plan is tailor made to cover such transition.

Plans

I start with the classic treatment of the topic provided by Miller *et al.* (1960) and then examine the way the concept of plan, along with that of script, was used in 1970s natural language programming. I then pick up the trail back to the present by considering goal-setting theory and, finally, some of the current work on plans, valence and goals.

Miller, Gallanter and Pribram

Miller *et al.* (1960) start by rejecting the classic concept of the reflex arc as the fundamental pattern for the organisation of all behaviour and their position is not that dissimilar to the opposition to stimulus–response psychology that I have already outlined in Chapter 1. They agree with Tolman that a concept is required to fill a gap between stimulus and response but feel that he fails to go far enough towards an account of action. The concept that they feel will capture the hierarchical organisation of behaviour and its representation (as a set of goals and subgoals which exist simultaneously at the molar and molecular level of description) is the concept of plan. This they define as follows:

> A Plan is any hierarchical process in the organism that can control the order in which a sequence of operations is to be performed. (p. 16)

Miller *et al.* (1960) declare an interest in the execution of plans and how this works. They see strategies as being concerned with the molar units in the organisation of behaviour, with tactics relating to the molecular level. The individual's knowledge of his or her life world, including the knowledge of plans, is termed the 'image'. I feel that this term has something in common with Lewin's *life space* and Tolman's *immediate behaviour space* and it serves to emphasise the cognitive facets of Miller *et al.*'s (1960) approach. Indeed, they say that the central problem of their book is 'to explore the relation between the Image and the Plan' (p. 18).

Perhaps their most famous contribution to this area was the articulation of a cybernetic feedback loop to describe what happens in the execution of a plan. They called this the TOTE unit, an acronym for *Test Operate Test Exit*. By way of illustration, I have drawn a simple TOTE unit for ironing a pile of clothes, in Figure 4.5. It is normally possible to express a TOTE unit algorithmically using one of the conventional control structures found in computer programming languages, such as Basic or Perl (a *do ... while* loop or something of that nature would do the trick).

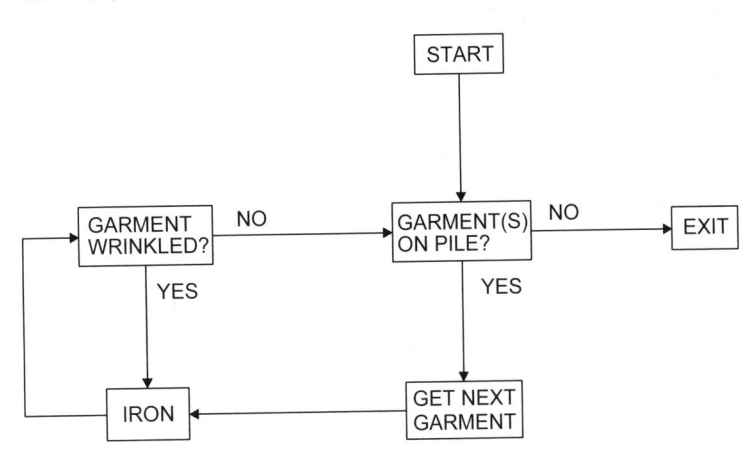

```
                    ┌───────┐
                    │ START │
                    └───┬───┘
                        │
                        ▼
  ┌──────────┐  NO  ┌────────────┐  NO   ┌──────┐
  │ GARMENT  │◄─────│ GARMENT(S) │──────►│ EXIT │
  │ WRINKLED?│      │  ON PILE?  │       └──────┘
  └────┬─────┘      └──────┬─────┘
       │ YES               │ YES
       ▼                   ▼
    ┌──────┐         ┌──────────┐
    │ IRON │◄────────│ GET NEXT │
    └──────┘         │ GARMENT  │
                     └──────────┘
```

Figure 4.5   TOTE unit for ironing clothes

As mentioned, the TOTE unit fills the gap between idea and behaviour for Miller *et al.* (1960). However, there are more things to consider in the representation of plans of action than TOTE units. A slightly richer model for the representation of states, goals, and the actions required to move from one state to the other is provided by Abelson's (1973) molecular metaphor.

Schank and Abelson's program for scripts and plans

Some forty years has passed since the publication of Miller *et al.*'s (1960) classic book on plans and that may be regarded as a very long time in the recent history of computing. A sense of just how long ago this was is provided by the fact that Miller *et al.*

(1960) were able to state in a footnote that John McCarthy had developed LISP at Massachusetts Institute of Technology but that the new programming language had not been published at that time (one of the important languages for artificial intelligence programming). Some twenty five years ago, Schank and Abelson (1977) attempted to merge a social psychological approach with artificial intelligence programming by concentrating on social scripts, plans and goals. They wrote computer programs to cope with talk and action within limited domains such as the restaurant. Their restaurant script was based upon the use of roles (customer, waiter, cook, cashier, owner) and it incorporated a number of standard props (tables, menu and so on). The script also broke the restaurant episode down into four scenes (entering, ordering, eating and exiting).

One of the reasons that I found Schank and Abelson's (1977) work so interesting was because they were using concepts which were at the heart of the dramaturgical approach developed by Goffman (1959) and endorsed by the ethogenic social psychology of Harré and Secord (1972). Although Schank and Abelson (1977) make no special mention of Miller *et al.*'s (1960) work, the latter do anticipate both natural language processing and the definition of role, based on the concept of plan. Abelson (1973) had already published a model for the representation of plans based upon a loose analogy with the way chemical molecules or atoms are represented on paper. In this it is shown how initial states may be linked to subsequent states and goals via the actions necessary to achieve them. This scheme does allow a number of useful aspects in the execution of action to be depicted in a clear fashion, (negative gating or the presence of enabling conditions, for example – see Chapter 2, also). A more complex approach to the representation of plans, using symbolic techniques which have a closer link to computer programming, is provided in Ableson (1975).

It is difficult to trace the successors of the early restaurant scripts in the 1990s. My impression (and I hasten to add that I have not worked in artificial intelligence or natural language programming) is that the large domain-specific programs do little once the excitement of the initial demonstrations that they work are over and done with. This is very different from the dynamic character of artificial neural networks which, once written, not only thrive on being given lots of data but modify their parameters in the light of this experience. The whole point about neural networks is that they can 'learn' to adjust to an optimal performance on the basis of the data fed to them. By comparison, the natural language approach produces programs (such as the restaurant script) which look huge, monolithic and static. Insofar as society evolves and changes, one could argue that programs like the restaurant script have a built-in predisposition to obsolescence from the moment they are completed.

For the moment I shall leave the link with artificial intelligence to one side, since I wish to examine the extent to which a research interest in goal-directed behaviour has survived into the 1990s, given the promising start made by Miller *et al.* (1960). My aim is not to provide a comprehensive review, but merely to furnish a sense of what is happening in this area of research. I will begin by giving a brief summary of the work on Locke and Latham's (1990) goal-setting theory.

Current work on plans, valence and goals

Locke and Latham's (1990) theory of goal setting has been developed mainly in the domain of industrial psychology and organisational behaviour, with Taylor's (1911/1967) approach to scientific management being cited as an important historical influence. Bandura, in a foreword to the Locke and Latham (1990) book, praised the way they give prominence to motivational functions in their attempt to link cognition to action. Locke and Latham (1990), in their Preface, reject both behaviourism and psychoanalysis as possible candidates for providing an explanation of human action on the grounds that:

> They [behaviourism and psychoanalysis] agree that people are not rational beings in that their thinking does not in any fundamental sense regulate their choices and actions. (p. xiv)

They would thus appear to be closely aligned to the TRA/TPB in their general orientation.

At the heart of goal-setting theory lies the assertion that 'there is a linear relationship between degree of goal difficulty and performance' (Locke and Latham, 1990, p. 27). This means that until a person reaches the limits of his or her ability at high goal difficulty levels (where the function levels off), the more difficult the goal, the better will be performance. Locke and Latham (1990), reviewing the research literature, indicate that approximately 90 per cent of some 175 studies provide supporting evidence for this linear function. They suggest that this may be explained by the fact that hard goals lead to greater effort and persistence than easy goals (p. 29).

A second finding is that goals that are specific and difficult lead to a higher level of performance than vague, non-quantitative goals such as 'do your best', or no assigned goals (which Locke and Latham interpret as being an implicit 'do best' condition). Their review indicates that approximately 90 per cent of some 200 empirical studies support the superiority of 'specific, hard' goals over 'do best' goals. They summarise the reasons for this by stating that specific, hard goals (as opposed to other types of goals):

1. Are associated with higher self-efficacy
2. Require higher performance for self-satisfaction
3. Entail less ambiguity about what constitutes good performance
4. Are typically more instrumental in bringing about valued outcomes
5. Lead individuals to expend more effort
6. Stimulate individuals to persist longer
7. Direct attention and action better and activate automatised skills
8. Motivate individuals to search for suitable task strategies, to plan and to utilise strategies that have been taught.
(from Locke and Latham, 1990, p. 108)

In sum, Locke and Latham (1990) review several interesting studies relating to goal setting and they relate the psychology of action to the industrial and organisational domain. Their research establishes the linear relationship between performance and difficulty and also confirms that specific hard goals yield better performance than 'do best' goals.

Brendl and Higgins (1996) present a discussion of valence, taking Lewin's work as their starting point. When approaching the hierarchical organisation of goals they acknowledge the work of both Miller *et al.* (1960) and Schank and Abelson (1977). When talking about levels of aspiration in low and high identity goals they touch base with Rotter (1942) and so much of the material discussed earlier in this chapter would appear to have some bearing on their general approach. Austin and Vancouver (1996) provide a review of goal constructs in psychology. They start with a quotation from James, and go on to acknowledge Miller *et al.* (1960) as some of the progenitors of research into goal structure and pay particular attention to the TOTE cycle as a conceptual replacement for the reflex arc. Karniol and Ross (1996) focus on the extent to which individuals might be pulled to behave by their conceptions of the future, as opposed to being pushed to act by their recollections of the past, but they also consider the power of responding to the here and now. Again, the importance of Lewin's concept of the life space is acknowledged at the start of their discussion. Palatano and Seifert (1997) focus their attention on pending goals which they define as intentions that are postponed by a planner because they do not fit into the current ongoing activity. They are particularly interested in how ways to facilitate the later recognition of opportunities for satisfying pending goals might be found. Buehler *et al.* (1994) bring to light a little-researched phenomenon known as the 'planning fallacy' which they define as ' the tendency to hold a confident belief that one's own project will proceed as planned even while knowing that the vast majority of similar projects have run late' (p. 366). Karoly (1993) provides a review of the systems view of the mechanisms for self-regulation. In sum, I feel that there is an abundant supply of excellent review literature which provides evidence to show that the concepts of goal and plan lie at the centre of an active research culture in the 1990s.

While I make no attempt to extend the scope of this review literature, I do feel the need to draw attention to one aspect in which it would appear to be deficient. I have noticed that the contributions from the perspective of critical social psychology have been largely excluded and this may be because the reviews have been written from within a fairly conventional scientific perspective. I am not asserting that the reviewers deal exclusively with material drawn from the positivist paradigm, since some theories considered by the reviewers, especially those concerned with motivation, stem from Freudian origins, and others, opposed to behaviourism, espouse systems theoretic or cybernetic approaches (especially those following Miller *et al.*,

1960). However, notwithstanding this, I have seldom seen any treatment within these reviews of material that might be regarded as providing a link to critical social psychology. Where there is discussion of the explanation of action, there is sometimes a link to accounting. Karoly (1993), for example, cites Schlenker *et al.* (1991) in this regard but makes no reference to the work of Antaki who has written extensively on accounts and explanations from the perspective of the new paradigm (see Antaki, 1988, for example).

The impression to be gained from this review literature is that there are many concepts and many theories which demand some form of integration into the research domain as a whole. There are many ways to cut this cake. Austin and Vancouver (1996) organise their review around the themes of goal structure, process and content. Bandura (1977), when introducing his comprehensive social cognitive theory, places human agency within an interdependent causal structure involving triadic reciprocal causation (discussed at the beginning of this chapter). Ford (1992) tabulates some thirty theories of motivation in terms of concepts relating to personal goals, agency beliefs, emotions and arousal, before dealing with his own motivational systems theory.

It is abundantly clear from Ford's (1992) summary that it is difficult to provide a definitive overview of all the various concepts and terms germane to the psychology of action. I doubt very much whether this is the sort of problem where there is just one correct solution. I am reminded of Wittgenstein's (1953) remark on classification:

> But how we group words into kinds will depend on the aim of the classification, – and on our own inclination. Think of the different points of view from which one can classify tools or chess-men. (p. 8e)

I shall delay putting forward my own classificatory framework until my concluding chapter (see Chapter 10).

Chapter 5
Agentic slips and errors

I will begin this chapter by briefly describing Freud's approach to the analysis of slips, errors and bungled actions in everyday life. I then move on to a more contemporary approach to everyday slips taken by Sellen (1994), a cognitive psychologist. This leads me to a consideration of Reason's (1990) work on human error and disaster. I shall devote rather more time to this topic than I do to the first two. Even then, I shall not be able to do justice to Reason's error model and I shall only attempt to outline some of its more important features. I shall not attempt a comprehensive review of any of this material, since I wish to devote time and space to a consideration of trans-paradigmatic matters in the last part of the chapter. For now, I turn to Freud.

The Freudian slip

The study of error in mundane situations was explored by Freud (1901/1975) in *The Psychopathology of Everyday Life*. Freud starts by considering why people forget proper names and he develops an answer to this question by analysing an instance of his own forgetting, coupled with the substitution of an incorrect name. During a conversation he was trying to recall the name of an artist called Signorelli, without success. At first two other names occurred to him: Botticelli and Boltraffio. He immediately rejected these as incorrect. Freud then takes the reader through a complex series of associations in order to demonstrate the process of psychoanalytic detection. Because he has encountered numerous cases of this nature, he arrives at the conclusion that 'by the side of simple cases where proper names are forgotten there is a type of forgetting which is motivated by repression' (p. 44).

Lest this sound somewhat mystical, I shall tease out the steps taken in Freud's analysis of the Signorelli problem. He linked the 'traffio' at the end of Boltraffio to the name of a place he had recently visited in the Tyrol, called Trafoi. Here he had dwelt on the fact that one of his patients, over whom he had taken much trouble, 'had put an end to his life on account of an incurable sexual disorder' (Freud, 1901/1975, p. 40). Meanwhile, he also established the non-psychoanalytic link between the 'Signor' in Signorelli and the German word 'Herr' on the basis of a straightforward translation.

Shortly before the forgotten name occurred in Freud's conversation, he had been talking about the customs of the Turks living in Bosnia and Herzegovina. He thus associates 'Signor' via 'Herr' to the first syllable of Herzegovina. Freud then reports that he was thinking of telling an anecdote to his travelling companion which concerned the value these Turks placed on sexual enjoyment and the fact that a colleague once had a patient who said to him: 'Herr, you must know that if that comes to an end [that is sexual enjoyment] then life is of no value' (p. 39). In this way Freud establishes the case for repressed thoughts about death and sexuality being tied into these word associations:

> Signor goes to Herr
> Herr ties in Herzegovina (and the material about death and sexuality)
> Herr is also the term of address used to the doctor in the story (again, death and sexuality)
> Traffio goes to Trafoi (suicide of the patient with a sexual disorder)
> Bosnia provides the link to both Botticelli and Boltraffio (via 'Bo').

So, the reason why Freud came up with the names Botticelli and Boltraffio instead of Signorelli was all to do with death and sex. This may well sound potty to anyone not familiar with Freud's work but these sorts of free association are all grist to the mill in the interpretation of dreams and so forth. In terms of the psychology of action, this particular example lies rather to the periphery of the field of interest. It is only of relevance if the forgetting of the name is somehow construed as an action requiring explanation (as opposed to something outside voluntary control). Freud analysed many other instances of forgetting, as well as slips of the tongue and pen and bungled actions. In more recent times, phenomena such as these have come under scrutiny from cognitive psychologists and I now move on to describe some of this work.

Cognitive slips

Sellen (1994) investigates the detection of error in everyday life in order to cast light on the way action is evaluated and in this way hopes to lay bare the mechanisms involved in action production. She defines error detection as 'knowing (either consciously or subconsciously) that an error has occurred' (p. 476). She is not concerned with how people recover from their errors. She worked with a data set comprising about 600 everyday slips and mistakes collected through a diary study. She then separated out about 140 of the 600 items as lapses involving memory failures. Many of these involved forgetting to do things (not posting a birthday card or not taking medication, for example). The others in this category involved a stalling of the action, such as opening the fridge door and then forgetting what it was that one had intended to take out. Most of these cases were easily remedied once the missing key was remembered.

The remainder of her data Sellen (1994) classified as either slips (errors in execution) or mistakes (result of ill-formed intentions). When she examines these instances in terms of what kind of information is used as the basis for detection, she finds some are action based, some are outcome based and some depend on detecting constraints in the environment. Action-based errors tended to be the types of thing whereby one catches oneself in the act, as it were: 'I was giving someone directions to turn left and saw that I was actually pointing to the right' (Sellen, 1994, p. 482). However, sometimes it is not until the actions have been carried out that the error is noticed and this is what Sellen calls outcome-based detection. She gives the following example, taken from her data:

> I planned to pour boiling water into a mug containing a tea bag. As I am accustomed to having tea in the afternoon (it was morning) I

poured coffee into the mug. I detected the error when I realised the tea bag was floating on top, and the contents in the mug smelled of coffee. (p. 485)

With regard to matters discussed in Chapters 2 and 4, the outcome state may be represented as an unexpected side effect in an Abelsonian plans molecule and, as such, it would feature in the cluster of accounts. However, it would have to be classed as a rogue or unexpected consequence of the attitude component in the TRA/TPB. As far as I am aware, the TRA/TPB has not been used as a framework for the investigation of error in everyday life. I think that the reason for this is that the predominant methodology in conventional studies is correlational in nature and the research paradigm is therefore ill-suited to the investigation of individual cases.

Sellen's third category involves detection through an external limiting function. This sounds to me like an unanticipated problem in the perceived behavioural control component in the TPB (see Chapter 2). One of Sellen's examples is as follows:

I planned to change out of my 'button-fly' jeans but reached down as if to pull down a zipper. Of course, there was no zipper to pull down. (p. 489)

Both the Freudian slip and these cognitive slips are usually found embedded in the trivia of everyday life events, and nothing too serious flows from them. However, some human errors, although perhaps no different in kind from these, have hugely significant consequences. In the next section, I consider errors which lead to disaster.

Human error and disaster

Error research, in its contemporary form, is concerned with the fallibility of human agents and the stimulus for investigation frequently comes from major disasters such as Chernobyl, the capsize of the *Herald of Free Enterprise* or the King's Cross tube station fire (see Reason, 1990; Zapf and Reason, 1994). The (fortunate) infrequency of such events places researchers in a difficult position. If they resort to laboratory simulation in order to solve their research problem, they open themselves up to criticism on the grounds of ecological validity. In this sense, error research shares some of the difficulties of other social psychological research into emergency situations, such as that carried out into bystander apathy by Latané and Darley (1970). While there may be a social dimension to disaster episodes, the human error research tends to have a cognitive focus and is not normally conducted from the perspective of social psychology.

Zapf and Reason (1994, pp. 427–8) work from a definition of error as the non-attainment of a goal and appear to go along with the assumption that such errors should be potentially avoidable. Reason's (1990) thesis is that errors arise as a result of cognitive abilities that otherwise stand us in good stead. He makes the point that error is intimately bound up with the notion of intention and can only be meaningfully applied to planned action. The relevance of his work to the psychology of action is self-evident.

Before I go on to consider Reason's (1990) model for error, I will briefly present one of his case studies in order to facilitate illustration and discussion. He summarises six cases in the Appendices of his book: Three Mile Island, Bhopal, *Challenger*, Chernobyl, *Herald of Free Enterprise*, and the King's Cross tube station fire. I shall focus on his account of Three Mile Island and, in addition, I will supplement this with material from another nuclear accident at the Toledo Edison power plant in Ohio, which Reason covers in slightly less detail.

Case studies in the nuclear power industry

Reason (1990) explains that in 1979 one of the turbines at the Three Mile Island nuclear power plant automatically stopped. The reason for this was that, owing to a recent maintenance fault, instrumentation incorrectly suggested that something was wrong. The explanation for this is technical but centres on the fact that the maintenance crew had inadvertently introduced a small quantity of water into the instrument air system, thus altering its pressure. The upshot of this was that the water flow to the steam generator was cut by mistake, due to the faulty information in the instrumentation. This, in turn, caused the turbine to trip.

At this stage the heat of the primary cooling system around the core could not be transferred to the cool water in the secondary (non-radioactive) system because the feedwater pumps had stopped. At this point the emergency feedwater pumps came on automatically. Unfortunately, the pipes from these pumps were blocked (valves had been left closed by mistake after maintenance work, a couple of days previously). Heat and pressure rose rapidly at the core and the reactor 'scrammed' as an automatic safety response. This stopped the chain reaction, but the radioactive materials that were still decaying continued to produce heat. The additional pressure was then relieved through a pilot-operated relief valve (PORV). This valve flips open, lets water down into a sump and then flips shut. On this occasion, however, the valve stuck in the open position. Reason (1990) summarised the situation as follows:

> This meant that the primary cooling system had a hole in it through which radioactive water, under high pressure, was pouring into the containment area, and thence down into the basement. (p. 190)

Reason (1990, especially Appendix) draws attention to a catalogue of errors in connection with this accident. Some he puts down to management failure. For example, maintenance crew had introduced water into the instrument air system on two previous occasions in the past yet no steps had been taken to prevent the reoccurrence of this error. Some errors were exacerbated by design problems. Thus operators failed to diagnose the stuck-open PORV for more than two hours, partly because they were hampered by a confusing control panel on which some 100 alarms were activated at once with no means of suppressing the unimportant ones. When training failures (I shall discuss this aspect in the sections below) were added into the maintenance problems and design flaws, a potentially lethal cocktail of errors was assembled which, in this accident, resulted in the release of small quantities of radioactive material into the atmosphere (Reason, 1990, states that no loss of life has been traced directly to the accident).

Reason (1990, pp. 180–2) also provides an extensive description of how the operators reacted to an accident at Toledo Edison's Davis-Besse plant in Ohio, 1985, where there was a serious loss of main and auxiliary feedwater. In this incident, the operators' training may have exacerbated the situation, since they were required to follow a rigid set of procedures laid out in an emergency manual. Reason (1990), quoting from the official accident inquiry report (NUREG, 1985), tells of the moment the operators heard the turbine stop valves slamming shut and how they knew then that the reactor had tripped:

> This 'thud' was heard by most of the equipment operators who also recognised its meaning and two of them headed for the control room... The shift supervisor joined the operator at the secondary-side control console and watched the rapid decrease of the steam generator levels... The assistant shift supervisor in the meantime opened the plant's loose-leaf emergency procedure book. (Reason, 1990, p. 181)

Apparently, consulting the plant's loose-leaf emergency procedure book, a hefty tome about two inches thick, did not solve their problem. Eventually the control room crew abandoned the rule book and, working on their own initiative, managed to restore the plant to a safe state within about 15 minutes

Reason (1990) provides the following rationale for his inclusion of the lengthy NUREG extract (of which I have reproduced but a small section):

> This passage is worth quoting at length because it reveals what the reality of a serious nuclear power plant emergency is like. It also captures the moment when the pre-programmed procedures, like the plant, ran out of steam, forcing the operators to improvise in the face of what the industry calls a 'beyond design basis accident'. For our present purposes, it highlights a further irony of automation: that of drilling operators to follow written instructions and then putting them in a system to provide knowledge-based intelligence and remedial improvisation. (p. 182)

The reference in the above quotation to knowledge-based intelligence provides a direct link to Reason's model for human error, and I summarise some of the main aspects of this below.

Reason's generic error-modelling system (GEMS)

Reason starts by classifying error into two basic types: first, slips or lapses where the actions do not go according to plan and, second, mistakes. Zapf and Reason (1994) characterise mistakes as planning failures: 'actions go as planned but the goals and/or plans are bad' (p. 428). Reason (1990) later acknowledges that while the slips/mistakes categorisation is useful as a first approximation, some well-documented errors fall between the two. For example, with regard to Three Mile Island (see above), the operators did not realise that the relief valve on the pressuriser was stuck open because the display on the instrument panel indicated that it was closed. Reason (1990, p. 55) argues that this can be construed, in part, as a mistake, since the episode involved an improper appraisal of the system's state. He also feels that this error contained the slip-like feature in that a 'strong but wrong' interpretation was involved, based on the application of inappropriate diagnostic rules: *'if (situation X prevails) then (system state Y exists)'*. Returning to my discussion of critical realism (see Chapter 3), the problem seems to be that the transitive features of the environment (in this case how a valve setting signal on an instrument display panel is interpreted) do not match up with the intransitive (the physical state of the valve represented).

Reason (1990) proposes a more flexible approach to classification in the GEMS which will take him beyond the simpler slips/mistakes dichotomy. He regards the execution failures of slips and lapses as being mainly skills based, whereas the planning failures contained in mistakes he sees as being either rule based (RB) or knowledge based (KB). Reason (1990) argues that this is an important distinction, grounded in the psychological literature:

> The key feature of GEMS is the assertion that, when confronted with a problem, human beings are strongly biased to search for and find a pre-packaged solution at the RB level *before* resorting to the far more effortful KB level, even where the latter is demanded at the outset. (p. 65, emphasis in original)

In RB problem solving, the person attempts to match some structural features of the current situation with a schema, script or template stored in the memory. I'm not sure that this would necessarily have to have been actually experienced, since presumably it could have been learned from a book of instruction, for example. In the case of the Toledo Edison plant at Ohio (see above), the script came in the form of an emergency procedure book, about two inches thick. Reason (1990) notes that rule-based mistakes can involve the misapplication of good rules or the application of bad rules. Further, he notes that the procedures contained within emergency manuals may involve highly elaborate branching structures or algorithms 'designed to differentiate between a set of foreseeable faults' (pp. 180–1). This obviously increases the possibility that a good rule for one situation may be misapplied to another.

At the KB level, problem solving gets down to first principles and a basic analysis of the situation is required. In the case of Three Mile Island, the supervisor arrived at a point where nothing seemed to be working or going as it should according to the manual; eventually he left his desk (and the procedure specified in the manual) to go and work out what was wrong for himself.

Towards the end of his book Reason (1990) distinguishes latent errors from active errors. The defining characteristic of latent errors is that their adverse consequences may lie dormant within the system for a long time (the effects of active errors are felt almost immediately):

> In general, active errors are associated with the performance of the 'front-line' operators of a complex system: pilots, air traffic controllers, ships' officers, control room crews and the like. Latent errors, on the other hand, are most likely to be spawned by those whose activities are removed in both time and space from the direct control interface: designers, high-level decision makers, construction workers, managers and maintenance personnel. (p. 173)

One of the strengths of acknowledging the presence of latent errors is that it provides a link out from the rather focused world of applied cognitive psychology to wider issues in society. For example, Reason (1990) points out that a problem similar to that at Three Mile Island, relating to a stuck-open (PORV) valve, occurred in 1977 at the Davis-Besse plant. However, the authorities investigating the accident did not collate the information and communicate it to the industry at large. The research may thus help to bring questions into focus regarding environmental politics, government accountability and the framing of industrial safety regulations.

Transparadigmatic considerations

Reason, an applied cognitive psychologist, might be regarded as operating within a research paradigm that was deeply divided from that of critical social psychology. While I am convinced that this is the case, I am not so sure that it necessarily has to be so. I shall therefore begin to explore the cross-fertilisation of ideas that might flow from bringing to bear an agentic perspective from the domain of critical psychology on the applied cognitive framework contained in GEMS.

In the first part of this section I shall focus on the concepts of rule and role, mainly drawing on the 1970s ethogenic paradigm. I shall then consider the potential for discursive and accounting approaches for human error research, before moving on to examine the way the use of narrative in applied psychology relates to the concerns of contemporary critical psychology.

The 4 Rs: rule, role, ritual and routine

I shall commence this exercise by considering Reason's (1990) description of rule-based matching: 'If (situation) then (system state), if (system state) then (remedial action)' (p. 65).

This may be compared with Harré and Secord's (1972) description of the general form of a rule:

> [In order to achieve A (the act)] do $a_1 \ldots a_n$ (the actions) when S (the occasion or situation) occurs. (p. 182)

What Harré and Secord call the act comprising of the actions $(a_1 \ldots a_n)$ is referred to as the remedial action by Reason. The inference of the system state from the situation for Reason is covered more generally by the occasion or situation in Harré and Secord's description. It is the concept of rule, above all else, which brings together these disparate psychological approaches.

Once the link between rule-based problem solving and the concept of rule in ethogenic social psychology has been made, it is a short step to extend this to include the concept of role put forward by Harré and Secord (1972):

> Role can be defined as that part of the Act-action structure produced by the subset of the rules followed by some individual defined as belonging to a particular category of person. (p. 183)

The applicability of the social psychological concept of role to industry is trivially straightforward: an industrial role (such as that for the operators in the control room at the Three Mile Island plant) may be regarded as being formally scripted in the job description. Further elaboration of roles may then appear, in liturgical form, embedded in training or emergency manuals in which procedures are laid down for actions to be taken in particular circumstances.

The concept of role needs flexibility of interpretation in order to be fully assimilated into the dramaturgical perspective where it must stand in for the more literary notion of character. However, once this distance has been travelled the (fuzzier) concept of role may do business within the scripts or schemas which stand as templates for the generation of prototypical action sequences or social episodes. In discussing the concept of plan and its relation to artificial intelligence I referred to Schank and Abelson's (1977) use of script (see Chapter 4), and this is another way in which the social psychological variants of the concept may be related, through cognitive science, to human error research.

Once the industrial operatives are seen to be carrying out sequences of rule-governed responses to emergency situations, the question arises as to how closely this activity matches the notion of ritual. Rothenbuhler (1998), in analysing this concept, emphasises the importance of the symbolic:

> So ritual is about the general, in a significant way. Ritual action is action oriented toward transcendence of the particularities of the situation in which it is performed. A ritual situation is one constructed so as to offer transcendence of the particularities of the social circumstances surrounding it... Presidential inaugurations are more similar than the presidencies they inaugurate... funerals

and funeral operations are more similar than the people they help bury... Why? Because in both cases, as in most rituals, the emphasis is on what is generally true, what has transcendent value, rather than on what is particularly true this time around. (pp. 60–1)

It is possible that industrial operators may construe rule-based safety procedures as quasi-rituals. Working at the purely symbolic level would allow quick equivalencies to be made between what was happening in a specific emergency and the general situation as set out in the manual. It is here that mistakes involving the misapplication of good rules may be made (cf. Reason's 'strong but wrong' errors). It is possible that training by simulation might encourage this. In simulation, everyone knows that there is no objective reality 'out there' beyond the dramaturgical frame of the simulation. One could argue that simulation might seduce trainees into a relativist view of the world (see Chapter 3) when, in the context of nuclear power plants, it is important that they keep a hold on the intransitive facets of their situation and, by implication, maintain a critical realist stance (I will discuss critical realism in more detail in the next section).

Harré and Secord's (1972) concept of routine is explicitly designed to capture the intransitive aspects of a procedure and the way human agency results in causal effects in the physical world, as opposed to achieving results merely by cultural convention.

> They [routines] are sequences of actions which are generated by the actors following rules, but in which the outcome is not related to the Act-action structure by a meaning-convention. A routine is performed simply by the faithful carrying out the required sequence of actions. The outcomes of routines are causally, not conventionally, related to the sequence of actions. For instance, servicing a car is a routine, a sequence of actions generated by following a set of rules, and the outcome, better running say, is causally related to the actions performed according to rule by the mechanic. (p. 201)

While ritual would appear to fit comfortably into a relativist discourse, the concept of routine seems to demand a realist perspective.

Critical realist issues

Gergen (1998) has recently explored the possibility of deploying both transitive and intransitive discourses, depending on what appears to be appropriate in the context. Here he equates the transitive with the constructionist perspective and the intransitive with a realist approach to the situation. He draws attention to the general points at issue as follows:

> And if the constructionist screamed, 'Run, there's a fire!' he or she would not wish others to look with suspicion and retort, 'Oh, that's just your construction'. Similarly, those who embrace tenets of realism may often draw arrows from the quiver of constructionism. Would the most committed realist wish to delete from his/her repertoire... 'This news report is slanted in favour of the government'. (p. 152)

Operators in the midst of a developing emergency (such as Three Mile Island) may need to use a discourse which is predominantly realist in nature while dealing with the crisis. However, when making sense of what happened after the event (perhaps when it is reported in the press or at an official investigation) a constructionist discourse may be more appropriate, especially if questions of bias arise in the reports. This leads me to the topic of accounting for the errors.

Accounting for human error

Another way in which the 1970s new paradigm social psychology is relevant to human error research is that in many real life cases (and possibly in laboratory simulations, too) the investigation may not stop merely at the establishment of the 'facts' but some comment will be required with regard to the apportionment of blame. An analysis of explanation in exoneration is given a somewhat broader and more contemporary treatment by Antaki (1994, especially Chapter 4). Antaki (1994) reviews Scott and Lyman's (1968) distinction between excuses (where the agent denies responsibility) and justifications (where responsibility is accepted but permissible reasons are offered for the action). Antaki (1994) then considers Semin and Manstead's

(1983) more detailed typology of excuses and justifications, which includes a sub-category of excuses for 'denial of intent'. In this category, appeal can be made to accidental or unforeseen circumstances. While this is only one among many categories where exoneration is considered in general, it becomes a focal category in terms of human error research and catastrophe. It is when Antaki (1994) moves on to the management of exoneration, drawing on examples from Atkinson and Drew (1979) and the analysis of courtroom talk and the work of Conley and O'Barr (1990) in their analysis of styles of accounting in a US small claims court, that the relevance to accident investigations and enquiries becomes apparent.

The way in which slips, lapses, rule-based and knowledge-based errors are handled may be examined from a discursive standpoint, in order to explore issues of facticity. After all, the applicability of the discursive approach to the press coverage of important events, political debate and the credibility of the principal protagonists in affairs of national interest has been demonstrated by Edwards and Potter (1992).

The case study as story

In providing descriptions of accidents in the form of case studies, Reason (1990) tells their stories. I think that narrative description is an extremely good vehicle for conveying a message and can act as a bridge between the more technical world of the theoretical/empirical psychologist's laboratory and the everyday setting inhabited by the clients of applied psychologists. Reason (1990) demonstrates that he is aware of the needs of different groups of readers when, in his 'skimmer's guide' to his book, he directs cognitive psychologists to some chapters and practitioners to others. Narratives, case studies, stories (the precise terminology is not important) have an important part to play in psychological consultancy, especially in the way they can be used to bring out the main message, from what otherwise might appear to be a morass of technical research points, to the non-specialist. In mainstream psychology, there is no real need to theorise the use of stories in the applied field; researchers/consultants can just go ahead and get on with it. Not so in critical psychology. The critical psychologist has to be reflexively aware of the rhetorical significance that the adoption of a particular narrative form (such as the story) may have. This is especially problematic for post-modernists who must not be seen to privilege their own (monolithic?) theoretical reading of a situation. I shall therefore take a post-modernist applied critical psychologist and compare the use of story in her work with that of the (implicit) use of story in Reason's (1990) work. The thing to remember is that, within the paradigm of applied cognitive psychology, there is no need for Reason (1990) to think about this as an issue and there is no theoretical framework which demands any form of explicit theorisation.

With regard to my point of comparison, I shall focus on a chapter written by Ruth Merttens in Parker's (1998) *Social Constructionism, Discourse and Realism*. Her inclusion in that volume indicates that she is regarded as a critical psychologist and her contribution suggests that her ideas are, indeed, radical. Parker's notes on contributors explain that she is a professor of primary education and the director of an international schools project whereby parents are encouraged to become involved in their children's learning of maths and English by participating with them in take-home tasks which are set by the teacher.

I am not especially interested in the substantive content of this project, but rather in how Merttens construes what she is doing and how she achieves interventions, as a professional educationalist. Merttens (1998) would appear to be coming from a broadly post-modernist position, given that she chooses to introduce her approach to educational intervention with references to Lacan, Derrida, Barthes and Foucault. She seems to have some good ideas about how to improve numeracy and literacy and these ideas would appear to be grounded in her knowledge and critical reading of the academic literature. On the face of it, she seems to be in a very similar situation to Reason who has good ideas about how to improve the training of operatives in the nuclear industry, for example, based upon his specialist academic knowledge. The difference is that Merttens, as a post-modernist, does not wish to be seen to be privileging the expert discourse of educational psychology. I shall explain how Merttens solves her problem, before I move on to discuss Reason's work in more detail.

Merttens (1998) solves her dilemma by using stories to implement her interventions into the school system:

> Stories, I shall argue, are useful, a cardinal notion in this argument. Their usefulness can take many forms: as cultural representations, as rhetorical devices, as therapeutic tools. But here we are concerned with the story as a means of generating both prescriptions and generalisations. (p. 64)

The stories that Merttens (1998) tells on the school project convey real experiences (born of real events or case studies) but they also may contain pieces of advice and instruction, whether overtly or covertly. One of her stories concerns a boy of seven who cannot read and who has had a troubled family background. This boy talked about his homework but never brought any in to school. The reader is drawn into sympathy for the teacher and possibly is led to believe that the child was lying and never actually does any of his homework. Later in the story, the child's mother arrives at the last moment to see the teacher at parents' evening and dumps a couple of carrier bags of homework out on the table, saying that her son had kept telling her she should bring it in and that then seemed like a good time to do that.

Merttens' story seemed like an old-fashioned fable to me. She resists stating what the moral of the story is, although it seems transparently obvious that it was something about not jumping to conclusions (that kids from difficult backgrounds don't do homework and possibly lie about it) and the prescriptive advice might be couched in terms of the negotiation of accounts ('always collect proper accounts and check them out'). For some reason, connected with her post-modernist position, she is blocked from making this explicit.

With regards to her story, I was surprised that it had none of the meta-fictional facets (see Waugh, 1984), none of the disruptions to plot or story line, and none of the deconstructive tendencies that might be expected of a post-modern story. In this respect, I found Merttens' position slightly paradoxical.

Merttens (1998) feels that transcripts or case studies do not enable her to explore possibilities as easily as do stories:

> What is important in the context of our initial dilemma is the ability of the story, unlike the transcript or case study, to afford a series of enabling potentials for action, prescription and interpretation. In the case of the transcripts described above, it is the inevitably deterministic nature of such accounts which fail to animate a vision of 'what might be' rather than of what is, or to provide a means of comparing possible (imagined) alternatives. (Merttens, 1998, p. 71)

In terms of the links between critical psychology at the millennium and the earlier 1970s 'new' paradigm, Merttens' concern with 'what might be' is highly reminiscent of Shotter's (1975) *Images of Man in Psychological Research* where he argues that psychology be regarded as a *moral* science. Be that as it may, I now turn once more to Reason's work.

Reason (1990), in his own way, also makes use of stories. I have already provided a quotation (see above) which he used to capture the unfolding drama of the incident at Toledo Edison's Davis-Besse plant in Ohio (NUREG, 1985). Although Merttens (1998) spurns the case study, I think the way that Reason (1990) conveyed the events at Ohio reads like a cracking good yarn, with lots of tension and excitement (think of the moment, in the above quotation, when the operators heard the turbine stop valves slamming shut and knew then that the reactor had tripped). I could almost feel the panic. It does not take much imagination to envisage the case study as providing the basis for an exciting TV drama documentary script.

Both Merttens (1998) and Reason (1990) use stories to provide a moral, only Merttens tries not to draw it explicitly. Both are concerned with important and pressing practical issues in the real world. Both need to reach out beyond their own particular expert discourses to those who live and work in the situations they study. By juxtaposing their work, I hope to have shown that there is some common ground between psychologists operating in mutually antipathetic research paradigms. I think that it can reasonably be argued that applied cognitive psychology and post-modernist critical psychology generate different language games. Because (at least in the cases I have discussed) these language games tend to be played out within the same tongue (English, in my examples), the idea of translation between the paradigms may seem perverse. After all, translation is normally something reserved for occasions when one wishes to move between different languages, not language games. However, I feel that not only is translation possible, but that it may well have heuristic pay-off.

Concluding remarks

I began by considering Freud's classic work on slips and bungled actions before describing the contemporary cognitive approach to such phenomena. I was able to make some links between Sellen's work and the TRA/TPB but this is hardly surprising since the TRA/TPB is primarily located in *cognitive* social psychology. The consideration of the severity of the consequences which flow from slips and errors lead to a consideration of the human error research relating to disasters.

While Reason's (1990) work is designed to be read as a piece of applied cognitive psychology, I found it interesting to attempt a reading from the perspective of critical psychology. It is important for me to stress that this does not amount to critique; it is more an exercise in heuristic eclecticism. This is a theme to which I shall return in Chapter 10.

Chapter 6
Weakness of will

My treatment of this topic moves back and forth between psychological and philosophical considerations and there are many links to material covered in earlier chapters (especially Chapters 2 and 4). For example, while weakness of will can be related to the philosophical discussion of willing in Chapter 2, its construal as self-regulation failure suggests that the discussion of the cybernetic and control theories of action, discussed in Chapter 4, will be of greater relevance. Weakness of will is sometimes referred to as akrasia in the philosophical literature and I use this term in order to group sub-topics relating generally to weakness of will in the first part of this chapter. This enables me to deal with further topics under the separate heading of procrastination in the latter part of the chapter. While I see procrastination as closely related to akrasia, I feel that it can be distinguished from it on the grounds that the passage of time is not an essential component of all phenomena capable of being categorised as akratic.

Akrasia

I start my treatment of akrasia with a consideration of some of the conceptual analyses put forward by the philosophers, before moving on to deal with some of the psychological research.

Definition and preliminary analysis

Mele (1992) defines weakness of will, or akrasia, as 'uncompelled intentional action that goes against the agent's consciously held better judgement' (p. 210). He then points out that this raises the question of how this kind of action is logically or psychologically possible and, if it is, how it might best be explained. Walker (1989), reviewing the philosophical literature on this topic, defines weakness of will, or what he refers to as last-ditch akrasia, in the following fashion:

> An agent, succumbing to last ditch akrasia, freely, knowingly and intentionally performs an action A against his better judgement that an incompatible action B is the better thing to do. (p. 653)

Providing the akrasia relates to doing something (*A*) when the intention is to refrain from doing it (*B*), as would be the case in giving up smoking or drinking, or not doing something (*A*) when the intention was to do it (*B*), as would be the case in the resolve to take regular exercise, for example, there would appear to be no impediment to using the theory of planned behaviour (TPB – see Chapter 2) as a framework for discussion. Where *A* and *B* are conceptually unrelated, the TPB is more awkward to use. For example, if the agent goes to the cinema (*A*) instead of working on a college essay assignment (*B*), the TPB would have to incorporate the outcomes flowing from not executing (*B*) as outcomes flowing from the execution of (*A*). This is a little cumbersome and is related to the general problem of the way in which the TPB is poorly suited for application to decision making between multiple choices.

Returning to the philosophical treatment of akrasia, one of the problems Walker (1989) considers is the *enslavement argument* which asserts that the agent's akratic desire to *A* is irresistible. Were this to be the case, the agent's action would not be free. Another objection, Walker (1989) notes, hinges on the interpretation of intentional action as being something that cannot, by definition, be against the agent's better judgement. If intentional actions are always done for a reason, then the akratic person who does *A* instead of *B* cannot be seen to be acting for a reason (since the reason is to do *B*, not *A*). But Walker (1989) contrasts this with the *backward connection argument*: if the person has done *A*, then the person will automatically have done what she or he thinks is best and so *B* could not have really been judged to be better, after all. When confronted with philosophical arguments such as these, the psychologists may have no alternative but to lock themselves in the broom cupboard and throw away the key. Still, Walker (1989) does attempt to resolve these philosophical conundrums. He distinguishes the sorts of evaluative reason which underlie a person's better judgement from the practical reasons (or directives) which determine what is to be done. The aim of evaluative reasoning is to determine what is desirable or good. Walker (1989) gives the example of the person who reasons that to drink another glass of wine would be bad (evaluation). The aim of directives is to determine what is to be done. An example of directive reasoning would be: 'Insofar as drinking will give pleasure, I am to drink'.

From the standpoint of cognitive psychology, Walker's (1989) ideas seem to imply parallel processing. In the drinking example, the evaluative cognition could be suppressed or repressed beneath the level of consciousness. From the psychoanalytic perspective, the evaluative reason sounds as though it should emanate from the superego, with the directive coming from the ego. Walker's (1989) proposal runs into some difficulty if a mainstream social psychological perspective is adopted since it is difficult to see how the evaluative and directive reasons could escape categorisation as dissonant cognitive elements in the theory of cognitive dissonance (see Festinger, 1957). Once the directive is turned into behaviour, the prediction would be an internal shift in the evaluative reason in order to reduce the dissonance engendered by the behaviour. Weakness of will has been addressed in a more direct fashion, within psychology, by Baumeister *et al.* (1994) and it is to a consideration of their approach that I now turn.

Self-regulation failure

Baumeister *et al.* (1994) construe akrasia or weakness of will as self-regulation failure. They see this, in epidemic proportions, as being at the heart of many of the social problems which at present bedevil society in the USA where people lack control over many diverse aspects of their lives: personal finances, weight, drink, sexual impulses, drugs and even the consumption of coffee or chocolate. Although there may be some points in common with the TPB or with self-efficacy theory, Baumeister *et al.* (1994) do appear to have a distinctive approach which focuses strongly on the process involved in the execution of action or the failure to act. Baumeister *et al.* (1994) argue that self-regulation prevents the occurrence of the normal, natural or learned response in a situation and substitutes another (which could be a lack of response) in its place (p. 7). Action must be construed as having multiple processes or levels, so that the lower level action can be overridden at the higher level. They use the term self-regulation to cover the more common terms of self-control and self-discipline and emphasise the inhibitory aspect of these processes.

> The original and rudimentary form of self-regulation is therefore what we call *self-stopping*: Intervention in one action or response pattern in order to bring it to a halt. (p. 7)

Baumeister *et al.* (1994) draw on the work of Miller *et al.* (1960), especially the notion of the TOTE (Test Operate Test Exit) unit (see Chapter 4). In the language of the TOTE, the goal or standard generated at the higher order level will be compared with the current situation and if there is an indication that the unfolding action is likely to move towards forbidden lower order goals, then an exit from that potential act will be effected before it occurs. If a person wants an alcoholic drink but judges or resolves not to have one, any behaviour which involves drifting towards a bar will have to be overridden at the higher order level. In this example, a shift in direction towards a coffee house instead of a bar would solve the problem. For this to work, there must be three things: standards for comparison purposes, the ability to monitor current circumstances in order to provide feedback and the ability of the agent to operate in such a fashion as to bring about the desired higher order state of affairs. Baumeister *et al.* (1994) feel that self-regulation requires sufficient strength on the part of the individual to override the lower order tendencies and they say that this concept of strength resembles the colloquial concept of willpower (p. 9).

Returning to Walker (1989) for a moment, when he talks of agents acting against their better judgement, it may be possible to think of this in terms of the better judgement fulfilling the role of the test standard of a TOTE unit. There is a slight tension in such an interpretation, since the better judgement in akrasia is normally tied into an ethical or moral ideal, whereas TOTE units tend to be associated with more mundane matters, such as Miller *et al.*'s (1960) illustrative example of hammering in nails. Walker (1989) considers Pugmire's (1982) discussion of the situation where an individual tries as hard as possible to resist caving in to desire, but in the end crumbles. Where all available resources are drawn upon but failure ensues, the enslavement argument will exonerate the individual from blame by saying that it is arbitrary to insist that the desire was resistible. Walker (1989) then points out that non-rational strategies such as not focusing attention on the desirable aspects of the akratic action could be deployed and that this would get round the enslavement interpretation.

Walker's (1989) mistake here might be to assume that not focusing attention on something could be done without drawing on available resources. This is a difficult issue to handle from a purely philosophical standpoint but it is one which can be approached in a more direct fashion by psychologists through empirical study and with advantage. Baumeister *et al.* (1994) review Gilbert *et al.*'s (1988) study of the cognitive aspect of self-stopping. Subjects watched a video of a social interaction and were subsequently tested on their understanding of it. The key to this experiment is that there happened to be a sequence of meaningless and irrelevant stimuli on the bottom of the video. When an experimental group were told to ignore the gibberish, they performed less well on the comprehension test than did the control group who had no instructions to engage in self-control. Baumeister *et al.* (1994) put this forward as an illustration that self-control consumes some attention, since how else could the poorer results be explained. After reviewing other related studies, they conclude that self-stopping may involve both mental and physical resources and suggest that the empirical evidence supports the use of the commonsense concept of willpower in these contexts.

Baumeister *et al.* (1994) then explore three reasons for unsuccessful self-regulation. First, chronic weakness in an individual may be seen as a character trait based on the notion of willpower. As such, psychologists would expect individual differences on this trait with reasonable consistency over time. Second, temporary depletions in the ability to self-regulate may be due to exhaustion or tiredness. Baumeister *et al.* (1994) make an analogy with muscle contraction and speculatively suggest that overuse in a short time-span may result in a depletion of resolve, even for the otherwise strong-willed individual.

The third category they consider is the unstoppable or irresistible impulse. It is this that bears closest resemblance to what Walker (1969) refers to as last-ditch akrasia. Baumeister *et al.* (1994) give the example of someone with a strong desire to go to the bathroom. It is true that willpower may be used to delay passing water but eventually the urge will become too strong to be stifled. I think that this, while being a vivid example, is an unfortunate one from the point of view of the psychology of action since the response crosses over from the realm of action into causally explained behaviour (the period of desperately wanting to go to the toilet being a rather fuzzy boundary between the two). The moral dimension of akrasia is a useful one to keep in mind. With Kant's dictum that 'ought implies can' there is little point in speaking of urinating against one's better judgement if one can do nowt about it. This is not to say that one might not feel guilty or embarrassed afterwards, but that is another matter.

Psychological inertia

Once started on a path of action it is sometimes difficult to stop. The example Baumeister *et al.* (1994) give is illicit sex. The first kiss may lead to a second and so on; it is much more difficult to stop the process after a period of passionate snogging by which time both parties may be in a state of undress and disarray. Inertia applies to the breakdown of the self-regulatory process within one particular episode. The case of kissing leading to sex can be thought of as a long chain, using Abelson's molecular approach to the representation of plans (see Chapter 4). Once started at one end, the action progressively and inexorably moves down the line to its orgasmic conclusion.

Baumeister *et al.* (1994) devote some time to the analysis of *lapse-activated causal patterns*. The point of interest here is to distinguish those occasions where a minor lapse might occur but the agent steps back promptly into self-regulated control (the person has just one pint of beer, for example) from those where the first step off the rails leads to a full-blown breakdown in control. These latter breakdowns are often referred to using the *snowball* metaphor. Snowballing mainly occurs in relation to impulse control where people break diets, go back on the booze, or whatever, in a highly indulgent fashion.

One of the things that Baumeister et al. (1994) cite as providing a difference between the initial lapse and the snowball run which follows is that the initial lapse may cause an unexpected emotional response which then fuels the snowballing effect. They suggest that a first act of extramarital infidelity may be undertaken as a minor fling, a one-off sexual adventure, but then the person may find themselves falling in love with the object of their transient desire. Guilt may be present as a response, too, and in the case of alcohol more of the substance may then be consumed in the hope that it will blot out the feelings of guilt which it, in the first place, occasioned.

It is the possibility that a first slip may lead to snowballing that leads Baumeister et al. (1994) to express reservations concerning 'zero tolerance' approaches. Zero tolerance is supposed to frighten people from taking the first step of transgression by catastrophising it. However, this may not work for two reasons: either the feeling may emerge that all is lost so the person might as well go all the way; or nothing particularly bad happens, so the authority of the zero tolerance regime is undermined since the warnings or threats appear to be without substance. Baumeister et al. (1994) liken this situation to the military strategy of putting all one's defences in the front line and leaving nothing in reserve.

Once snowballing has started, it may be perpetuated if there is a reduction in monitoring and this is quite likely to happen with the consumption of alcohol. Lack of monitoring will effectively break the TOTE unit, since there will be no point of comparison. One further issue considered by Baumeister et al. (1994) is that people may sometimes acquiesce in their own failure to regulate their behaviour. This could be important on moral and legal grounds: if people lose control because of the power of irresistible urges, then it is possible to argue that they cannot be held responsible. If they acquiesce in this loss of control, then the responsibility sticks with them. There is no doubt that this is a grey area. Baumeister et al. (1994) tend to think that in general there will be some acquiescence in self-regulation failure, since most situations are not of the sort where we have to respond to stimuli automatically (like when the knee jerks in response to the doctor's tap or the eye blinks to the puff of air administered by the optician in a test situation). The issue of acquiescence returns us full circle to the philosophical problem of last-ditch akrasia.

Last-ditch akrasia

The application of akrasia to matters broader than the ethical is considered by Gosling (1990):

> Since morality tends to embody overall judgements about the way it is best to live, that way into the problem will at least incline one, although it does not require one, to see akratic cases as ones of acting against some wider all-embracing judgement. (p. 197)

He then goes on to explain that, if not confined to ethics, the problem can be seen as a conflict between 'shorter- and longer-term, or narrower and more all-embracing sets of considerations' (p. 197).

Gosling's (1990) analysis brings akrasia more closely into the category of irrational behaviour, as opposed to that of sin, and thereby provides a better connection with the psychological approach to action which has its origins in Miller *et al.*'s (1960) work on plans. Gosling (1990) emphasises the fact that for anyone to count as a rational agent they must engage in long-term projects requiring a certain amount of planning from time to time. This enables him to get away from the short-term passion examples which tend to proliferate in discussions of akrasia. From this point of view, it is not so much the particular choice of the agent that makes him or her appear akratic on a particular occasion but the fact that if this was *generally* characteristic of the agent, the person's rationality would be called into question.

The choice of the alternative which runs counter to the agent's better judgement is thus regarded as an irrational choice in some sense. One thing that renders the akratic paradoxical is that the person appears to be serious about a set of reasons on which they do not in fact act, even though they do what they do deliberately. Gosling (1990) suggests that the problem arises partly because we can expect language users to articulate their goals and 'in general know what they are about' (p. 198). When we are faced with someone who does not act in accordance with their declared reasons, it is unclear as to what is happening. Returning to my interpretation of the TRA as a rule governing the intelligibility of clusters of statements (see Chapter 2), this is precisely the state of affairs described by a mismatch between intention and behaviour where the intention is supported by a balanced TRA equation, given no other extraneous factors.

Gosling (1990) pushes the sense of irrationality involved in the akratic situation a little further when he suggests that:

> For anyone to count as a rational agent it does seem that they have to display some tendency on occasion to pursue relatively long-term projects involving a certain amount of planning, even if not necessarily on the akratic occasions. The closer we get to someone supposedly never planning beyond the immediately accessible in the immediate environment, the more doubtful it becomes that we have a rational agent at all. (pp. 198–9)

Gosling's (1990) philosophical analysis seems consonant with the view that I put forward in Chapter 2 that the TRA equation may be regarded as the formal expression of a rule of intelligibility whose application to virtual linguistic communities may be demonstrated empirically. It also squares with Harré's (1983) view that the self-concept is, indeed, a concept and as such has much in common with the concepts we find in scientific theories which often depend on models or analogies to underpin them. Harré (1983) suggests that it is the way persons are indexed, the sorts of things that are attributed to them, and the fashion in which they feature in the talk and conversations of particular socio-linguistic communities that provides the model for the concept of self. He illustrates his argument by drawing on social anthropological data and linguistic analyses in a comparison of the concept of self in Maori and Eskimo cultures, where the Maori self-concept is seen to be much more powerful and individualistic than its Eskimo counterpart. Harré (1983) speculates that this may be due in part to formal aspects of the language, especially where the language makes it difficult to attribute psychological properties to individuals (through indexicals or pronouns, for example). The fact that not all human beings are accorded full status as persons or agents is institutionalised in law, at least in western culture. The obvious examples are minors and the insane. In some cultures turbulent passion is more readily acknowledged to take the individual out of the realm of rational agency (on a temporary basis) than in others (the French category of *crime passionnel* would be a case in point). Even in sub-turbulent cases (where the individual may be extremely depressed, for example), there may be some grounds for regarding a particular occasion as involving an atypical lapse where for the time being the individual's claim to 100 per cent personhood is set aside. Gosling (1990) argues that because of the range of possibilities surrounding akratic behaviour, it would be a mistake to assume that there might be some form of irrationality which would account for all cases.

Gosling (1990) foregrounds the situation where the agents are capable of responding to reason and know what they are about to some degree, as may be evidenced from their sincere declarations of intent. This situation, Gosling (1990) argues, provides the norm from which the puzzling cases of akratic behaviour deviate. These cases are difficult to understand because they are not the cases where a complete failure or breakdown in rationality has occurred with loss of responsibility and control. They lie in a disturbing grey area where if the individual's pattern of behaviour was generalised from the particular case in question to their actions in general, we would be forced to conclude that that particular individual could not be counted as a rational agent. Gosling (1990) seems to think that this grey area is likely to exist, given the background norm, unless there was to be a total change in our view of rational agents. My impression, from reading Gosling (1990), is that the background norm is something that may be regarded as relatively enduring and that it provides a stable, if difficult to articulate, criterion.

Procrastination

Procrastination is a phenomenon closely related to akrasia, as may be discerned from Sabini and Silver's (1982) definition:

the procrastinator is... someone who knows what she wants to do, in some sense can do it, is trying to do it – yet doesn't do it. (p. 126)

An essential element in procrastination is the delaying of action to or past the point when it is too late to successfully execute the intended act. Procrastination may therefore be regarded as a sub-category of akrasia, since it is not always necessary in akrasia for delay to be the primary feature (there may be no delay in swiftly downing the double whisky against one's better judgement). I shall start with a discussion of Sabini and Silver's (1982) conceptual analysis of the topic, prior to considering some of the positivist questionnaire approaches. I shall then compare the positivist and post-positivist approaches and indicate where I think there may be some potential for a fusion of both strategies.

Conceptual analysis

Sabini and Silver (1982) argue that procrastination is irrational, and therefore they have to set aside those cases where someone puts off doing a task with a rational reason. This would apply to someone who puts off an onerous task where there is a reasonable chance that by so doing they might get out of doing it altogether. Having tested out their ideas on some entertaining illustrations (a student who doesn't do an essay but goes on a date instead may be not so much irrational as sinful if she knowingly assigns her essay to a lower priority than her date, for example), they conclude that the irrationality of procrastination lies in the fact that the procrastinator knows what they ought to do. They acknowledge that the irrationality in procrastination is parasitic on rationality. I prefer the later analysis by Gosling (1990) who links the irrationality of akrasia via the implications of generalising from the particular case to the individual's standing as a competent agent (see my discussion earlier in this chapter). However, Sabini and Silver (1982) do discuss four interesting aspects of procrastination, which I shall now briefly describe.

Non-interchangeability of actions

The first of Sabini and Silver's (1982) categories covers the situation where someone does something like clean up the house instead of writing a college essay. Borrowing from ethology, I like to think of this as engaging in a displacement activity. Sabini and Silver (1982) point out that strategies which involve some degree of substitution among sub-plans need not necessarily be irrational. They provide the example of taking an alternative route to a location, which could be done in order to avoid traffic or some such thing. But cleaning houses and writing essays are not interchangeable. The outcome of housework is a clean house whereas that of not doing the essay may be a failed university course and these are quite different things: the less important obligation is met in order to procrastinate on the more important obligation.

Frittering

Sabini and Silver's (1982) second strain of procrastination is where 'a person sacrifices a substantial pleasure to his obligation but finds he has frittered away the time, entrapped by some minor pleasure' (pp. 139–40). Thus a student may decline to go out for the evening on a date or with friends in order to write an essay. Because this is not an enjoyable activity for them, they turn on the TV just for ten minutes (something that would not in itself have any great detrimental effect on the essay project). However, at the end of ten minutes, the decision is made to extend the watching for just another ten minutes and so on, until the evening has been frittered away with nothing having been done on the essay. What is sad about this is that the individual might just as well have gone out in the first place.

The primary problem is that the frittering away of time on minor pleasures has the cumulative potency of frustrating a temporal enabling condition for the execution of the target activity. This is not dissimilar to Baumeister *et al.*'s (1994) notion of a breakdown in self-stopping or snowballing. The difference is that the goal which is frustrated by, say, drinking one whisky after another is that of not drinking at all. The goal which is frustrated when one game of pinball is played after another is not the negative goal of *not playing pinball*, rather it is the positive goal of writing an essay. Playing pinball repetitively could be an extremely good alternative to drinking beers repetitively; it's just not a good alternative to the extended activity of writing an essay. Although it might be possible to analyse the pinball/essay example using the TOTE unit, it is easier to see it in terms of a computer program loop. Instead of a single loop being specified, it is as if the person gets stuck inside a loop with no exit test written into it and so they go round and round until the program crashes (and time has run out for all activity, except for bed).

Procrastination field

The third of Sabini and Silver's (1982) variations involves maintaining what they refer to as a 'procrastination field'. Here the procrastinator is always at readiness to work but gets sidetracked by things that require only ephemeral involvement, such as tidying up the spice rack, reading obscure sections of the newspaper, watering the plants or whatever (again, I construe this sort of thing as displacement activity). Sabini and Silver (1982) make the link with Goffman's (1959) notion of dramatisation. This brings out the distinction between acting in order to achieve a goal and the situation where the individual has some props and can simulate the activity from a dramatic point of view without actually engaging in it seriously. So someone might take some academic books with them on holiday, tell their friends that they can't come out to play because they are writing their academic paper, sit in a chair surrounded by books (some open at credible places), even put pen to paper from time to time, and yet no work is actually done (and this is where the spice racks or newspapers come in handy).

Right commitment, wrong plan

The fourth aspect of akrasia, discussed by Sabini and Silver (1982) is, for me, the most subtle part of their analysis. They advance the view that it is not rational, in some situations, to make all decisions rationally. Sometimes, in situations where there is the choice of following many paths but no one path appears to be the obvious choice to take, a person may start on one (perhaps because they know how to go on in this direction) and then they get stuck on this track thus persevering in an inappropriate fashion. Sabini and Silver (1982) give the example of a woman wanting to write an essay on the French Revolution but not knowing where to start. The problem is not her intelligence or commitment but she can't find the right plan for the essay. A less able student might be content with a rather coarse plan for the essay which involved collecting together a reasonable number of facts and stringing them together in chronological order. Sabini and Silver (1982) use cooking as a metaphor to explain the problem:

> There is a way of making stew by combining in any order whatever is at hand… it has a simple recipe and a tolerant criterion. Bordelaise sauce, however, has a stricter criterion, allows less substitution, and requires each ingredient to be treated in its own way in the proper order; the recipe is correspondingly demanding. (p. 138)

For the student who does not know what to do next, and who has no recipe but wants to produce something a little better than the basic stew, the situation is difficult and may well promote anxiety. Sabini and Silver (1982) suggest that if a flash of insight is not forthcoming then one solution is to acknowledge that doing one thing may be as good as doing another and therefore some kind of random trial and error approach might be the best. Unless the student acknowledges this, she may well fall into perseveration. This could take the form of never stopping the preparatory stage of prior reading, never stopping the collection of facts and so on. Of course, at some point there could be a switch to the previous form of akrasia with the introduction of frenetic spice rack alphabetising.

Procrastination questionnaires

The fact that procrastination might best be regarded as a failure in agency has not prevented its investigation by positivist psychologists. Questionnaires have been developed to measure procrastinators and these are similar to trait or attitude questionnaires. For example, the Aitken Procrastination Inventory, reviewed in Ferrari *et al.* (1995), comprises 19 items using a five-point true/false response scale to yield a total procrastination score. It was designed to distinguish chronic procrastinators from non-procrastinators among college undergraduates. Some sample items are as follows:

> I delay starting things until the last minute
> I am often late for my appointments and meetings
> I overestimate the amount of work that I can do in a given amount of time
> (Reported in Ferrari *et al.*, 1995, p. 53)

All that is happening here is that, through self-reporting, an assessment of the frequency or likelihood of an individual's procrastination, in general, is obtained. This is regarded as a measure of trait procrastination and it differs from Sabini and Silver's (1982) approach which tends to focus on particular examples of acute procrastination in order to develop a more complex analysis of the concept. Positivist researchers do frequently break down concepts but they do so usually through the development of sub-scales or through the search for underlying factors (using the statistical techniques of factor analysis). For example, Ferrari *et al.* (1995) indicate how the items in the Academic Procrastination State Inventory (APSI) can be subdivided into categories loading separately on the three factors of *Procrastination, Fear of Failure,* and *Lack of Motivation*. Of course, once a scale has been developed, it is then very easy to research its relation to other known scales. Thus Ferrari *et al.* (1995, p. 87) were able to report that the Procrastination sub-scale of the APSI correlates 0.60 with trait procrastination, and the Fear of Failure sub-scale correlates 0.66 with a measure of test anxiety.

As might be expected from the positivist approach, once basic measures of procrastination have been developed they may then be put to use very effectively in research designed to examine general trends within populations (such as university students). Tice and Baumeister (1997) administered procrastination questionnaires in two studies to groups of students taking health psychology courses. They found that procrastinators obtained significantly lower grades than non-procrastinators both for their course work ($r = -0.29$) and for their exams ($r = -0.64$). This dispels the myth that massive inspiration and creative energy kicks in to save the day for procrastinators who play chicken with approaching deadlines, at least for the sample in general. Another of their findings was that, although the procrastinators reported fewer symptoms per week on average than the non-procrastinators at the beginning of a semester, the position was reversed as course work deadlines approached at the end of the semester with the procrastinators reporting more symptoms (r = 0.65), more stress (r = 0.68), and more non-routine visits to the healthcare professionals (r = 0.37). This is an important study, since it links procrastination not only to academic performance, but also to levels of sickness and stress in the student population.

Of course, the statistical maxim that correlation does not imply causation applies to Tice and Baumeister's (1997) research and there could be some underlying factor which was responsible for the poor performance. The obvious alternative explanation is that the procrastinators are in fact less intelligent than the procrastinators but this view is rejected by Tice and Baumeister (1997) on the grounds that previous studies (Taylor, 1979; Ferrari, 1991) have found no relation between procrastination and intelligence. They also consider the possibility that procrastination leads to stress and illness and it is the latter that then causes the poor academic performance. They acknowledge that their study does not yield data that can directly address such a possibility.

Paradigmatic triangulation in procrastination research

I have considered research drawn from two very different approaches and, in my view, the work can be separated paradigmatically into the positivist and post-positivist. Sabini and Silver's (1982) work is much closer to the conceptual analysis offered by the philosophers, than is that of Ferrari *et al.* (1995). However, conceptual analysis alone is incapable of providing the sort of interesting evidence obtained by Tice and Baumeister (1997), for example. Within paradigms, it is not unusual for researchers to deploy complementary techniques in their research and this is sometimes referred to as methodological triangulation. Tice and Baumeister (1997) did this by using the McCown and Johnson Adult Inventory of Procrastination questionnaire (1989, cited in Ferrari *et al.*, 1995) in their first study, followed by the Lay (1986) General Procrastination Scale in their second study. I think that the study of procrastination could benefit from an element of paradigmatic triangulation. The positivist research of Tice and Baumeister (1997) alerts us to potential problems in terms of academic procrastination, for the performance and health of the students. The conceptual analyses, whether from the philosophers or from the post-positivist psychologists, provide many clues as to where the problems may lie in specific cases of (acute) procrastination. In order to marry the two it may be necessary to engage in detailed case studies of procrastinators and non-procrastinators (identified through the positivist scales) as they attempt to execute their projects. In the case of academic procrastination that would presumably involve tracking individuals in their completion of course work assignments and preparation for examinations. In this regard, an approach based upon the psychology of action and the execution of plans (discussed in Chapter 4) could yield specific advice and recommendations as to how to resolve the problem (see also Chapter 7 for a discussion of time management). Where individuals seem to be condemned to chronic procrastination across many projects of varied types, they may need to work on their self-concept, possibly with the help of counselling. This is the point where the psychology of action meets that of personality or character.

Lay (1986), discussing Sabini and Silver's (1982) analysis, acknowledges their point that the irrationality in procrastination hinges on the fact that one is not doing what one thinks one ought to do. He then points out that although such moral obligation may be related to what others think we ought to do, in the case of his own data, there is some suggestion that procrastinators are less responsive to what others think they ought to do than are non-procrastinators. Furthermore, with regard to Sabini and Silver's (1982) point about individuals needing to draw on their past experiences in order to judge the duration of time required to complete specific tasks, he feels that in his research there was good indication that procrastinators lacked the necessary organisational tendencies for such fine tuning in the timing and scheduling of their activities. While procrastinators may be able to make plans linked to their important life projects and even prioritise on a day-to-day basis, Lay (1986) thinks that their Achilles heel may be in the waiting stage between sub-episodes of extended activity where they may omit to keep their priorities uppermost in their minds or actively engage in behaviour which does not correspond with these priorities.

> This link between priorities and goal-associated behavior may be viewed as an inherent part of the defining of procrastinatory behavior. The premise here would be that one should spend the most time, or the most adequate time, on tasks that are viewed as most important. Failure to do so would constitute procrastinatory behavior, viewed in both the short-run and the long-run as a failure to act on one's priorities. (pp. 493–4)

If moral condemnation comes with this interpretation it does sound a little harsh. The analysis gets its bite from an individual's priorities being known and clearly articulated, and this may not be the case for many people. Indeed, this is precisely the sort of area where individual differences might be expected. However, if the co-ordination of everyday plans of action and the integration of higher order goals into daily, weekly and longer-term schedules are regarded at heart as agentic skills, then there should be some scope for an improvement in expertise, through education, experience and practice.

Concluding discussion

The philosophical debate about weakness of will is brought into stark focus when the extreme situation of last-ditch akrasia is considered. I have argued that it may be possible to describe this phenomenon drawing on the terms readily available within the TPB. However, where weakness of will is seen to be a self-regulation failure, the cybernetic approach offers a better descriptive framework, especially when the TOTE unit is invoked. Some of the psychological research suggests that something akin to willpower, in the ordinary sense of the term, may be required if akrasia is to be avoided. There may, on occasion, be times where the act in question crosses the threshold into causally explained and law-governed behaviour; here there is little sense in speaking of weakness of will, since the concept of agency will no longer apply. In some circumstances, one minor lapse may, through a snowballing effect, lead to a fullblown breakdown in control. Even here, individuals may acquiesce in their own failure to regulate their own behaviour and some things, such as the consumption of alcohol, may contribute to this result by reducing the person's capacity to monitor what is happening. The discussion of last-ditch akrasia drew me into the territory of rationality and the criterion for rational agents within linguistic communities. In this regard, I was able to return to ideas I had previously developed in relation to the TRA/TPB construed as a rule for intelligibility (see Chapter 2).

With regard to procrastination, I was taken with Sabini and Silver's (1982) analysis. They present their material in a fashion which lacks some of the formality of the contemporary philosophical approaches to the topic, but their views are nonetheless informative. I was reminded more of the armchair psychology of James as they illustrated their points with hypothetical case studies drawn from a credible world of mundane reality. They also have something in common with Goffman in this regard. While I am happy to admit that I like this approach, I also acknowledge that it cannot do the same job of work that the questionnaire-based positivist studies do. And I am not prepared to dismiss these out of hand merely because they reside in my non-preferred paradigm. It seems to me that the notion of trait procrastination which ties into the positivist's questionnaire research in empirical psychology is of direct relevance to the philosophical debates concerning last-ditch akrasia. This is what led me to advocate a fusion of the positivist and post-positivist approaches in future research on the topic.

In this chapter, I have been concerned mainly with conceptual and research matters. However, where procrastination, akrasia or agentic impotence in general becomes a problem for particular individuals, it may have to be addressed through some form of counselling whether self-administered on the basis of DIY manuals or dispensed by the professionals. I discuss both of these therapeutic strategies to agentic improvement in the next chapter.

Chapter 7
Agentic improvement

I shall start with a rather crass analogy between agentic and home improvement. If I wish to improve the plumbing in my house or put in some additional bookshelves, I can do it myself or I can get in the professionals. I am happy to take on minor tinkering with a DIY approach but anything major, involving structural alterations, has me phoning for a plumber or a builder. Agentic improvement, too, can be accomplished through DIY and there are numerous manuals on sale in the popular psychology shelves of the larger bookstores which can be used to good effect in this context. These range from the broadly programmatic lifestyle classics of Smiles (1859/1969) on *Self-Help* or Carnegie (1936/1998) on *How to Win Friends and Influence People* to a host of books providing a more contemporary focus on narrower topics such as time management (for example Fontana, 1993) or assertiveness training (for example Smith, 1975). I shall deal with both the DIY and the professional approaches to agentic improvement, although this chapter will not be a therapeutic manual in miniature; my goals lie closer to deconstruction and critique. I shall start with a consideration of time management and will leave my discussion of professional counselling until the latter part of the chapter.

Time management

I shall focus my discussion of time management on one particular manual (Fontana, 1993) which is written for professionals to use in a fashion that will cover all aspects of their lives, not just the demands emanating from the working environment. I have chosen this manual on the grounds that it has some degree of endorsement from the psychological establishment (given that it is published by the British Psychological Society).

Fontana (1993) regards good time management as a skill that can be learned. His approach to the topic is based on research in psychology and management. Given that this book falls within the genre of the self-help manual, it is not surprising to find that he demands of the reader a degree of commitment and perseverance. As a reader, I may have been atypical in this regard since I had half an eye to critique, if not actual deconstruction. Still, I am happy to acknowledge that I took away several tips to try out in my own everyday life and these, somewhat reflexively, had an impact on how I organised my time to write this book.

Opening gambits and metaphors

Fontana (1993) starts with a quote from Lewis Carroll's *Through the Looking Glass* and thereby makes the assumption that the readers will be familiar with Carroll's book and, furthermore, will empathise with Alice's predicament of having to run just to stay still. While this may be a reasonable assumption, given that the primary readership targeted would appear to be British professionals and managers, it backfired with me; I really disliked the Alice stories when I was a child.

Fontana (1993) then moves to a financial metaphor in order to illuminate what happens when things go wrong. He argues that time is *capital*; it is not renewable income. When we draw on time it dwindles away until it is gone, just like capital does. And once gone, it is gone forever.

> The upshot of this is that any programme designed to help us manage our time efficiently must start with our realization that time is precious, consequently motivating us to use this finite asset with the same care we would devote to the spending of gold coins. (Fontana, 1993, p. 3)

To pursue this analogy further would tug against the liberal humanist mission statement (see Stainton Rogers *et al.*, 1995) and the sense of optimism which runs through much of the self-improvement literature. After all, one can hardly escape the conclusion that bankruptcy equates with death, voluntary liquidation with suicide and debt with living on borrowed time. I'm not sure that time in a prison cell, time waiting in line at the supermarket checkout or time on a factory production line is best captured by the gold coins metaphor since, here, time can drag. Fontana (1993) lets such gloomy conclusions hover in the background, largely unstated, while he coaxes the metaphor to work on the level of a moral imperative.

Setting this aside, I will proceed on the basis that the point of Fontana's (1993) metaphor is to get the reader into a suitable frame of mind to start a programme of time management; there is no hypothesis to be critically appraised.

The right frame of mind

According to Fontana (1993), the benefits of time management are increased effectiveness and efficiency, higher productivity, increased leisure time, enhanced job satisfaction, reduced stress, more opportunity to switch off after hours, more room for forward planning and for long-term solutions and higher creativity (p. 5). He contrasts these with what it is not: Type A behaviour, a ruthless selfish approach to life, efficiency gone mad, being inflexible or uncreative (p. 6).

Fontana's (1993) exhortation to develop the right attitude of mind is so clearly a moral statement that no attempt is made to derive it from empirical investigation. Fontana (1993) engages in storytelling in a way which is similar to how Reason (1990) talks about the events in the NUREG accident report or Merttens (1998) builds tales out of what happens in her professional experience (see Chapter 5). Fontana (1993) tells a story about an advertising executive called Morgan who has the wrong attitude to his chronically disorganised lifestyle and then uses the story in order to illustrate what can go wrong. Fontana (1993) then offers a psychological explanation for what happened in the story.

> We all have the power to think clearly, to show decisiveness, to be single-minded and so on; the main reason we fail to show these qualities more consistently is that they require a certain amount of effort. (p. 10)

It could be argued that this assertion flies in the face of the very considerable individual differences that are found when populations are tested on verbal, mathematical or logical reasoning tasks (especially the sort included within IQ tests). No evidence is put forward to support the claim that frequency and consistency in clear thinking is a function of effort for given individuals. No clue is given as to the nature of this 'effort'. James' dread heave of the will describes a mental effort but one deployed in the execution of an intention where procrastination or akrasia have to be overcome (see Chapter 2). The effort to think clearly may be something quite different.

Fontana (1993) considers whether temperament might play a part in time management ability but, having discussed the nature versus nurture debate, he concludes that although there is likely to be a genetic component one should not use this as an excuse for failure. He summarises his main message as follows:

> The more we tell ourselves that we don't have 'the kind of mind' necessary to manage time, the more we condition ourselves into believing we haven't. The evidence from sports psychology and from certain areas of occupational, clinical and educational psychology (Fontana, 1988) is that the ability to think positively about our abilities has a profound effect upon our performance. (p. 13)

From a rhetorical standpoint this is a sweeping conclusion which grounds itself in the scientific reputation of professional and applied psychology. It occurs to me that Bandura's (1997) magnum opus, published after Fontana's book, would provide further support for this claim. I acknowledge that Fontana can hardly be expected to produce both a critical appraisal of the relevant research literature *and* a programmatic volume on time management in a popular psychology series aimed at professionals, since there is not space for him to do both.

Strategies for improvement

It is not my intention to move slavishly through Fontana's (1993) book, chapter by chapter; I shall cover only a sample of his recommended techniques. He advocates the keeping of a diary record of the use of time on a day-to-day basis in order to obtain data for a more detailed analysis of the way the person uses their time. The diary record has been used extensively in time budgeting research (see Szalai, 1972) and it also features prominently in the slips and errors literature (see my discussion of Reason, 1990, in Chapter 4).

Fontana (1993) also includes a personality-type quiz which enables the reader to assess where the main problems lie in terms of their time on-task. These are divided into three main areas: issues relating to the doing of the tasks (trying to do more than one thing at once, rushing to meet deadlines and so on), problems linked to self or personality (procrastination, distraction, poor memory, inability to relax and so forth) and the social dimension (difficulty in delegation, difficulty in saying 'no' to other people's requests and demands, poor performance at dealing with interruptions from other people). When I did this exercise I found that I had virtually no problems with the mechanics of task execution but that there were a number of things relating to myself and my dealings with other people that could be improved. In order to illustrate the approach adopted in explaining the virtues of good time management, I will take an example from the section which deals with planning the workload and the statement of relevant objectives.

Objectives identify and stipulate the goals that we wish to achieve, and in managing our workload their presence allows us to (Fontana, 1993, p. 31):

- identify clearly what needs to be done
- plan how we are going to do it
- monitor our progress while we are doing it
- assess the extent of our success when we have done it
- learn more effectively from the experiences it has offered us.

Fontana (1993) argues that this advice is based upon psychological research and cites Pearson and Tweddle (1984) in support of his case. Whether such advice transcends common sense is an open question but, as one psychologist to another, I'm not going to start calling kettles black.

It would appear that the management of time is a skill that may be learned and improved by monitoring how time is spent and putting into effect strategies that will eradicate inefficiencies and wastage. Personal organisers (paper or electronic), planning schedules and so forth can all be brought to bear upon the executive facet of agency. Some problems, such as poor self-efficacy beliefs or ineffective interpersonal skills, may require deeper solutions. For example, where the problem requires a revision of the person's self-image, therapeutic techniques which go beyond time management may be necessary. This is the point where referrals may be made to counsellors or individuals may voluntarily seek therapeutic help. I move on, then, from the DIY into the domain of the professionals.

Counselling

Given the constraints of space, I have had to be selective when singling out counselling techniques for discussion in the context of the psychology of action. I have chosen to focus on behaviour modification because, as explained in Chapter 1, it is the concept of behaviour that sits competitively against the concept of action and it is behaviourism which is most diametrically opposed to the notion of agency.

I mount a critique of behaviour modification from an agentic perspective and provide an alternative interpretation of what it involves. In order to do this, I adopt a rhetorical standpoint as the basis for my critique. I conclude the section on counselling techniques with a discussion of rational emotive behavioural counselling because I see this approach as occupying a mid-way position between behaviour modification and some of the work on plans and goal setting I discussed in Chapter 4.

Rhetoric

Cockroft and Cockroft (1992) emphasise, in their definition of rhetoric, that words can be used not only to form attitudes but also to induce actions in other human agents. It is this latter function that leads me to a consideration of behaviour modification and other therapeutic techniques from a rhetorical standpoint.

The aim of deliberative oratory is to persuade or dissuade the listener with regard to possible future projects or lines of action. It is thus relevant to the rhetorician to be aware of what is likely to motivate a person. Aristotle's (1926) view concerning this is close to a conventional hedonism:

> Men, individually and in common, nearly all have some aim, in the attainment of which they choose or avoid certain things. This aim, briefly stated, is happiness and its component parts. (p. 47)

There is some embarrassment in now looking back from a distance of some two thousand years at the way Aristotle then proceeded to operationally define the concept of happiness:

> Let us then define happiness as well-being combined with virtue, or independence of life, or the life that is most agreeable combined with security, or abundance of possessions or slaves, combined with power to protect and make use of them; for nearly all men admit that one or more of these things constitute happiness. (p. 49)

Setting aside Aristotle's reference to slaves and his endorsement of materialist greed, the inclusion of a hedonistic element in his approach to rhetoric makes it easy to relate it to some of the theories discussed in the earlier chapters of this book, especially the expectancy-value theories dealt with in Chapters 2 and 4. For example, Aristotle makes the point that since nobody deliberates about what is certain, it is the merely *probable* that provides more scope for the orator. Probability beliefs lie at the heart of the attitude component in the TRA/TPB.

Behaviour modification

I now propose to use the link that hedonism provides between rhetoric and expectancy-value models as a vehicle for developing an agentic interpretation of learning theory and its therapeutic techniques. It is the concept of reinforcement that makes this possible.

Mapping reinforcement on to the rule for intelligibility

The link between Rotter's social learning theory and the TRA/TPB may be discerned in Rotter's definition of reinforcement (see also Chapter 4). Although he expresses this definition in the form of an algebraic equation, it may easily be stated in plain English. Rotter (1982, p. 245) says that the value of a reinforcement in any particular situation will be a function of the expectancies that that reinforcement will lead to other reinforcements (this is very similar to the probability of the consequences of intention in the TRA) and of the values of these other reinforcements (this is very similar to the evaluation of consequences in the TRA).

With regard to the selection of the reinforcers, Nemeroff and Karoly (1991) acknowledge that what is a reward for one person may not necessarily be so for others. While I can see that this is a sensible point for them to make, there may well be some things which most people would agree were rewarding and it should be possible to discover this empirically (see the discussion of Tolman's modal matrix in Chapter 4). A reward may be defined as a positively evaluated TRA outcome. Nemeroff and Karoly (1991) suggest the adoption of the Premack principle which they describe as the rule of 'using a relatively high-probability behavior to reinforce a lower-probability behavior' (p. 147). The attention to probability provides the tie-in to expectancy-value theory.

Nemeroff and Karoly (1991) advocate that rewards should be administered immediately, contingently and consistently to maximise effectiveness. They also suggest using a variety of different reinforcers to minimise the loss of potency due to satiation (if music be the food of love...).

There are a number of points I wish to make at this stage. In terms of an Abelsonian plans molecule, the therapist, in arranging the schedule of reinforcement, is grafting a number of arbitrary side effects on to the target behaviour. The positive valence of these side effect outcome states is taken as given (on the basis of prior observation, common sense, or whatever). It is the probability of their occurrence that has to be learned by the protagonist and integrated into the existing plans schema. Other things being equal, it may be assumed that the subjective probability estimate (expectancy belief) held by the protagonist will be in line with the way in which the therapist chooses to administer the reinforcement. Nemeroff and Karoly (1991) advocate starting with a schedule of continuous reinforcement to bring the target behaviour to optimal frequency and then to shift to partial reinforcement 'to minimize loss of potency of the reinforcer and to increase the durability of effects' (p. 147).

In terms of the rule for intelligibility (see Chapter 2), I assume that the grafting of the reinforcing side effects (be they positive or negative) on to the Abelsonian plans molecule can be arranged to produce an imbalance in the TRA/TPB equation unless the client switches her or his intention to the desired direction. In other words, in addition to the rewards or punishments involved, there is the meta-consideration that the client could be acting in an unintelligible fashion, as defined by the rule for intelligibility, unless they go along with the therapist. I have elsewhere (see Smith, 1987) considered the possibility that in some settings (such as psychiatric hospitals) this could carry serious meta-consequences in the form of electro-convulsive therapy, the administration of psychotropic drugs or whatever, should the client appear to be acting irrationally by failing in the therapeutic regime. I shall not pursue this here; I merely note that, in the language of the movies, they may be given an offer they can't refuse.

At this point I will pause to recapitulate the academic position. I have taken my critique of the TRA/TPB and applied it to behaviour modification. The reason why this is possible is because reinforcement can be described as an expectancy-value consequence flowing from the target behaviour. Although a strict behaviourist would not speak of the client's intention, that does not mean that I am debarred from doing so. In this way the therapeutic situation is easily translated into the language of the TRA/TPB. Once this is achieved, anything I say about the TRA/TPB must be applicable to behaviour modification.

Power and control

Nemeroff and Karoly (1991) set out recommendations for implementing a number of specific operant techniques. The language they use to describe this is, in itself, interesting. They talk of equipping the applied behaviour analyst with 'a full arsenal of concepts' (p. 147) and elsewhere say that these principles will 'continue to find a place in the clinician's armamentarium' (p. 155). The weaponry metaphor is appropriate, since it highlights the issue of power and coercion, an issue which always lies seething beneath the surface of any behaviour modification technique.

Behaviour modification will only work if the therapist has sole control over the reinforcers. If this is not the case then the protagonist could independently obtain the benefits of the reinforcer not as a side effect which is contingent on the target behaviour but as a primary goal in and of itself. Where this happens, the principle of the contingent administration of the reinforcers will be violated. The potency of the reinforcer is likely to be diminished, although its valence could remain intact (sweeties may still taste nice, even if you can have them *without* having to do something you don't want to do to get them).

There are at least two ways to look at this from the standpoint of power and control in the therapeutic situation. First, the therapist must be able to control not only the situation where the target behaviour is likely to occur but also the wider life space of the protagonist in such a way as to prevent free access to equivalent reinforcers. Only in this way can the therapist hope to control the schedule of reinforcement and to maintain the potency of the reinforcers. Second, from the point of view of the protagonist, it can be seen that the obtaining of the reinforcer is likely to be regarded as the target behaviour.

Looked at this way, the therapist has to do two things. First, she or he must ensure that perceived behavioural control is zero with regard to the protagonist's ability to reach the reinforcers, except by executing the behavioural intention targeted by the therapist as an intermediate step. I find it helpful to think of the target behaviour (from the therapist's point of view) as being embedded in an action-state chain which culminates in the reinforcement. Second, the therapist must have such total control as necessary to block all routes to the reinforcer save the one she or he sets up via the target behaviour. It is therefore of little surprise that behaviour modification works best in closed institutions such as psychiatric hospitals or schools. In less optimal situations, Kazdin (1981, p. 70) suggests that the domain of control can be extended if the therapist can recruit secondary agents such as psychiatric aides, parents, teachers and others.

Punishment

Nemeroff and Karoly (1991) state that when positive control and non-physical forms of punishment are ineffective in changing behaviour, the use of response-contingent aversive stimulation (RCAS) may, if used within guidelines they set out, work best. RCAS may be an acronym for a string of technical terms but what it stands for is *punishment*. Sandler and Steele (1991) say that by far the bulk of the operant aversion therapy literature 'involves the use of stimuli that are physically unpleasant or even painful' (p. 214). They list water spraying, foul odours, uncomfortable sounds, slaps, hair pulls and electric shocks applied to the limbs as examples of aversive stimuli, with the latter being the most common. Apparently, an appropriate technology has been developed to deliver to the practitioners the instruments of therapeutic torture as and when they require them.

> A number of shock delivery devices are commercially available for use in aversion therapy, the most practical of which are battery operated, portable instruments. (Sandler and Steele, 1991, p. 215)

The use of punishment may be regarded as stacking the expectancy-value computation more strongly in favour of the desired behaviour. I have already suggested that a client, when faced with an impressive array of positive or negative reinforcements, may well take the rational path and go along with the required responses, unless there are other extraneous reasons not to. Such reasons might be grounded in religious, moral or political principles (see Chapter 2).

Self-injurious behaviour

Therapists may sometimes be faced with clients whose situation can only be described as dire and for whom the full range of commonsense attempts at problem solving has afforded no relief. Some particularly striking examples come from children engaged in self-injurious behaviour (SIB). Sandler and Steele (1991), reviewing practical applications of aversion methods, discuss two 6-year-old identical twin girl clients reported in Wesolowski and Zawlocki (1982). These girls were diagnosed as totally blind and profoundly mentally retarded. The problem was that both girls frequently pushed their fingers up into their eye sockets, causing tissue damage around their eyes. The aversive techniques used involved auditory time-out periods and response interruption by holding down the girls' hands (perhaps not the most aversive of aversive techniques). Sandler and Steele (1991, p. 221) state:

> By far the most extensive application of aversion therapy with discrete problem conditions has involved the use of painful shock, contingent on head banging and self-mutilation in children. There are now a sufficient number of observations that confirm the effectiveness of such procedures, especially when compared with nonaversive techniques, in terms of rapid suppression of the behavior.

It is easy to give the impression that behaviour therapists are the devils incarnate with untold powers over their clients who languish incarcerated within corrective institutions while being subjected to all manner of aversive stimulation, selected from their therapist's armamentarium which, in turn, is stocked with an abundance of potential terrors including electric shocks, water spraying, visual screening (blindfolds), foul odours, uncomfortable sounds, slaps, hair pulls, shouts and reprimands (see Sandler and Steele, 1991, p. 214). As a general impression this may be unfair but it is nonetheless grounded in reports in the therapeutic literature.

Agentic modification

Behaviour modification takes place in a social episode or series of episodes (but I shall refer to the singular case henceforth). The context within which that episode takes place may vary in terms of the extent to which the client is free to operate independently outside the episode. In this sense, the boundaries of the episode may vary in permeability from the reasonably open, in many everyday life settings, to the relatively closed, in the case of locked psychiatric wards or prison environments (see above discussion). It is likely that the imbalance of power in favour of the therapist, relative to the client, will be greater the more closed are the boundaries of the episode. To my knowledge, there is no specialist therapeutic vocabulary within the agentic perspective and therefore any interpretation born of that perspective will have to make do with the extant terms and concepts available.

Agentic modification might sensibly start with a meta-account as to why any modification is required in the first place. It is at this point that any one of a range of moral stances might be applied to the episode. If the protagonist (client) has sought out the change agent because of a desire to change, the therapist may be seen as an agent of the protagonist in the same way a piano teacher or a personal fitness trainer might be. In these cases, it may be odd to hold the therapist responsible for the client's experience of negative reinforcers, providing that the receipt of negative reinforcement was openly acknowledged in the therapeutic contract (actual or implied). The issue of responsibility here is not dissimilar to that in hypnosis, masochism and obedience situations (see Chapters 8 and 9).

The situation where the protagonist has been referred to the change agent by some authority (such as the courts) is slightly different. In this latter situation, the protagonist may be a less than willing participant in the therapeutic episode. This could happen where the therapeutic regime is presented as an alternative to a prison sentence or as part of a deal involving a less extreme form of incarceration than would otherwise be the case, for example.

A number of problems are thrown into relief by these considerations. If the modification episode is not construed as therapy, then the rewards and punishments tied into the episode must be understood in terms of other practices in society. I shall briefly consider two underlying models for the therapeutic episode: circus training and wage labour. I put these forward in competition to the medical model.

The administration of rewards or punishments may be construed in terms of training animals to perform tricks and this is close to the mark in terms of the historical development of learning theory. In this model, the client will be construed *qua* animal, not as a human agent. Given that the client is not accorded full status as a person, incarceration or other control over the client's freedom will not appear as an abuse of that person's human rights.

The second model I wish to put forward is one based on wage labour. Here the client acts in a manner not dissimilar to someone at work (especially in the service sector). A client who is rewarded for being polite to people in social situations (perhaps at school, in the hospital or in the community) has some similarity with service industry workers who instruct their customers to 'have a nice day'. In other words, behaviour modification can be seen along the lines of labour being sold for a price. The parallel is particularly close to the mark in terms of token economies (see Kazdin, 1977) where tokens equate to performance related pay. It may be noted that in this model the client is regarded as a rational agent and is expected to behave appropriately.

Flogging, the administration of electric shocks to the body and other diverse forms of corporal punishment are no longer condoned in the majority of western democratic societies. The mystery is how punitive behaviour modification techniques elude accountability. The answer to that question may lie partly in the historical association of therapeutic techniques with the medical profession and the hospital setting. The therapist may thus be shielded by the institutional power and status accorded to doctors and surgeons. Such exemption from accountability is not afforded by the agentic interpretation of behaviour modification, since there is no way in which what happens can be seen as medical or therapeutic. The administration of an electric shock in behaviour modification is to be regarded more like a smack on the bottom than an appendectomy. The application of an agentic perspective to behaviour modification decouples the latter from its pseudo-medical cover story and aligns it more closely with circus training or wage labour as underlying metaphors. I move on now to consider an approach which is closer to the agentic perspective but has some affiliation with behaviourism.

Rational emotive behavioural counselling

Although cognitive-behavioural counselling (CBC) and rational emotive behavioural counselling (REBC) take the modification of behaviour as part of their central concerns, they differ from behaviour modification in a number of ways that suggest a closer affinity with the agentic perspective. Dryden and Yankura (1995) introduce REBC by suggesting that it is not so much particular events that people may find disturbing as the views they take of these events. While this could be open to the criticism that it is an inherently conservative approach, seeking to adjust individuals to the prevailing status quo, there would appear to be a commitment to using therapy as a catalyst to change where change is possible. The reason why some people may be disturbed by events may be because they hold irrational beliefs about them. In REBC, irrational beliefs are those that are rigid, inconsistent with reality, illogical and which interfere with the person's wellbeing. The foundations of REBC can be described in terms of four rational–irrational belief pairs and I comment on each of these in the sections immediately below.

Preferences versus musts

Dryden and Yankura (1995) give the examples of someone who feels that they absolutely must pass their driving test or absolutely must not get into trouble with their boss. I think that the imperative nature of *must do* beliefs takes them beyond the theory of reasoned action, since the consequence of transgression is too dreadful to even contemplate. What REBC seems to be doing here is moving the *must* into the realm of the TRA whereby the negative outcomes and probabilities of not complying to the must are given a more measured assessment as against some of the positive outcomes that might also accrue. The emphasis in REBC on the therapist demonstrating logical inconsistencies and so forth is very much in tune with my interpretation of the TRA as a rule governing intelligibility. It also emphasises the rhetorical nature of REBC (see my discussion, above).

Anti-awfulising versus awfulising

Once the link with the expectancy-value model is made (see, above, regarding preference versus must) then the REBC focus on *anti-awfulising* can be seen as directed primarily to consequence evaluations of the TRA. The aim is to get the negative consequences which are thought to be right off the end of any scale imaginable into a more realistic appraisal as merely being *very bad.* The use of the colloquial term 'anti-awfulising' reminds me of the way Berne (1964, 1972) chose somewhat folksy names for the games and pastimes which he catalogued in transactional analysis. For example, 'anti-awfulising', as a descriptive term, is evocative of Berne's pastime *Ain't it Awful.*

High frustration tolerance versus low frustration tolerance

In this category, low frustration tolerance beliefs are grossly exaggerated (so the person in Dryden and Yankura's, 1995, example would find their whole world disintegrating were they to fail their driving test). Again, I think that the REBC strategy is merely to help the person to bring the situation under a more relaxed appraisal of the expectancy-value consequences. Once again, the strategy meshes well with the TRA and the rule of intelligibility.

Self-/other-acceptance versus self-/other-downing

The main point here is to acknowledge the complexity of the self and to move away from globally damning assessments of oneself such as *I am bad, I am a failure* and so forth. In terms of agency, mistakes and failures in specific activities and projects must not be allowed to generalise to the agent as a person but should be construed very much in the limited context of action where the mishap or failure occurred. The complexity of the concept of self is something which Harré (1983) deals with at some length but it is not a primary feature of expectancy-value models such as the TRA/TPB.

These four rational and irrational belief pairs are an important part of the ABCDE of REBC. Dryden and Yankura (1995) claim that this simple, alphabetical mnemonic appears in most books written about REBC. The letters stand for:

Activating event (this triggers the irrational beliefs)
Beliefs (this involves the four rational–irrational pairs already listed)
Consequences (it is this aspect which seems to be most directly related to expectancy-value models)

Disputing (this is what the therapist does with the client to eradicate the irrational beliefs)
Effects (Dryden and Yankura, 1995, characterise this in terms of the outcome of therapy and all the changes that flow from this).

In terms of the concerns of the present chapter, it is the 'disputing' aspect of REBC that establishes it as a rhetorical practice. Dryden and Yankura (1995) provide advice about how the therapist should go about their disputing, based on a model put forward by DiGiuseppe (1991). Without going into the full model, advice on the type of disputing argument to be used covers logical, empirical and pragmatic approaches. The style of disputing is discussed in terms of Socratic, didactic, humorous, metaphorical and self-disclosing techniques. Various warnings are given to therapists: *watch your pace, refrain from being overly persistent* and so forth.

It would appear not unreasonable to extend Aristotle's (1926, p. 33) three kinds of rhetoric (deliberative, forensic and epideictic) to include the therapeutic. Dryden and Yankura (1995, Chapter 1) talk about choosing the right style. For some clients it may be best for the counsellor to adopt a formal relationship, with others a more informal interaction may be best. Similarly, the counsellor may vary in terms of the extent to which he or she presents as an expert or depends on a more personal style for impact. In a parallel fashion, Aristotle (1926, Book II) gives advice as to how the speakers can create a certain impression of themselves and put the listener into a certain frame of mind. In this Aristotle emphasises the necessity of the speaker convincing the audience of his or her trustworthiness. I think that both Aristotle (1926) and Dryden and Yankura (1995), by emphasising the importance of trust, counter the notion that rhetoricians might be best regarded as rather shallow high self-monitors (see Snyder, 1987). Dryden and Yankura (1995) say:

> As long as we are genuine, we can become what Arnold Lazarous (1981) calls an 'authentic chameleon' in our work with our clients. (p. 6)

Establishing a more explicit link between REBC and rhetoric means that training for counsellors might be extended to include the study of the sorts of rhetorical device that are listed in Cockroft and Cockroft's (1992) Appendices. What I have in mind here is something akin to rhetorical workshops for counsellors. This would be categorically different from, but not mutually exclusive to, the deployment of discourse analysis in the counselling situation. The way the latter might work is for the counsellor to work on a transcript of a session with the client (or at least watch a tape) and then to develop a discursive analysis of it. This would be something quite different, although anyone who has completed training as a sensitivity training group (T-Group) leader (see Smith, 1980) would be tuned up for delivering the sorts of functional and process comment that might arise from discursive analysis in real time, as opposed to the infinitely slower response rate which flows from producing transcript of interactions.

Before I leave the topic of REBC, I will say a few words about the importance of planning in this approach. Dryden and Yankura (1995) stress the importance of goal setting, partly in relation to what client and counsellor wish to achieve from the therapeutic sessions, and partly in relation to 'homework' assignments and so forth. There tends not to be any direct link between the goal-setting literature in the domain of industrial psychology (see my discussion of Locke and Latham's, 1990, work in Chapter 4) and goal setting within the therapeutic context. I can see no reason why there should not be closer integration here. Indeed virtually all the material I covered in Chapter 4 could usefully be integrated more closely into the therapeutic forum, including the work on plans, their representation and their execution. Because of limitations of space, I am not able to deal with cognitive-behavioural counselling (CBC) in the context of this chapter (see Scott *et al.*, 1995, for an introduction to CBC). However, given the emphasis that CBC places on working with the way the client construes their problematic situations, there are close parallels between this approach and REBC. I feel that many of the remarks I have made concerning REBC could equally be applied to CBC.

Concluding discussion

In approaching the topic of time management I adopted the pragmatic strategy of focusing on one particular DIY manual, one which I felt had some endorsement from the British psychological establishment. Although my treatment may not have amounted to a fully fledged deconstruction, I did pay attention to some of the rhetorical tactics and strategies employed by the author. Any DIY manual must contain directives concerning the reader's future conduct if it is to be worth its salt, and Fontana's (1993) book is no exception. The challenge for the author of DIY material is how to persuade the reader to submit to such directives. I think that Fontana's (1993) use of storytelling (such as *disorganised-Morgan*) or his deployment of colourful metaphors (such as *time-is-capital*) were more potent in providing warrants for the directives, arguments and prescriptions contained within the manual than were the somewhat vague references to research in sports, occupational, clinical and educational psychology.

The use of storytelling is something that I noted in Chapter 5 in the context of Reason's (1990) and Merttens' (1998) work in applied psychology. Perhaps there are lessons to be learned with regard to the way undergraduate psychologists are trained. An ability to read the runes of a three-way interaction in the analysis of variance would seem to be of limited use compared to a thorough grounding in fable, allegory or parable when it comes to proselytisation. I say this with only a modicum of flippancy, since deliberative oratory provided me with a base from which to develop my critique of behaviour modification.

In Chapter 1, I dwelt on the tension between the concepts of behaviour and action and indicated that they spawned separate and competing paradigms in psychology. I wanted to choose a professional therapeutic technique for detailed analysis in the latter part of this chapter, and I chose behaviour modification on the grounds that it emanates from the behaviourist stable. In developing my critique of behaviour modification, I did not seek to challenge its efficacy. Rather, I sought to understand it from an agentic standpoint.

Having established the connection between expectancy-value theories and the concept of reinforcement, I was able to apply my agentic interpretation of the TRA/TPB to the operant techniques and I illustrated this with reference to self-injurious behaviour in children. The agentic viewpoint brings the issues of power and control sharply into focus and nowhere is that more evident than when considering the part punishment plays in behaviour modification. There can be no justification of the use of punishment on medical grounds when the agentic interpretation is invoked; the behaviour therapist must therefore be held to account for his or her therapeutic practices in much the same way that parents, teachers or prison warders would be held to account for their conduct.

An approach which has some superficial resemblance to behaviour modification is REBC. In fact this was found to be much closer in spirit to the agentic paradigm and this flows from the importance it accords to the client's rational and irrational beliefs. REBC also lends itself to a rhetorical analysis of its preferred style of therapeutic disputation. The idea that clients would subject themselves to such verbal battering or, for that matter, would do as the therapist bids them when carrying out their homework assignments suggests that client and counsellor enter into an agentic contract with one another. The notion of an agentic relationship is something I explore in more detail in the next chapter where I consider the topics of hypnosis and obedience.

Chapter 8
Control: hypnosis and obedience

In many ways this chapter and Chapter 9 may be read in parallel since the ordering of topics between the two chapters has been somewhat arbitrary. I regard all the substantive topics (hypnosis, obedience, masochism and suicide) as raising difficulties for the agentic perspective. I start with hypnosis.

Hypnosis

Marcuse (1959) defines hypnosis as 'an altered state of the organism originally and usually produced by a repetition of stimuli in which suggestion (no matter how defined) is more effective than usual' (p. 21). Harmless as this definition may seem, it harbours controversy. The problem stems from the way hypnosis is characterised as involving an altered state of consciousness and, related to this, may require a special ritual called an induction process in order to bring the hypnotic subject into the so-called altered state.

One of the difficulties in advancing a state definition of hypnosis is that in laboratory investigations a range of hypnotic phenomena can sometimes be observed or produced in cases where the person is not hypnotised but merely pretending to be or is simply doing what is asked by an experimenter. If this is the case, then there is no need to postulate a special state of consciousness, since the phenomena can be manufactured without recourse to such a state.

Another problem is that some of the shifts in consciousness which are reportedly related to hypnosis are frequently experienced in everyday situations which would not normally be regarded as hypnotic. For example, someone may drive to work and yet, on arrival, have no recollection of the journey. Experiences of this nature may have something in common with introspection. Indeed, Stout (1898/1938) describes the first stage of introspection as the development of explicit self-consciousness.

> The mere transition from the objective to the subjective point of view, as when a man, previously engrossed in watching the waves beating on the shore, begins to notice that he is watching them. (p. 38)

It may be argued that while the hypnotised subject does not gain explicit self-consciousness (in Stout's sense) of what takes place during the hypnotic episode, he or she will, nevertheless, be able to experience the events at the primary level. The hypnotist sometimes issues an instruction to the subject that he or she will not remember what has taken place during the hypnotic episode. From an introspective standpoint, this may be seen as an exhortation not to bring the flow of events into self-conscious experience. If these events are the equivalent of the journey to work in the driving example, such an exhortation may be unnecessary; the subject would not be able to remember any of the detail even if she or he wanted to.

The split between explicit self-consciousness and subconscious action is formalised in the concept of dissociation. This concept underpins both the neodissociation model and the dissociation control model of hypnosis (reviewed by Kirsch and Lynn, 1998) and I move on to consider these theories.

Dissociation theories

Hypnotic suggestions, as reflected in standardised scales of suggestibility, cover ideomotor, challenge and cognitive domains (Kirsch and Lynn, 1998). Some examples would be arm raising for ideomotor suggestions, arm rigidity for challenge suggestions and amnesia or hallucinations for cognitive suggestions. In order to account for these hypnotic phenomena, dissociation theories postulate the division of consciousness into different parts. Kirsch and Lynn (1998) consider two theoretical variations: Hilgard's (1986) neodissociation theory and Woody and Bowers (1994) theory of dissociated control.

Neodissociation theory postulates an executive ego split by an amnesic barrier into two portions which then interact with sub-systems concerned with movement, pain perception and memory; one portion of the split ego is unavailable to consciousness. This can be used to explain self-hypnosis on the grounds that the conscious ego may be construed as the agent making the suggestions to the unconscious part. Furthermore, in the case of ordinary hypnosis (hetero-hypnosis, as opposed to self-hypnosis), it is possible to think of the hypnotist as taking over the role of the subject's conscious ego, along the lines that Miller *et al.* (1960) proposed. In this way, the hypnotist would gain control over the subject's plans (I discuss this in greater detail later in this chapter). The problem with the neodissociation model, as Kirsch and Lynn (1998) point out, is that there is nothing in the theory to explain how dissociation might be brought about and how the amnesic barrier might be erected.

Dissociated control theory is different from neodissociation theory and works best for well-learned or automated behaviours. The example I gave earlier of driving on a regular journey would be a case in point. It postulates no unconscious splitting of the ego and thus no amnesic barrier. It does, however, propose an altered state of consciousness which is similar to that found in patients with frontal lobe disorders. Hypnosis is thus seen to bring about a weakening of frontal lobe control, enabling cognitive sub-systems to be activated directly. However, one problem with dissociated control theory is that hypnotic phenomena are by no means well learned or automatic; many of them are novel for the hypnotic subjects. Kirsch and Lynn (1998) also comment that the extensive search for a distinct physiological condition corresponding to the hypnotic trance state has not been fruitful. The existence of a trance state has been a sore running through the academic debates on hypnosis for many years. Recently, an interesting initiative to deal with this problem has been offered by Wagstaff (1998) who argues that proponents of the hypnotic trance state may be committing a category mistake. I find this an appealing move and shall therefore devote some time to a consideration of this idea.

The hypnotic state as a category mistake

Wagstaff's position is that it is unhelpful to postulate an altered state of consciousness which will tie in the disparate hypnotic phenomena such as ideomotor suggestions (for example arm lowering), the phenomenological feeling of being hypnotised, the perceptual distortions (positive or negative hallucinations), memory effects (amnesia), clinical effects (for example treatment of warts) and suggested analgesia (including levels of anaesthesia). He feels that no one particular state can be invoked to cover everything. Instead, we may need to draw on a wide range of processes including motivation, relaxation, imagination, absorption, expectancies, attitudes, beliefs, concentration, suggestibility, placebo effects, selective attention, stress reactions, role enactment and compliance with instructions (see Wagstaff, 1998, pp. 153–4).

The conventional view of hypnosis has been that, although some response to suggestions and instructions might be observed in the waking state, the person will only be truly hypnotised when in the special 'hypnotic state'. Wagstaff (1998) argues that to do this is to make a category error. Ryle (1949/1963) explained what is meant by a category error using the concept of a university by way of illustration. Thus, one might begin showing the university to a visitor from an alien culture by starting with the classrooms, and then go on to point out the laboratories, the library, the administrative buildings, the students' halls of residence and so forth. At the end of this, it would be very puzzling to then be asked by the visitor 'But where is the university?'. The visitor would be making a category error by thinking that the 'university' was yet another component alongside all the others, instead of being the superordinate category or the higher order concept which integrates and gives meaning to the lower order components. Wagstaff's argument hinges on mapping the various categories and components of the hypnotic phenomena on to the components of the university in Ryle's illustration.

The success of Wagstaff's claim is also dependent on accepting that the hypnotic state bears the same relation to the hypnotic phenomena as the university does to its components (as I have already set them out). Woody and Sadler (1998) do not think that Wagstaff succeeds. They point out that it is not illogical to look at a pile of bricks, wood and so forth, and ask where the house is. Wagstaff's reply is that it would be illogical to look at all the separate components of an assembled house, name and point to them and yet still ask 'Where's the house?' There is not going to be any agreement here. Woody and Sadler (1998) obviously think that Wagstaff's description of all the bits and pieces of hypnosis is equivalent to the raw materials of an unassembled house, whereas Wagstaff sees the description as one of a fully assembled one. And, unfortunately, the difference between built and unassembled in this analogy is supplied by the notion of an altered state of consciousness in the case of hypnosis. I think I'm with Wagstaff, on balance, but looking at the dispute this way does suggest that the notion of a category mistake is not going to provide a handy solution.

The altered state of consciousness can be seen as something that may or may not come along with the hypnosis on a particular occasion. Some subjects may report entering an altered state more than others. Perhaps some hypnotists have greater success in facilitating reports of altered states than others, although one would have to be very careful of demand characteristics in any attempt to check this out. Perhaps it's one of those things where the chances of it happening may be diminished by trying too hard or by attempting to bring the phenomenon under conscious control (a paradox to which sex therapists alert their impotent male clients, I believe). I think that to use the trance state as a defining characteristic of hypnosis is to place too much of a burden on something which might better be described as an occasional, ephemeral or transitory hypnotic peak experience.

The hypnotic subject as planless agent

Miller *et al.* (1960) consider the way we organise our plans in everyday life and note that elaborate plans are usually monitored by our inner speech. The imperative to act often comes from listening to ourselves speak the order, sub-vocally. This is very similar to James' declaration that he should get out of bed and get on with the day (discussed in Chapter 1). It is also very close to Harré's (1983) ideas on how we learn to obey orders.

According to Miller *et al.* (1960), the reason why the hypnotised subject listens and goes along with the hypnotist's plans, when a waking observer would not be expected to do so, is that the hypnotised subject has stopped making plans and therefore has none to conflict with those articulated by the hypnotist. Miller *et al.* (1960) interpret induction procedures based upon relaxation as creating situations similar to those when we go to sleep at night, and sleep they see as an excellent way to shut down planning activity. The same argument could be used with regard to relaxation and meditation techniques involving the repetitive recitation of mantras or the concentration on reduced perceptual fields, such as candle flames or whatever.

An alternative strategy for taking over the planning function is for the hypnotist to give difficult or conflicting instructions at a rapid rate. Miller *et al.* (1960) say that, in the resulting confusion, the subject may find the hypnotist's plans a welcome relief. Rossi (1996) suggests that this tactic was used by Erikson, although the motivation was to put the client in touch with their own unconscious plans and not necessarily to have the client submit to those of the hypnotist.

When explaining some of the more dramatic hypnotic phenomena, such as anaesthesia, Miller *et al.* (1990) suggest that this may be the result of the suspension of 'stop rules'. This is something that I last considered in Chapter 6 in relation to Baumeister's ideas on the breakdown of self-regulation. Neodissociation theory is not incompatible with a plans approach, since the conscious self could be seen as generating plans for the unconscious. However, I shall leave the concept of plan for the time being since I now want to explore the extent to which Billig's (1997) ideas on the dialogic unconscious might be related to neodissociation theory.

Neodissociation and the dialogic unconscious

Billig uses discursive psychology and conversation analysis to provide a novel interpretation of the psychoanalytic concept of repression. Drawing on Drew (1995), he makes the point that conversational structures are so normatively powerful that they set the boundaries of what happens in conversational interaction. However, by focusing only on what is said, Billig feels that the conversation analysts are committing themselves to dealing solely in the relations between (often transcribed) utterances either forward or backward in time from the focal speech act. The problem with this is that conversation analysts can say nothing about what is left out of a conversation. The approach is thus unable to deal with repressed material.

Billig (1997) comments on the fact that ethnomethodologists and conversation analysts have stressed the importance of reciprocal politeness as a guiding and pervasive norm in everyday intercourse. More strongly, politeness is seen as a code of morality. Billig turns his attention to the other side of this particular coin:

> One might stipulate that the possibility for 'doing politeness' depends upon the capability for 'doing rudeness' and, thus, that there is a permanent flaw in the apparently agreeable, co-operative structure. Developmentally, politeness and rudeness are linked. If politeness is routinely taught, as it must be for the skills of conversational turn taking to be acquired, then so must rudeness. (p. 149)

Billig's (1997) idea is that in telling a child not to say something because it is rude, the child also learns what is rude. For example, if daddy says 'Don't say "shit", it's rude' then daughter may learn not only not to say 'shit' but also that if she wants to be rude she should use this word. Furthermore, she may routinely add 'shit' or an equivalent item to her knowledge base of rude words whenever such learning opportunities arise within mundane conversational episodes. Billig (1997) then goes on to say that it is not just an impulse for rudeness that can be formed in dialogue of this nature; the possibility for repression to take place is also on the cards:

> The child who learns the codes of discursive politeness, which are integral to learning to talk, learns how to change the subject, to avoid questioning ('it's rude to ask'), to turn threatening topics into humour, and so on. In learning these dialogic skills the child is acquiring routines, which can be applied to their own individual mental life. (p. 156).

There are at least two ways in which Billig's (1997) idea of the dialogic unconscious may be applied to the topic of hypnosis. In the first place, the norms of conversational politeness may exert some weight in the induction process. For example, if the hypnotist says that the subject's arm is getting heavy or that she or he is feeling tired or sleepy, it might be construed as rude for the subject to disagree. Hunt (1979), reporting on her subjects post-experimental comments after they had witnessed a defiant confederate disrupt and walk out of an experimental group hypnosis session, commented on this aspect of the situation.

> All of the subjects in group 3 [defiant confederate group] said that they were not prepared to get up and follow the confederate out of the room. For most this was because they regarded his behaviour as *rude*. (p. 25, emphasis added)

The dialogic skills of repression may be triggered into action to deal with any thoughts which challenge the hypnotist's assertions. 'Your arm is getting lighter and lighter, lighter and lighter, it's floating upwards into the air, upwards into the air, light as a feather', says the hypnotist. Any notion born on the uncertainties of proprioceptive feedback can be dialogically sorted out through the tactic of switching attention away from the rogue twitches of muscle fatigue brought on as the subject's arm jerks puppet-like in a skywards direction. In other words, the dialogic skills of repression, learned over the passage of a lifetime, provide the amnesic barrier between the conscious and unconscious segments of the ego postulated by neodissociation theory.

A second application of Billig's (1997) ideas relates to the way normally repressed behaviours, thoughts and rudeness might be given a controlled avenue for release within the hypnotic episode. Billig argues that the existence of such repressed items owes much to the powerful conversational norms pervasive in everyday interaction. If a different set of conversational norms are seen to operate within the hypnotic episode then this will have implications for repression. Hypnosis may be seen as an unusual sort of social episode, with its own local conventions. Within that frame the stage hypnotist may give permission to the subject to be rude or vulgar in atypical ways; the subject may be persuaded to make the sound of a farting hippopotamus, much to the amusement of the audience. In a similar fashion, the hypnotherapist may grant the subject leave to speak ill of loved ones or to talk about aggressive or sexual desires and other sundry embarrassments that might well be better left unsaid in the hurly burly of everyday life. On this view, it should come as no surprise to find waking simulators producing a reasonably similar set of responses to hypnotised subjects, providing it is assumed that the simulators have grasped and have adjusted to the shift in conversational norms implied in hypnosis.

Hypnosis as ritual

Rothenbuhler (1998) points out that ritual is established by convention. If hypnosis is construed as ritual, then the search for causal explanations will be largely misplaced. I want to develop the idea that hypnosis is seen as ritual but, in doing so, I shall keep my distance from dramaturgical considerations. Sarbin's (1950) ideas concerning role perception and role-taking aptitude are of relevance to my argument only indirectly. Rather, I shall turn to speech act theory (see Chapter 3) to provide my point of departure.

Speech act theory draws attention to what can be accomplished by talk. When all the right parties say the right things at the right time and in the right context, the deed will be deemed to have been done (the ship will have been named, the couple will have been married or whatever). In terms of my present purposes, I need to interpret what is meant by talk in a fairly broad fashion. In Chapter 3, I pointed out that semiology was one of the foundations of discourse analysis. If semiology is also assimilated to speech act theory, then even the minimalist ideomotor response of the little finger can be construed as a sign which may qualify as a legitimate signal within the hypnotic episode. Thus the use of non-verbal responses to show agreement or dissent (and any other binary choices) within hypnosis can be counted as legitimate fodder for analysis within a speech act theoretic perspective.

Accordingly, if the words spoken are 'You are feeling tired and sleepy, tired and sleepy' and if the response is a drooping of the eyes, then something like an hypnotic adjacency pair will have taken place. Harré and Secord (1972) speak of the liturgical aspect of formal episodes (many marriage ceremonies are conducted in a fashion dictated by the written liturgy, for example). In the case of hypnosis, the hypnotic suggestibility scales (see, for example, Barber and Wilson, 1978) may be seen as analogous to a formal liturgy. When the adjacency pairs have proceeded in an orderly fashion through the liturgy, hypnosis will have occurred.

As ritual, the internal experience of bride or hypnotic subject is irrelevant to the accomplishment of the act. In the case of marriage, providing the bride goes through the ceremony in a proper fashion (saying 'I do' at the appropriate time and so forth) she will be married at the end of it, like it or not. If, during the ceremony, her thoughts dwell upon what an awful person the groom is, or upon how she doesn't really want to marry him, her inner experience might be used as grounds for a pessimistic prognosis as to the future marriage but it would not alter the fact of the marriage one jot. Similarly, if the hypnotic subject upholds his or her side of the bargain, hypnosis will have taken place and the presence or absence of an altered state of consciousness becomes irrelevant.

When bride or groom walks out of the marriage ceremony, no wedding is deemed to have taken place. So too with hypnosis, should the subject exit the script before the end of the session (see my discussion of Hunt, 1979, above). In both cases, the pressure to stay within the script once it has begun may be great. If hypnosis is seen as scripted ritual, then the fact that simulators can 'do' hypnosis in the experimental laboratory is about as surprising as the fact that people can behave passably well at a wedding rehearsal (providing they know or are given a reasonably flexible and forgiving script). Context is enough to ensure that neither simulated hypnosis nor wedding rehearsal counts as the real thing. This renders less interesting the experimental findings that simulators can perform in a fashion that is markedly similar to hypnotised subjects. I acknowledge that the script may sometimes be paired down to a skeletal version. Some clinicians, obsessed with the causal aspects of hypnosis, may be disposed to skimp on the ceremony; I take this to be bad style, bad taste. I am no minimalist when it comes to dramaturgy.

Interim summary

Obedience in hypnosis moves beyond the mundane where altered states of consciousness are postulated, and I considered the neodissociation and dissociation control theories in relation to this. Dissociated control theory can be criticised on two fronts. First, given that the theory is built on an analogy with frontal lobe disorders, its credibility is stretched when it is acknowledged that hypnotic phenomena are not necessarily well learned. Second, no distinct physiological condition corresponding to the hypnotic trance state has so far been identified.

Neodissociation theory I found more appealing, partly because of its potential for integration with the concept of plan and the account put forward by Miller *et al.* (1960) and partly because I thought it might be possible to draw upon Billig's (1997) ideas concerning the dialogic unconsciousness. However, despite Woody and Sadler's (1998) objections, I did lean towards Wagstaff's (1998) view that both these dissociation theories might be dismissed on the grounds that to postulate an altered state of consciousness is to make a category mistake.

I associate Billig's (1997) emphasis on the importance of the norms of conversational politeness for repression with the structural aspects of the hypnotic episode. Once these are regarded as being established by convention, it is a short step to go on to construe hypnosis as ritual. Drawing on the 1970s new paradigm in social psychology, this construction enabled me to place a liturgical interpretation on the hypnotic susceptibility scales developed for use in positivist experimental investigations of the topic. Two further points flowed from construing hypnosis as ritual. First, inner states of consciousness (whether altered or not) become marginalised in terms of their relevance. Second, it is possible to set to one side questions of causal explanation as being merely of indirect concern to hypnosis.

If hypnosis, as ritual, is to be achieved then the hypnotic subject must, by scripted definition, yield to the will of the hypnotist. It is this aspect of hypnosis that brings it close to the topic of obedience to authority.

Obedience

Because Milgram's (1974) classic experiments concerned with obedience to authority have been so widely disseminated and, indeed, are covered in most introductory social psychology texts, I shall provide only a brief description of them. I shall, however, spend a little more time talking about Milgram's (1974) explanation of the obedience behaviour that was manifested by his experimental participants. As for the ethical issues raised by these experiments, and questions relating to their internal and ecological validity, an excellent discussion may be found in Colman (1987, Chapter 4). Colman also considers various problems concerning the applicability of Milgram's findings to the way in which the Nazi's obeyed orders to exterminate the Jews in World War Two; he deals with this issue in a direct and illuminating fashion.

Milgram's basic experiment

Milgram (1974) carried out a series of experiments where a naive subject came to the laboratory to participate in an investigation into the effect of punishment on learning. On arriving at the laboratory with a second subject (in fact the experimenter's confederate), lots were drawn to see who would be the teacher or the learner; this was always fixed so that the naive subject was allocated to the teacher's role. The teacher was required to test the learner on a paired associates memory task. The learner was hooked up to an electric shock generating machine (although unbeknown to the naive subject no shocks were in fact administered and the confederate was a professional actor who merely pretended to receive the shocks). The experimenter instructed the teacher to administer a shock to the learner every time a mistake was made on the memory test. Each subsequent mistake required the teacher to press the next lever on the shock generating machine so that the shocks increased each time by another 15 volts. The highest shock level was 450 volts. Milgram carried out many variations on the basic theme of this experiment, but the main study revealed that 65 per cent of the subjects obeyed the experimenter to the end and administered the full 450 volts.

Milgram and the agentic state

Milgram (1974) starts from the platform that the co-ordination of individual members of species, through some form of hierarchical social organisation, will give that species the edge in terms of evolutionary survival and may thus be bred in. Furthermore, dominance hierarchies within groups will, through regulating intra-group relationships, reduce internal violence. Milgram does not rest content with a simple Darwinian account, since to explain obedience through reference to instinct does not get us very far. He therefore turns to cybernetics to provide a model.

Milgram (1974) starts by considering autonomous subhuman organisms roaming a shared environment. Unless some form of inhibiting mechanism is built into them, they will not distinguish their fellow organisms from other items in the environment and eventually they will simply eat one another out of existence. Taking that principle forward a little, Milgram (1974) applies it to the human situation:

> The presence of conscience in men, therefore, can be seen as a special case of the more general principle that any self-regulating automaton must have an inhibitor to check its actions against its own kind, for without such inhibition, several automata cannot occupy a common territory. (p. 128)

Given the occurrence in the twentieth century of two world wars and the countless conflicts of a more localised nature, many involving acts of genocide, I find it difficult to take this principle as axiomatic. Leaving that aside, Milgram (1974) points to the presence of a superego to provide the inhibitory checks to stop most people hurting or killing one another 'in the normal course of the day' (p. 128). At this point I will simply note that the invocation of the superego and attendant inhibitory mechanisms opens up the possibility of forging an interpretation based on Billig's (1997) notion of the dialogic unconscious (see my discussion of hypnosis, above).

Milgram (1974) next proceeds to consider what happens when individuals are tied into a hierarchical organisation. The most important fact is that an individual's control has to be ceded to a superordinate controller (the armed forces provide good examples of this). When an individual receives orders or directions from an authority higher in the hierarchy, those orders will not be evaluated against the internal standards of the superego (as might be expected to happen, were the individual to be operating in autonomous mode). For Milgram (1974), it is the shift from autonomous to systemic mode that holds the key to obedience behaviour.

> Specifically, the person entering an authority system no longer views himself as acting out of his own purposes but rather comes to see himself as an agent for executing the wishes of another person. (p. 133)

Milgram describes the switch from autonomous to systemic mode as entering the agentic state and he provides definitions of this state from both cybernetic and phenomenological standpoints:

> From the standpoint of cybernetic analysis, the agentic state occurs when a self-regulating entity is internally modified so as to allow its functioning within a system of hierarchical control. From a subjective standpoint, a person is in a state of agency when he defines himself in a social situation, in a manner that renders him open to regulation by a person of higher status. In this condition the individual no longer views himself as responsible for his own actions but defines himself as an instrument for carrying out the wishes of others. (pp. 133–4)

When considering the antecedent conditions that foster obedience, Milgram (1974) notes that within the family parental injunctions are not merely the source of the child's moral rules but they also provide the means for the inculcation of a generalised obedient attitude. With Milgram, an order such as 'Don't hit your little brother' yields a specific moral rule and an opportunity to 'do' obedience. This is not dissimilar to Billig's (1997) ideas on repression and politeness. 'Don't talk like that, it's rude' provides a specific rule on rudeness and paves the way for the child to 'do' repression.

Milgram (1974) then notes that at school and later in the world of work, the individual is socialised into institutional systems of authority and, in modern industrialised societies, many of the authority figures will be impersonal and unknown to the individual, being identified by insignia, uniform or title. In this way the social order is internalised:

> Just as we internalize grammatical rules, and can thus both understand and produce new sentences, so we internalize axiomatic rules of social life which enable us to fulfil social requirements in novel situations. In any hierarchy of rules, that which requires compliance to authority assumes a paramount position. (p. 138)

Milgram (1974) goes on to make some interesting remarks concerning the immediate antecedent conditions for obedience. In the first place we must perceive the authority figure as legitimate within the domain in question. This does not mean that the person in authority has to be particularly impressive in terms of their prestige. For example, at the cinema or the theatre an usher would fit the bill. Milgram comments that the trappings of authority, such as uniforms, will help to define the situation. What Milgram has in mind here is very close to Goffman's (1959) dramaturgical notion of personal front (which would cover the person's bearing and demeanour, as well as their uniform) and front (which would refer to the physical setting and the props contained within it).

Milgram suggests that although people may comply with orders under coercion, the obedience phenomena often have an internalised basis where submission to the legitimate authority is voluntary. It is at this point that Milgram (1974) touches base with the social sciences when he suggests that the individual will need to subscribe to an overarching ideology within which particular acts of obedience may be legitimated:

> The inquisitor of sixteenth-century Spain might have eschewed science, but he embraced the ideology of his church, and in its name, and for its preservation, tightened the screw on the rack without any problem of conscience. (p. 142)

One thing that happens when people move into the agentic state is that they become tuned to the authority figures and the signals from others become muted. The obedient subject is therefore more likely to accept the definition of the situation, which is provided by the legitimate authority. Any suspicion that the definition put forward by the authority may be nothing more than a social construction placed upon reality (in the sense brought out by Berger and Luckman, 1966) must be guarded against. This is why propaganda may be necessary to shore up the background ideology in order to make it appear as acceptable and compelling as a law of nature. Only when the submissive subject is exposed to the process of deconstruction and political critique might the dominant definitions of the situation be weakened. And this is where critical psychology comes into its own. Stainton Rogers *et al.* (1995) speak of the activity of deconstruction as generating perturbations, and this is a good way to think of what might happen.

The loss of responsibility can be seen, then, as something that the individual gains from subscribing to the overarching ideology. However, such a loss does not mean that morality ceases to apply to the obedience situation. What happens is that the focus takes on a radically different slant, with the moral issues hinging on questions of loyalty, duty and discipline. This applies to the behaviour of the obedient subject.

Once the person enters the agentic state, he or she may become trapped in it through various binding factors. For example, Milgram (1974) points to the sequential nature of the action where having got started it is easier to continue than to break off the flow (this idea is similar to the *snowballing* discussed in relation to Baumeister's analysis of self-regulation failure; see Chapter 5).

Milgram (1974) acknowledges that he has to account for disobedience as well as obedience, in his experimental situation. This he does by accepting that there will be strains within the situation that may outweigh the effects of the antecedent predisposition to obedience and which may result in the overcoming of the various binding factors surrounding the obedience episode. The sources of strain in Milgram's situation covered a wide range: the negative emotional response of the subjects to the cries and protests of the victim, the conflict that the behaviour had with existing values and norms which would not allow for the administration of powerful electric shocks to innocent victims and the incompatibility of the subject's callous behaviour with their self-image as caring individuals. Some of these sources of strain may be rendered less potent by placing buffers into the situation. For example, when the victim is placed in a remote location, hidden in a cubicle, the cries of pain will appear less immediate and possibly less personal. If the obedient subject is required merely to pass on the order to administer the shock to another person, he or she thereby gains some distance from the primary aggressive act and in this way it can be seen that highly bureaucratic systems contain their own buffers. Milgram (1974) makes the point that it may only be necessary to select a relatively small number of hardened cases to do the dirty work, while larger numbers of people contribute their acts of obedience in ways that do not expose them to the final act which they might otherwise find too emotionally upsetting.

Blass (1991) provides a recent review of the obedience research and does so with the distance of two or three decades since the original studies. In his view, the academic reaction to the obedience research was to downgrade personality explanations in favour of situationist accounts of such behaviour. He reports that there is some evidence to suggest that subjects operating at the higher levels in terms of Kohlberg's (1969) stage theory of moral development were more defiant in Milgram's pilot studies. This is a comforting finding and squares with the notion that a more morally developed person would be less likely to accept definitions of a situation as veridical merely because an authority figure attempted to impose them. However, I am conscious that I may be letting some of my own warm liberal humanist sentiments influence my interpretation here since the force of this account is parasitic on the strength of Kohlberg's theory and this has been severely criticised in the past (see Trainer, 1977).

Of direct relevance to the psychology of action is the finding that there has sometimes been an association reported between obedience and Rotter's (1966) measure of internal–external locus of control. Blass (1991) suggests that it is the internals who resist influence and disobey to a higher degree than the externals. On similar grounds, one would expect high self-monitors to be more responsive to the demands of an experimental obedience situation than the low self-monitors. For me, this is an attractive idea, since it highlights the dramaturgical aspect of the obedience situation. Blass (1991) does consider Mixon's (1979) role-play replications of the Milgram experiment but he homes in on the personality trait of trust when drawing his conclusions about this work. This is not something that I would focus on as being of primary interest. I will briefly describe Mixon's (1979) work.

Mixon (1979) found that by altering the extent to which information present in the role-play script challenged the assumption that safeguards to protect subjects from harm in the experimental situation were in place, he could generate complete defiance *or* complete obedience from his subject groups. He maximised the likelihood of obedience by removing cues that indicated serious consequences might flow from administering the electric shocks (no printed warnings on the shock generator, no verbal feedback from the victim). He maximised the likelihood of defiance by scripting in not only the warnings and the feedback but, additionally, a worried and agitated concern on the part of the experimenter. In other words, he undermined the assumption that no serious harm could flow from participating in a psychology experiment.

Blass (1991) interprets Mixon's work as indicating that 'trust in the benign purposes of the experimenter is the key to understanding the obedient subject's behaviour' (p. 403). He thus brings the personality trait of trust to the fore. Mixon points out that in some situations information might be mixed, contradictory or conflicting and, in such situations, there will be a lot of scope for individuals to arrive at different interpretations. While I can see that there is some potential in looking for individual differences in interpretation in terms of personality differences (along the lines suggested by Blass, 1991), I think that discursive or semiological approaches might be more interesting since context and meaning lie at the heart of the latter perspectives.

Concluding discussion

In my discussion of hypnosis, I noted that neodissociation theory retains the conventional agent/patient dichotomy, with the person-as-patient removed beyond the amnesic barrier to an unconscious region. In self-hypnosis, agency is located at the person's conscious ego; in hetero-hypnosis it is lodged with the hypnotist. This account bears some resemblance to Milgram's (1974) concept of the agentic state. The notion of agency which is brought into focus by this interpretation is close to the way the term 'agent' is deployed in a number of legal and commercial senses. For example, in English law, the executor is charged with the responsibility of executing the wishes of a dead person, as set out in the will. In the case of running a business, it is the job of an executive to carry out the wishes of the board of directors. Within the world of commercial transactions an agent is deemed to act for and on behalf of the principal, in accordance with the terms of the contract.

Agency, with its association with the world of work, draws on the concepts of servant, factotum, worker and, at the extreme, even slave for its meaning in this context. The extent to which overt coercion operates within these categories may vary from the more blatant and brutal in slavery to the more subtle and indirect in service. A common thread is that all require, to some extent, submission and obedience to the will of the principal (individual or institution). Freedom to act, to act creatively and to show initiative within the bounds of the contractual (economic or social) domain of the relationship may be a necessary component of executive agency. The degree of such freedom may, as a rule of thumb, be assumed from the hierarchical level at which the goals are specified. A principal who says 'Maximise my profits' to a broker gives the latter much scope. The instruction 'Buy £500 of Bloggo's shares at no more than £1.50 per share', issued to a stock exchange clerk, leaves little room for manoeuvre. The problem with specifying these differences is that, as with most hierarchies, the differences will be relative. The instruction to a sergeant to 'Take that hill' contains more freedom than the instruction to the private soldier to 'Shoot the sniper currently hiding behind the tree directly ahead'. But this is a problem that runs through the whole of agency. One way to capture the distinction, while still acknowledging the implicit relativity of the description, is to deploy the terms 'macro' and 'micro'. As the brief taken on by an executive agent moves towards the macro, so more and more responsibility comes with it.

In Chapter 4, I discussed the contrast between working towards 'do best' goals and hard specific goals. The level of specificity would appear to be inversely proportional to the degree of freedom left to the agent. In general, although a macro goal could be specified tightly, there will be vagueness left as to how the micro sub-goals should be specified and achieved.

Once again, where there is a lack of specificity, there will be the assumption of responsibility attaching to the agent.

Whereas, above, I discussed the concept of agency in relation to the taking on of active responsibilities in the world of work, I now wish to consider the possibility that this concept could suffer hermeneutical seepage from that of automaton, robot or cyborg. With inanimate agents (I am tempted to call them quasi-agents) things can sometimes get done in much the same way as they would if the agents were human. Discerning the difference between mechanical and human agents is becoming more and more difficult as computer science, robotics and artificial intelligence programming improve. At the macro level, it can make life easier if terms and explanatory concepts are borrowed from the realm of human action when dealing with automata. For example, a sequence of repetitive robotic movements might be best described using the higher order computer program language concept of a *for-do loop* which is much closer in spirit to talk of human plans than it is to machine code and the binary pulses of electronic circuits.

The situation appears to be that I have generated a number of distinctions which, while being related to one another, are not synonymous. Agency, linked to its commercial sense, I will refer to as executive in order to distinguish it from the mechanical sense which I will call robotic. Although the executive and the robotic distinction echoes that between agent and patient, from the point of view of teleological and causal explanation, neither are usefully applied to the human *qua* patient. The issue in Milgram's (1974) obedience situation (and the massacres and atrocities which it is designed to model) is whether the person is best described as an executive or as a robotic agent. If robotic, then no responsibility sticks and, therefore, no moral condemnation is appropriate. If the person is construed as an executive agent, then they will not be able to duck the issue of responsibility and will remain accountable for what they do. One hypothesis to flow from this is that the person in authority will maximise the likelihood of submission and obedience in the subject by specifying the orders at the micro level. However, as the orders move further down the hierarchy, away from the macro level, so too will the subject's relation to the authority shift from executive agency to robotic.

In hypnosis, conventional induction procedures and the normal progression of events from light to deep trance (as operationally defined within hypnotic suggestibility scales) could be described in the above terms. Hypnosis could be regarded as moving from the micro suggestions ('Your eyelids are getting heavy') which force the subject into the robotic role, through to macro suggestions ('When you next want a cream cake you will find something non-fattening to eat') which demand a more executive role from the subject, in the latter stages. Moving into the robotic state could be construed as a necessary rite of passage en route to the executive. Ritual, in general, works best when robotic agents blindly perform the acts required of them in a state of existential bad faith. An obsession with detail at the micro level is good for ritual.

It is normally important that ritual is witnessed. This is because the meaning of the ritual is established by convention within socio-linguistic communities. On this count, self-hypnosis becomes problematic. The right words may have been intoned and the correct responses given, but it is not clear that the hypnotic speech act has been properly performed.

An analogy may be used to bring out the limitations of the equivalence between hetero- and self-hypnosis: for most people, it is nigh on impossible to tickle oneself successfully. I am not suggesting that self-hypnosis is as hopeless as self-tickling, I am using the latter to mark out an extreme. In the next chapter I shall be discussing masochism and Phillips (1998) argues that sexual masochism is essentially a social activity (she is mainly discussing recreational masochism). I think that this is closely bound up with the part played by ritual in recreational masochism. Setting that aside, self-flagellation and other self-administered punishments may go at least half the distance in this regard, perhaps being more successful than self-tickling but less so than auto-hypnosis.

Hypnosis creates problems for the psychology of action partly because in the philosophical approaches to the explanation of action it is usual for agency to be located at one unique location in what Harré (1983) refers to as the array of persons. Both the neodissociationist's interpretation of hetero-hypnosis and Miller *et al.*'s (1960) view that the planning function is taken over by the hypnotist require that the explanation and execution of action be spread across more than one location in Harré's array of persons. Drawing on another of Harré's (1983) concepts, it may be helpful to think of the hypnotist and subject as joined in psychological symbiosis. A dissociated self may be construed as a multiple personality. While the dual selves may inhabit the same physical body (and thus be forced to share a common trajectory through the spatiotemporal matrix, to borrow further from Harré, 1983) they will be identifiable as different locations in the array of persons. This enables the same conceptual framework to be used for both self-hypnosis and hetero-hypnosis. In terms of my earlier discussion, the symbiosis could still be described in terms of the executive and robotic models of agency. What is clear is that, whether in executive or robotic mode, agency requires a degree of obedience if the symbiotic union is to be successful in its own terms. The manifestation and management of dominance and submission lies at the heart of masochistic symbiosis, and it is to a consideration of this topic that I now turn.

Chapter 9
Enigmas: masochism and suicide

Masochism

The masochist appears to desire punishment and humiliation; this is odd since most folk don't. Were the normal values attached to pain and punishment loaded as consequences into a TRA/TPB expectancy-value computation, the person would appear to be in transgression of the rule for intelligibility (see Chapter 2). Thus masochism presents a problem for rational action. If masochists are allowed to have their own private positive evaluations for pain and punishment, their behaviour would be rendered intelligible according to the rule for intelligibility but they would appear to be deviant in holding such positive values. I think that this helps to explain why masochism has sometimes been regarded as tantamount to a psychiatric disorder. I shall start by considering a view totally opposed to such an interpretation. Masochism, as theatre, tends to be sexually charged and conducted among consenting adults, almost as a recreation. This is a far cry from viewing masochism as a personality disorder, where the person may be tied into an abusive relationship. I shall examine this later in the section.

Masochism as theatre

Baumeister (1997) sets aside a number of views relating to masochism as being mistaken. He rejects the notion that masochism should be declared a diagnostic category in the context of the *Diagnostic and Statistical Manual* (DSM-IV) of the

American Psychiatric Association (1994) on the grounds that research suggests that practising masochists exhibit few signs of psychopathology or deviant behaviour patterns outside their masochistic activities. He also dismisses the assumption that masochism is self-destructive since, while masochists might welcome the opportunity to experience pain, they avoid injury. Indeed, he makes the point that some couples use pre-arranged code words so that the masochist can signal to the dominant partner that a particular activity is approaching a point of harm and should be discontinued. Baumeister (1997) also firmly resists the temptation to use the term 'masochism' to apply to non-sexual behaviours which are in some way self-defeating or self-destructive:

> My position is that the term masochism should only be used in its original meaning, which referred specifically to the patterns of sexual behavior marked by pain, relinquishing control, and embarrassment or humiliation. (pp. 135–6)

This reluctance to allow masochism to be deployed as a description of non-sexual behaviours is shared by Phillips (1998) who would also endorse Baumeister's (1997) views that masochism is about controlled pain rather than serious injury. Phillips (1998) goes to some lengths to explain that sadists seldom make ideal partners for masochists. Because the sadist seeks a victim, she or he is likely to be disappointed by the pleasure masochists may find within the sadomasochistic episode. Speaking of the masochist's partner, Phillips (1998) says:

> The opposite number is someone who can be convinced or charmed into acting the role of torturer, not a brutal heavyweight... No sadist is any good for a masochist, since each is disqualified from dancing to the other's tune, with the result that both are wrong-footed. The perfect choice may be another masochist. (p. 12)

Phillips (1998) also makes a firm distinction between being a masochist and being a victim. A victim is the object of violence, assault, bullying or whatever against his or her will. The masochist, on the other hand, initiates a dramatic scenario involving bondage, pseudo-domination, spanking, restraint, humiliation or degradation.

Both Baumeister (1997) and Phillips (1998) draw attention to the contractual and dramaturgical aspect of contemporary masochistic behaviour. Phillips (1998) defines masochism as 'the agreement between two people to explore the roles of master and slave by acting them out for a specified time period' (p. 25). To some extent the contractual nature of masochism has become institutionalised through the emergence of S&M clubs and the dramaturgical potential has probably been facilitated by the wider availability of fetishistic clothing and equipment, all of which can be pressed into service as props to give the event an air of what the experimental psychologist might call ecological validity. The somewhat theatrical trappings of masochistic activity may also be described in terms of Goffman's (1959) concepts of front and personal front; it is as if they help to frame an episode or a period of time, separating it from the mainstream of everyday life. The process may have something in common with play and, perhaps, just as play fighting can sometimes turn into real fighting, so may play sadomasochism spill across its dramaturgical frame into something quite different where real harm and injury ensues. A reading of Baumeister (1997) suggests that such slippage may be rare. And, of course, real torture is quite another thing. As Phillips (1998) says:

> Master and slave scenarios, chains and whips in the bedroom are completely compatible with membership of Amnesty International. To think otherwise is to claim a false innocence, an ignorance of sex and of the imaginative engagement it demands. (p. 53)

The picture I have painted, so far, shows masochism almost as a recreational activity (as I am sure it is for some people); a highly charged sexual activity. However, not all academics agree to treat it as such. I turn now to a consideration of psychological masochism, construed as a central facet of a person's identity.

Masochism as essential identity

Warren (1985) adopts a completely different approach to the topic and explicitly focuses on what she calls non-sexual masochism. She is concerned with people who seem to sabotage their chances of pleasure and success and who bring unnecessary pain and misery upon themselves. It seems to me that Warren (1985) has in mind the sort of person Berne (1964, 1972) describes as a victim in transactional analysis. Many of Berne's games involved both victims and persecutors. A classic game for the victim would be *Kick Me*, while *Now-I'll-get-you-you-son-of-a-bitch* (NIGYSOB) requires a persecutor for its protagonist. It has been said that a marriage made in hell might consist of one partner predisposed towards NIGYSOB with the other obligingly taking the victim's role in *Kick Me*.

Warren (1983) suggests that while some people might initially desire pain as a means to some end or other, they eventually seek it out because the experience of pain has become an essential part of their identity. She defines masochists as:

> individuals who desire and actively seek pain – apparently for its own sake – and who play a role in causing themselves much unnecessary pain. (p. 106)

Warren (1985) goes on to consider some of the standard explanations of masochism in terms of the external and internal rewards that may accrue to the masochist as a consequence of the behaviour. In passing, it may be noted that it should be possible to accommodate these explanations within the framework of the theory of reasoned action (see Chapter 2).

In terms of possible external rewards, Warren (1985) thinks that illness, anxiety and exhaustion may excuse the masochist from unpleasant duties or may enable him or her to get out of irksome situations. Suffering may also increase the masochist's power over others, especially if it makes those other people feel guilty. When this happens, they may even be drawn into playing the part of rescuer (another of Berne's, 1972, roles). In this way, the suffering and the humiliation may carry the benefit of securing the protection of the powerful other. Where attacks from others are expected, they may be forestalled by the tactical use of self-inflicted injuries ahead of time. This is a strategy not dissimilar to self-handicapping in attribution theory. Similar effects may be achieved through self-deprecating humour.

Warren (1985) then goes on to consider internal rewards. One possibility is that punishment relieves the masochist's sense of guilt. Furthermore, by suffering greatly, he or she can feel justified in demanding attention, care and sympathy from others. Warren (1985) also comments on the curious desire of some people not to inflict discomfort or suffering on others in any situation where there might be the slightest choice between hurting themselves or hurting others. An example might be the overprotective parent making endless personal sacrifices for his or her offspring.

Having discussed these possibilities, Warren (1985) concludes that masochistic behaviour is not odd enough to be interesting if it *can* be explained away on utilitarian grounds, either in terms of internal or external rewards. I think that if the utilitarian explanation is invoked then it must be possible to accommodate the behaviour in the ordinary way (as evaluated consequences), in the attitude component of the theory of reasoned action. Warren (1985) is inclined to reject this view. She points, for example, to the case where children seeking attention may, where they cannot get praise, go for punishment. This conjures up the appalling situation where getting verbal or physical abuse is better than being ignored for the child.

The other possibility that Warren (1985) considers is that desiring pain as an intrinsic end (and not as a means to some other internal or external reward) is too odd to be comprehensible. While acknowledging that relatively trivial pains could be found to be interesting, she rejects the idea that most people could find truly awful pains to be so. Therefore, she stays with the idea that pain is, by and large, something negative and challenges the means–end mentality of psychological hedonism. Her point is that 'one may desire something as an essential (necessary) part or aspect of a more encompassing intrinsic end' (p. 112). Pain thus becomes an integral part of something bigger; it's not normally possible to run a marathon or give birth without it.

Moving beyond psychological hedonism, Warren (1985) regards pain as an essential part of the masochist's identity. If this is so, then part of what it is to be who you are will, for the masochist, involve being a sufferer. Warren (1985) sees three routes into this situation. First, the person may have been victimised in the past and then, if this begins to form a regular pattern, gradually come to identify themselves as a victim. This is very close to Berne's (1972) idea in transactional analysis that people may become scripted into the victim role from an early age. Second, the masochist may come to see him or herself as an evil person, deserving punishment. Once people start labelling someone as evil, there is much scope for the operation of a self-fulfilling prophecy. Third, the masochist may begin to see her or himself as someone who can take a lot of pain and suffering, almost with pride.

Warren (1985) allows for the possibility that some masochists may not be aware that they are contributing to their own pain and that they might not know what to talk about should they be deprived of their pain and suffering. Pain provides the structure for their mundane reality. For the self-conscious masochists, however, opportunities for pride abound through self-inflicted pain. Not only will this foster the illusion that they are in control of their lives but, also, they may with good cause feel that they have power over the other folk who are touched by their lives. As Warren (1985) points out: 'One says to others: "You are powerless to stop me, or to comfort me, or to make me like myself; I am stronger than all of you"' (p. 115). The self-conscious masochists, therefore, arrange for their lives to be governed by predictable series of no-win situations in order to ensure that they may continuously take a sense of pride and accomplishment in their pain and suffering.

In order to achieve their masochistic identity, Warren (1985) suggests that many masochists have to be 'doubleminded'. She defines doublemindedness as 'a second-order desire to have conflicting first-order desires' (p. 118). She illustrates what it would be like to lose one's doublemindedness by imagining that in a mind transplant the person be required to give up seeing themselves as a victim. This would involve a change in identity which might not be welcome. The masochists will not feel like themselves. They may have to substitute new character traits, central beliefs and activities for those currently in place. They would have to give up self-hating activities, such as constantly listing all their errors or spending as much time as possible with those who berate them.

Looked at from Warren's (1985) perspective, masochism can be seen as a problem relating to personal identity, a problem which any counsellor worth their salt might relish. I have already mentioned Berne's (1972) transactional analysis in this context and one defence that a masochist might use against the efforts of a do-gooding liberal humanistic counsellor would be to engage in Berne's (1964) game 'Why don't you – Yes, but... ' (YDYB – Berne's acronym). In this game, the victim (the masochist in this context) seduces the therapist (or friend or relation) into taking on the role of the 'rescuer'. The myriad pains and sufferings are paraded enticingly in front of the rescuer with the demand for some indication as to how they might be alleviated. Yet every suggestion put forward ('Why don't you... '), no matter how creative or pragmatic, is met with an objection ('Yes, but... ') from the masochist. Although masochists might be expected to prefer to be losers, on this count they would find themselves, paradoxically, as winners. But the winning is grounded in the fact that the therapist/rescuer is forced to acknowledge that the masochist's position is hopeless. Presumably this will give the masochist some comfort.

The view of masochism as an essential aspect of identity leads me to psychoanalytic approaches to masochism, built on the notion of dissociation.

Dissociation in masochism

The doublemindedness, referred to by Warren (1985), has some similarity to the DSM-IV category of dissociative identity disorder which was formerly known as multiple personality disorder. The essential feature of dissociative identity disorder is the presence of two or more distinct personality states that recurrently take control of behaviour. The primary identity may be rather passive, guilty, depressed and dependent. The alternative identity may, by contrast, be hostile, controlling and self-destructive. The individual may also be prone to amnesia and memory gaps relating to the alternative identity. The features associated with dissociative identity disorder include self-mutilating and suicidal behaviour. People with this disorder may report experience of physical and sexual abuse in childhood and/or be involved in a repetitive pattern of relationships involving such abuse as adults. They may also manifest symptoms relating to post-traumatic stress disorder (such as nightmares or flashbacks). Finally, they have been found to score near the upper end of the distribution on measures of hypnotisability and dissociative capacity (see American Psychiatric Association, 1994, for a fuller exposition of these diagnostic criteria). I have already discussed dissociation in the context of hypnosis (see Chapter 8) and there are some similarities in the way the concept is used in both domains. However, when dissociation has been applied to masochism, the framework seems to have taken on a more overtly psychoanalytic cast.

Howell (1996) discusses the link between dissociation and masochism (she also touches on psychopathic sadism). She approaches the topic from a contemporary psychoanalytic perspective. She sees masochism as a post-traumatic adaptation based on defensive dissociation of rage and aggression. This provides the masochist with a victim-self state, together with the self-observer/narrator state. The third state of perpetrator is dissociated. By way of contrast, the sadist dissociates the victim-self state. Howell (1996) explicitly ties the self-observer state to the hidden observer of hypnosis. Functionally, she sees this state as similar to that of the dreamer of the dream, as the narrator/observer of the characters and their activities.

Howell (1996) defines masochism as 'the tendency to be abused or tortured by oneself or others' (p. 429). She resists any account of masochism based upon drive theory, since that leads to the view that victims are victims because they want to be victims. She points out that the cause of the suffering is unlikely to be the victim, especially in clinical cases where this will tend to be the abuser (a spouse, for example). The problem is not, therefore, that the masochist is causing the suffering but that she or he does not or cannot leave the situation or the relationship.

Howell (1996) looks to trauma theory for an explanation of masochism. She notes that the lack of will and agency found in the masochist's submission to the abusive partner's commands is similar to that found in the hypnotic situation. She also feels that the masochist's sense of helplessness is similar to that of the victims of trauma and abuse. The experience of involuntariness seems to be at the core of all three forms of experience (the traumatic, the hypnotic and the masochistic).

The way Howell (1996) links masochism to trauma may sound fanciful to anyone unsympathetic to the psychoanalytic perspective, but I will describe it in order to bring out the importance of dissociation in this particular form of explanation. The masochist stays in the adverse setting of abuse because she or he lacks information vital to their self-defence and to their ability to manage the situation. This state of affairs has come about because the masochist has dissociated the pain to which, as a victim, he or she was exposed. The rage that may have been present at the time of the original abuse will also have been dissociated and this, Howell (1996) thinks, is what makes the masochist so passive.

Self-torture is, according to Howell (1996), explained in terms of a self-fragment splitting off to become organised around the function of vigilantly protecting the individual 'by demanding proper behaviour in a dangerous world' (p. 436). The protector fragment turns into the internal persecutor because it has no attachment which can bind it to love. The persecutor can only control and express hatred or aggression. This tyrannical facet of self can then be projected on to others in the real world, thus providing a rationale for the masochist's submissiveness towards the object of their projection. Howell (1996) uses the spell as a metaphor for masochistic behaviour.

> There is an utter involuntariness about the victim of the spell: there is nothing he or she can do about it. Individuals may spend their lives trying to break the bad spell. (p. 438)

Howell (1996) then goes on to speak of vampires, but at that point I bale out and rummage for the garlic.

I shall briefly pause to comment on some aspects of Howell's (1996) analysis of masochism, before returning to Baumeister (1997) who takes a very different approach. Howell's (1996) idea that being a masochist might be like being trapped by a spell for life reminds me strongly of Berne's (1972) life scripts in transactional analysis, particularly because he makes frequent use of the persecutor and victim roles within his portfolio of common scripts and games. It is perhaps no surprise that there is some overlap between Howell (1996) and Berne (1972), since both draw loosely on psychoanalytic theory. Howell's (1996) use of the fairy tale analogy with the concept of spell, together with the vampire myth, brings her into some alignment with narratological approaches put forward in some areas of contemporary critical psychology (see Murray, 1995).

I am happy to explore the notion of dissociation in masochism, although I am more comfortable when this is done from the standpoint of cognitive psychology rather than psychoanalytic theory as has been the case with regard to hypnosis (see Chapter 8). The problem with a heavyweight psychoanalytic account is that it becomes more and more difficult to swallow once one gets away from extreme examples. I would be reluctant to posit an abused childhood as the prerequisite for the sort of masochism described by Phillips (1998) which could almost be defined as *recreational* in character. As I have already indicated, Baumeister (1997) puts forward an explanation of masochism that has no recourse to psychoanalytic concepts.

The escape from ordinary identity

Baumeister (1997) advances the view that masochism offers a set of techniques which may be deployed to escape self-awareness. The advantage of this temporary loss of the person's normal identity is that some relief may thereby be obtained from the stresses and strains that surround the modern western forms of self-hood. This is an attractive idea which relates the phenomena of masochism to a cultural context, as opposed to grounding it in individual psychopathology.

Baumeister (1997) points out that there are three ways in which masochism is baffling: most people would avoid pain rather than seek it, most would desire more rather than less control and most would prefer to avoid humiliation or embarrassment rather than welcome it. I think that Baumeister (1997) is saying that masochists, *in their normal primary identities*, will also want to avoid pain and humiliation and will want to have control over their situation. This is why he rejects explanations of masochism that invoke deep psychopathologies; he sees none there. Masochism is therefore used as a device to temporarily topple ordinary identity. The humiliation that a male masochist undergoes by being made to crawl around the floor, dressed in women's clothing, may violate levels of minimum dignity required if their normal identity (as an executive or member of parliament, for example) is to be taken seriously. Interestingly, the leverage of humiliation to disrupt the ordinary identity will be stronger the more conventional is the baseline self. If someone holds extremely liberal and eccentric views about these matters, then the degrading activities will have less to bite on in order to generate humiliation.

Baumeister (1997) sees the quest for control as a pervasive feature of ordinary identities. The self cannot function normally if, in submitting to bondage, the masochist relinquishes all control to the dominant partner. Bondage, obedience and submission combine with humiliation, embarrassment and degradation to provide a powerful cocktail for dislodging the individual from their normal identity. Pain assists this process in a slightly different fashion. By capturing attention urgently and immediately, pain draws it away from any concerns that are not present in the 'here and now'. Thus awareness of a meaningful identity (tangled up with a web of ongoing plans, commitments or problems) is forced out of consciousness; in pain, there is just the immediate sensory experience. This is why it makes little sense to speak of betrayal in relation to anything that the torture victim might say or do. In the prolonged, excruciating and vile variations of pain that our torturers generate around the globe, the identity of their victims will be consumed in those moments of pain. But this is a far cry from recreational masochism, with its safe word codes and conventions.

Baumeister (1997) argues that masochism as a phenomenon is not pan-cultural and is of relatively recent origin. He claims that the incidence of sexual masochism is confined almost exclusively in Western Europe and the US. While it was pretty much non-existent prior to 1500 it had become well established by the 1800s. He bases this conclusion on a study of sex manuals, drawn from different cultures, and from research literature on what sorts of service prostitutes provided for their clients.

> The early modern period (1500–1800) in Europe witnessed the emergence of a historically and culturally unusual form of selfhood, in which the expectations of autonomy, individualistic uniqueness, and self-promotion were much higher than in traditional societies. If masochism is indeed an escapist response to those demands, then masochism would presumably have increased at that time and place. (pp. 141–2)

Baumeister (1997) concludes with the speculation that the emergence of masochistic practices in Asia and other places may be related to the increasing globalisation of western culture.

Grammatical considerations

One of the puzzles that masochism throws up is knowing how to make sense of sentences such as 'I am torturing myself'. This is because it is more normal for the person doing the torturing to be different from the person being tortured. I shall approach this from the perspective on personal being put forward by Harré (1983).

Harré (1983) advances the thesis that the first person indexical 'I' does not so much refer to a speaker as label a speech utterance as 'mine'. For Harré (1983), individuals are like locations in the primary array of persons. This array can contain former persons as well as possible persons.

> I believe the personal pronouns by which persons identify themselves as 'speakers of the moment' are a lexical system parallel to the 'here' and 'now', 'this' and 'that' of physical space and time. The study of the logical grammar of 'I' and 'we' should therefore reveal the referential grid for psychological and social reality. It is the array of persons since it is to persons that utterances are anchored by the pronominal indexicals by using 'speaker' as the utterance label. In the primary structure persons are not like things, they are like places. (p. 61)

Psychological phenomena like thoughts and feelings are not seen as attributes of people, rather, they are seen as entities located at people.

In Chapter 8, I indicated that Harré's theory provides a way to understand what is involved in dissociation in hypnosis. I will elaborate on that theme, this time in relation to masochism. The dissociated speaker issues utterances which hearers would normally locate at a unique address in the array of persons (the identification of this address being made through the body of the speaker). In the case of the dissociated speaker, however, the problem is that these utterances need to be located at more than one location in the array of persons. The observer is constrained by the operation of the rule: one physical body, one person. Interestingly, such constraints are relaxed in some situations where communication takes place over the internet. Here, the location of a person is primarily tagged to their internet id. The use of aliases and 'handles' may facilitate the deployment of multiple identities by any given corporeal being. In Goffman's (1959) terms, there is greater scope for impression management in web-mediated communication (see also Buchanan and Smith, in press).

Harré's (1983) ideas can be applied to Baumeister's (1997) analysis. The thoughts, feelings, behaviours and speech utterances that go to make up acts of humiliation, degradation, torture and abuse are psychological phenomena which will be located at an alternative location in the array of persons to that normally occupied by the masochist. The dominant partner acts as an agent of redirection. The masochistic contract demands that the linking or tying together of these two separate locations be resisted, or at any rate be kept hidden. The potential for blackmail by an unscrupulous third party feeds on this secrecy.

Interim summary

In Chapter 1, I introduced the concept of agency, partly by drawing the distinction between agent and patient. In some ways the masochist can be construed as patient. This is especially true where, restrained or bound, she or he is made to suffer passively what happens to them. Where, however, the masochist does the dominant partner's bidding, there may be elements in common with the phenomenon of obedience (see Chapter 8 for a discussion of the distinction between robotic and executive agency). The idea that some form of dissociation may take place within the masochist squares with what some theorists argue happens in hypnosis (see, again, Chapter 8). Another point of similarity is that dramaturgical interpretations would appear to be as apt for some masochistic episodes as they are for the hypnotic.

Warren (1985), Howell (1996), Baumeister (1997) and Phillips (1998) all seem to think that there are people who are consistently masochistic over time. Masochists thus produce coherent sets of behaviours in a reliable fashion. Masochism cannot therefore be explained on the grounds of chance. Masochism is a force to be reckoned with when human rationality is asserted; it breaks the mould. The view that humans are rational can be retained only if something can be done about the case of masochism. If masochists are defined as insane, then there will be no problem since they are then out of the frame (no one expects fully rational behaviour from mad people). If this step is not taken, then further efforts need to be made to account for their behaviour. Dissociation allows the belief in ordinary rational explanation to be upheld at the cost of adding complexity to commonsense notions of the person. This can be accommodated through grammatical considerations by teasing apart personal being from strict one-to-one notions of embodiment (see my discussion, above, of Harré's, 1983, position).

I am reluctant to abandon psychological hedonism since this solution may well generate more problems than it solves (see my discussion of the weight of evidence in support of the TRA/TPB, in Chapter 2). One area where theories of action based upon the hedonistic calculus have a part to play is that of suicide, if it is to be considered as a rational act, and it is to a discussion of this topic that I now turn.

Suicide

Werth (1996) uses 'suicide' as a verb, in order to free himself from phrases which are constructed with the modifier 'commit'. This is because the word 'commit' is redolent with connotations of crime. I intend to follow his example, and shall try not to feel too guilty about tweaking the English language in this fashion. In general, Werth (1996) takes a stand against a number of commonly held views: that suicide is a crime, that suicide is a sin, that suicide is a manifestation of insanity. This enables him to develop the argument that it is possible for people to make a rational decision to suicide. As a counsellor, he has worked with people suffering from AIDS and this practical background has informed his theoretical position.

The *Oxford English Dictionary* defines suicide as 'the intentional killing of oneself'. It is the intention that brings suicide into the realm of action and distinguishes it from mere behaviour. The distinctions discussed in Chapter 1 between action and behaviour are crucial in the context of suicide. Consider, for example, a body which falls from a high building and spatters on the pavement below. A medic or physiologist will be able to give a convincing causal explanation of the death. It may be much more difficult to establish how the death is best construed. In order to establish the event as suicide, simple causal explanations which could account for how the chain of events got started must be ruled out. Were things put down to a freak gust of wind, that would be the end of the matter. Next, it may be necessary to rule out the possibility of foul play. If the dead person suffered at the hands of another then, in the language of agency, the person would be a patient; the death would be something that happened to him or her and not something intended. Setting aside murder, another possibility is that the death occurred by accident or misadventure. For example, someone might lean over a very steep cliff in order to pick up a stone or fossil, only to lose balance and subsequently hurtle to his or her death. In terms of my discussion in Chapter 5, the intention would be clear but the action would be bungled. In terms of the molecular representation of plans (introduced in Chapter 2), the accidental death would appear as an unfortunate side effect. With suicide, as opposed to accidental death, the death takes centre stage in the plans molecule as the primary goal of the intention.

The reason why suicide deserves special attention in the context of the psychology of action is that it has obvious but devastating consequences for the agent. When the agent suicides successfully, he or she dies. Suicide, as an act, has uniquely transcendent properties: it is the only act which destroys the agent. According to the *Oxford English Dictionary*, an agent is 'a person or thing that exerts power or produces an effect'. In suicide the essential property of agency is nullified through a display of agency. Successful suicide, through death, will also terminate the person's opportunities for being a patient (in the agentic sense of the term). It is possible, however, in the case of a failed or bungled suicide attempt, for the person to remain alive while being effectively incapacitated, perhaps through brain damage or paralysis. There is a sense in which such a suicide may be regarded as partially successful. This is because the suicide, by rendering the person incapable of agency, succeeds where it matters most. As a human 'vegetable', the person can only exist as a patient (with the agentic and medical senses of this term moving closer together). However, this condition could occur naturally as, for example, the outcome of a progressive terminal illness. Where the probability of this happening is high, this may, for some individuals, provide grounds for a rational suicide attempt. I turn to a more detailed consideration of Werth's (1996) position on this.

Rational suicide

Werth (1996) uses a definition put forward by Siegel (1986) to provide an orientation to the topic.

> The defining characteristics of a rational suicide are: (1) the individual possesses a realistic assessment of his [or her] situation, (2) the mental processes leading to his [or her] decision to commit suicide are unimpaired by psychological illness or severe emotional distress, and (3) the motivational basis of his [or her] decision would be understandable to the majority of uninvolved observers from his [or her] community or social group. (p. 407)

Much of this definition can be related to the terms of the TRA/TPB (see Chapter 2). The first characteristic speaks to the attitudinal component and covers the person's realistic evaluation of likely consequences and their attendant probabilities of occurrence. As is often the case with the TRA/TPB, the way in which the intention is framed is a little awkward. The assessments are best calculated from the point of view of what would happen if the person were *not* to suicide. The second characteristic can be seen as a safeguard that the person is in a fit state to do such computations. The third characteristic relates indirectly to the subjective norm component of the TRA/TPB. However, not all theorists construe suicide as the outcome of a rational decision process. Baumeister (1990) regards it as impulsive behaviour, far removed from the realm of rational action.

Suicide as impulsive escape

Baumeister (1990) advances the theory that suicide can be seen as 'an ultimate step in the effort to escape from self and world' (p. 90). He does not mean this theory to cover all forms of suicide (altruistic self-sacrifice, ritual suicide and honour suicide would, for example, fall outside his remit). There are six steps in this theory.

The first step reminds me of Miller *et al.*'s (1960) TOTE unit (see Chapter 4) and postulates a mismatch between current circumstances and expectations. The reason for this might be that expectations are set too high or that some recent problems or setbacks have occurred. Baumeister (1990) points out that suicide rates tend to be higher in nations with higher standards of living and, also, higher in locations where the weather is better. He suggests that favourable external conditions produce high expectations.

The second step concerns the way the person accounts for the mismatch which is perceived in the first step. He suggests that the person will make internal attributions which will have negative implications for the self. The idea behind this is that when times in general are bad, people will tend to attribute their problems to external causes but when things are going well, people will tend to see their problems as being their own fault.

The third step is the occurrence of a state of high self-awareness. This is seen as a direct consequence of the comparison between how the self is doing in practice with how the self should ideally be doing (in Step 2) and is due to the self-blame for the recent disappointments in performance. Reviewing some of the indirect evidence, Baumeister (1990) notes that war has the effect of reducing suicide rates. The suggestion is that in times of war, personal identity becomes less important than a social identity based upon the nation state and that this reduces self-awareness.

The fourth step is that the heightened self-awareness produced by the unfavourable comparison of self with high standards results in negative affect, especially depression and anxiety. Anxiety may be linked to guilt over letting people down and depression may be tied to the sense of failure and loneliness of many who experience divorce, romantic rejection or who lose their jobs.

The fifth step encapsulates the most creative aspect of this theory. It postulates a state of cognitive deconstruction as a result of the preceding four steps. This involves a subjective shift to less meaningful ways of thinking about what is happening. Baumeister (1990) describes what is involved:

> Deconstructed ('low-level') awareness means being aware of self and action in concrete, short-term ways, focusing on movements and sensations and thinking only of proximal immediate tasks and goals. The essence of cognitive deconstruction is the removal of higher meanings from awareness. (p. 92)

Cognitive deconstruction is tantamount to a shift from action to behaviour. Baumeister (1990) emphasises that passivity will be a consequence of cognitive deconstruction and this lends weight to the view that the person moves from being an agent to being a patient (in the philosophical sense of the word, discussed in Chapter 1). The importance of cognitive deconstruction in the context of suicide is that it acts to remove or dampen the negative emotion, owing to the fact that such emotion arises from the meaningful interpretations that the person places upon his or her situation.

In the mental state produced through cognitive deconstruction, the person may then take the sixth step and go on to suicide. Baumeister (1990) sees this as being increasingly likely on the grounds that inhibitions which might prevent such a response will be reduced through the cognitive deconstruction in the fifth step. Suicide, according to Baumeister's (1990) theory, thus provides an escape from self through a route characterised by irrationality and disinhibition.

Responsibility

Werth (1996) and Baumeister (1990) sit on opposite sides of the fence with regard to suicide. Werth (1996), speaking primarily from the standpoint of counsellors and the caring professions, puts the case that the responsibility for suicide should not necessarily be laid at the professional's feet. He sees this situation as becoming anachronistic, especially with the recent changes in society arising from the spread of AIDS. He argues that for some people suicide can be a rational decision and, in doing so, he is effectively arguing that responsibility for the suicide be shifted from the professional to the client.

In Baumeister's (1990) escape theory, rationality survives in the first step, since expectations are compared to the unfavourable situation in reality. I think that, given the client makes internal attributions, it can also be said to survive into the second step. The high self-awareness of the third step and the resulting negative affect produced in the fourth can both be tied into a rational response to what is happening in the real world. It is only at the fifth step of cognitive deconstruction that rationality is lost. This would appear to be the point of agentic bifurcation which sets Baumeister (1990) against Werth (1996). Baumeister (1990) sees the transition from agent to patient at this stage, with suicide being an impulse coming through disinhibition. Werth (1996), focuses on the possibility that the person can weigh up the situation, formulate an intention and then generate an explicit plan to suicide (possibly with medical assistance).

I do not think Baumeister (1990) or Werth (1996) are putting forward their views to be applied pandemically across the whole domain of suicide, and so there is no sense in which one has to choose between them. However, in any particular case, the rational and escapist accounts will be mutually exclusive.

Szasz (1986) not only rejects the image of suicide as a combination of sin, sickness and crime but also deplores the tendency to regard it as implying irrationality, incompetence and insanity. He argues that suicide be construed as 'an act of a moral agent for which that agent himself or herself is ultimately responsible' (p. 806). By adopting this position, Szasz (1986) is driven to emphasise the distinction between agent and patient when considering the vexed question as to how mental health professionals might discharge their duty to prevent suicide.

> If one person is to prevent another person from killing himself or herself, the former clearly cannot, and should not be expected to, accomplish that task unless he or she can exercise complete control over the suicidal person. But it is either impossible to do this, or would require reducing the so-called patient to a social state

beneath that of a slave. The slave is compelled only to labor against his or her will, whereas the suicidal person would thus be compelled to live against his or her will. Such a life is not the life of a person or human being, but only that of a human organism or 'living human *thing*'. (p. 808, emphasis added)

It is interesting to note that both Szasz (1986) and Baumeister (1990) are concerned with the suicidal person's agentic status as a patient. With Szasz (1986) this is something that would have to be achieved by the mental health professional through coercive suicide prevention. For Baumeister (1990) it just happens all by itself as the patient reaches the fifth and sixth steps of the suicidal process.

On the surface, there would appear to be some similarity between the positions of Szasz (1986) and Werth (1996). This comes from the fact that both construe suicide as rational. However, Szasz (1986) develops his arguments on the basis of a general moral principle without drawing upon the expectancy-value computational model that underpins Werth's (1996) position.

> If on moral and political grounds we decide that we oppose a social policy authorizing coercive mental health interventions vis-à-vis so-called suicidal persons, then the mental state of any particular suicidal person becomes irrelevant to judging whether, in that specific case, such a policy should or should not be implemented. (Szasz, 1986, p. 810)

I think that this could be interpreted to mean that there is no point in looking into the extent of the hopelessness of the person's situation in order to make a decision as to whether it passes muster on the basis of Werth's (1996) first characteristic (see above discussion). Szasz (1986) would not be drawn into any arguments about whether someone with terminal bone cancer should be regarded any differently to someone who was bankrupt. His argument is not dependent upon the outcome of TRA/TPB style deliberations for any particular case.

Concluding discussion

There is a clear similarity between Baumeister's theory of masochism and his theory of suicide. In both cases the activity involves an escape from self. In recreational masochism this is achieved on a temporary basis. Restraint, bondage and obedience all serve to shift the person away from the active agentic state into the passive state of the patient. In suicide this happens as a result of cognitive deconstruction. Pain, in masochism, focuses attention on the here and now and this constricted temporal perspective is close to that postulated by Baumeister (1990) in the suicidal phase of cognitive deconstruction. Consciousness becomes empty and devoid of meaningful content with regard to the person's position in everyday life and broader autobiographical context.

Szasz (1986) also sets aside the person's inner experience, although admittedly to make a different point. For him, the higher order moral principle does not require an examination of the experiential details of specific cases. Szasz (1986) is neutral as to mental experience. The person's mind could be emptied out through cognitive deconstruction or full to bursting point with the sorts of computations demanded by the TRA/TPB; it makes no difference.

There are some points of comparison between suicide and some of the other topics I have considered in this and the previous chapter. Szasz's (1986) disregard for subjective experience is something to which I drew attention when discussing hypnosis as ritual (see Chapter 8). Exploring the link with hypnosis a little further, self-hypnosis is to hypnosis as suicide is to assisted suicide. Of course, if the subject were to be hypnotised unwittingly, or against his or her will, then the appropriate comparison might be between suicide and murder. Baumeister's (1990) concept of cognitive deconstruction involves a great deal of theoretical speculation. I think that this concept is not dissimilar to the state postulated by dissociation control theory (drawing a parallel with frontal lobe disorders). The possibility of the suicide being carried out impulsively but still under rational control arises if, instead of pushing the analogy with dissociation control, it is forced with the neodissociation theory (see Chapter 8 for a discussion of these approaches to hypnosis).

There is no doubt that suicide presents a difficult, if not intractable, problem for the researcher. There is no way of knowing how many deaths classified as undetermined, accidental or by misadventure may have been successful suicides, in fact. Furthermore, it is technically possible, although perhaps unlikely, that some deaths are misclassified as murder when in reality they were suicide and vice versa. Be that as it may, the number of real suicides may never be known and therefore empirical researchers can never be confident of starting from an unambiguous data base.

Of the real suicides, a proportion may have left notes or may have talked to surviving friends, relatives or professionals. If these data are available, they may provide evidence that, in particular cases, the suicide was rational. Where such evidence is not forthcoming, a number of alternative interpretations are possible: the suicide may have been one of escape from self involving cognitive deconstruction; it may have involved dissociated control; there may have been a neodissociated state of mind. Admittedly, some circumstantial evidence may support one of these interpretations rather than the other, but it is difficult to see how this could result in little more than guesswork.

As for the failed suicides, these cases do, in principle, offer the possibility for *post hoc* data collection. The difficulty here is that there is likewise no way of knowing whether, for example, escape-from-self suicides are overrepresented among these cases. The argument could be made that rational suicides might have a better chance of success since they will have been better planned; this would result in their underrepresentation among failed suicides. Of course, the counter argument that there is no guarantee that the person would not baulk at the execution of the suicide plan (when compared with the cognitively deconstructed person in a state of disinhibition) can just as easily be made.

The ambiguous nature of suicide research data may ensure that crisp empirical resolutions to what are essentially moral or legal dilemmas in professional practice will never be found. I am dealing with this topic primarily from the perspective of the psychology of action and not from the standpoint of the caring or legal professions. This means that I can set aside some considerations which are especially pertinent to the professionals. For example, Pritchard (1995) is keen to puncture the myth that death might be a beautiful thing for some talented young poets or painters who end their lives in idealistic suicides for the sake of their art. He singles out the case of a young poet (Chatterton) who poisoned himself in his London garret in 1770.

> We eschew the elevated notion of self-death, for, cruelly, the physical reality is of a vomit-choked face, of the hideous distortions of a twisted rope, of the grotesque multiple fractures of a shattered body, of a stinking bloated cadaver whose rotting remains are thrown back by a rejecting sea. (p. 2)

In terms of the TRA, these are the outcomes of the intention to suicide which should properly enter into the attitude component and should feature within a rational suicide decision. If they do not (and the young person is naive about the consequences, perhaps), then this is regrettable but does not provide any form of embarrassment to the theoretical position. In practice, on the other hand, a mismatch between myth and reality could be used in one of two ways by counsellors, social workers and other professionals. If the professional's mission is to prevent, then demystification and education should result in a more realistic appraisal of consequences and this, in terms of the TRA/TPB, might result in a change of intention on pain of transgressing the rule of intelligibility, as it were. Preventive strategies, apart from altering the contents, expectancies and values in the attitude component of the TRA might also involve working on the perceived behavioural control element in parallel. The professional who believes in rational suicide, and who is able to act on this within the law (or, at least, within his or her own conscience), will need to work with the client in order to provide reassurance that the consequences of suicide can be pulled closer to the idealistic myth and that the horrors of the description offered by Pritchard (see above quotation) are not the reality to be expected. The most obvious path is to guarantee that the client will have the means, through 'medication', to enter a deep, peaceful and final sleep. I am conscious that I have used the word 'medication' and that not only is this a euphemism for poison but also, in doing so, I have drawn on the medical model of suicide. It goes without saying that 'sleep' is a euphemism for death. The more technical expression 'physician-performed euthanasia' is more neutral in tone but the medical model still seethes beneath. It is difficult to see how this can be circumnavigated, since straight talk about taking poison leads directly to murder as an underlying metaphor.

With regard to the psychology of action, where suicides are construed as an escape from self (as in Baumeister's, 1990, theory), I feel that they fall outside the boundaries of action. I see such events as unfortunate behaviours. Rational suicide seems to me to be a paradoxically superordinate demonstration of agency. It is the act by which, in all but the most exceptional circumstances involving loss of freedom, the individuals can claim their personhood and assert their being. It is the last thing that a person can do where there is nothing else of any meaning that can be done by the person. There are many extreme circumstances which may trigger some sort of empathic understanding for the plight of the person who decides to suicide.

External circumstances might relate to the individuals incarcerated under corrupt, coercive, cruel and oppressive regimes: the torture chambers, the concentration camps, the filthy prison cells sprinkled across the globe with what seems like random abandon. Physiological circumstances might involve terminal medical conditions: bone cancer, Alzheimer's, AIDS, to name but three. Psychological circumstances are hard to specify without falling into the trap of DSM-IV classification: depression, anxiety, the products of domestic abuse, the family home turned prison cell. The working environment offers many opportunities to receive abuse, bullying and ostracism; and through financial ruin or job loss: the spectre of homelessness, starvation for self and loved ones, a trashed reputation. The physical environment may seal our fate with barren hope: starvation through famine, failed crops, draught; pollutions of the conventional kind; the unknown pollutions to come, be they derived from radioactivity, genetic mutation or chemical weaponry. And then there is war, bloody war. The fact that suicide rates are reportedly lower in wartime is a fact from which I draw no comfort. It seems to me that there are plenty enough grounds for rational suicide; it's a tribute to human resilience, resourcefulness and sheer bloody-mindedness that there is not more of it about.

Chapter 10
Conclusion

I shall start by drawing together some of the themes and threads covered in the book. I shall do this chapter by chapter, making links where appropriate. Eventually, this will bring me back to the topic of suicide on which I concluded the last chapter. I am aware that I painted a grim picture of the life world at that point and, although I shall dwell briefly on this negative picture once again, I shall move on in a more optimistic fashion by briefly considering communitarianism (Etzioni, 1998) and third way politics (Giddens, 1998). Then, staying with the broad perspective, I shall explore the way agency may benefit from eclecticism or what I like to think of as fusion psychology. I therefore conclude the chapter by putting forward a framework for agentic psychology, in order to provide a way of imposing some order over the large array of concepts and considerations facing the researcher in this domain. I do this in the hope that it will be interpreted as a heuristic tool, to be adapted flexibly as situations demand, rather than as a definitive statement set in stone.

Recapitulation and broader issues

In Chapter 1, I considered the difference between agent and patient and the importance of this distinction has arisen time and again throughout the book. Similarly the distinction between action and behaviour has been crucial in many ways. I wear my academic heart on my sleeve and I am sure that the fact that I side against the behaviourist stance has been made readily apparent. I remain convinced that action can be accounted for and I still find much of value in the work of Peters (1949, 1960) on reason and, also, the work of Harré and Secord

(1972) on the collection and negotiation of accounts. It is through the concept of negotiation that accounts (and thereby action) can be related to critical sociology, especially through the earlier work of Giddens (1979):

> Power is expressed in the capabilities of actors to make certain 'accounts count' and to enact or resist sanctioning processes; but these capabilities draw upon modes of domination structured into social systems. (p. 83)

In Chapter 2, I examined the theories of reasoned action and planned behaviour, together with self-efficacy theory. I felt that these represented good theories of action within the positivist mode. My strategy was to force a discussion of them in the context of conceptual analyses taken from the philosophy of action. This encouraged me to develop a critique of the TRA/TPB, while acknowledging the firmness of its empirical support. Thus I arrived at a paradigmatic relocation of the positivist theory by construing the theoretical equation as a rule governing the intelligibility of clusters of statements that might be made about a given action. Anticipating matters discussed later in the chapter, I see this as an example of fusion psychology. This paradigm shift invited and required different methodological techniques and I put forward some suggestions, based on the notion of attitudinal semantics, as to how the rule might be checked, refined and extended. One bonus to come from this was the possibility of establishing a better link with the concept of plan through the use of Abelson's (1973) molecular scheme for the representation of states and actions.

It was my aim, in writing this book, to develop a post-positivist psychology of action. I therefore felt duty bound (in Chapter 2) to consider the discursive action model of Edwards and Potter (1992). I have no quarrel with the model but I feel that it is rather limited in its application, dealing as it does solely with speech acts. When I broadened my consideration to discursive psychology in general and the critique of the earlier ethogenic paradigm, I found myself in disagreement with most of the criticisms that had been advanced. I have not, therefore, condemned or jettisoned the observational method or the negotiation of accounts and would wish to avail myself of such techniques within post-positivist agentic psychology.

CONCLUSION

I took some time out, as it were, to consider the rhetorical style and reflexivity in a number of critical psychology texts. It was interesting to note some of the ways the authors had built a certain amount of deconstruction into their own texts. In this book I have not used dialogue with imaginary interlocutors, nor have I resorted to graphical devices such as boxed text in order to provide a deconstructive meta-commentary on the main text. The amount of autobiographical material that I have included has been held to a minimum (and in this sense I did not follow Armistead, 1974). Looking back, I have produced a fairly conventional text. It strikes me that this may be because my feelings never run more strongly than lukewarm when I think about post-modernism or relativism. This could account for the fact that I have not felt especially committed to engage in reflexive deconstruction.

I looked at the relativist position held by some of the prominent discursive psychologists and was by no means converted; for me, the furniture is still there to be thumped, and death remains as real as ever. This forced me to meander through some linguistic considerations and I have to say that I was surprised by the extent of my reluctance to embrace the discursive standpoint on these issues. However, my interpretation of the TRA/TPB seemed to fit reasonably well with the stance I took at the end of Chapter 3. This also meant that I was in no position to dismiss out of hand some of the other material in mainstream psychology on the concept of plan, nor did I want to.

I very much enjoyed tracing the academic roots of the expectancy-value models (in Chapter 4). Bandura's work led me back to that of Rotter. I was surprised by the extent to which I was able to relate Rotter's work to the post-positivist developments in social psychology; both the 1970s ethogenic paradigm and the 1990s discursive approach provided points of contact. Once back to Tolman and Lewin the concept of plan began to assume greater importance and this enabled me to spend some time discussing Miller *et al.*'s (1960) classic work. The use of the concept of plan in artificial intelligence programming was an interesting development in the 1970s but it was not sustained to any appreciable degree beyond that time. On the other hand, a lively contemporary research literature appears to support work on plans and goal setting.

The bulk of the material I examined in relation to the concept of plan in Chapter 4 could by no stretch of the imagination be classified as critical psychology or critical social psychology. The concept of plan was central to the earlier 1970s new paradigm but does not feature in any obvious way in the later discursive psychology of the 1980s and 90s. I feel that there should be a place for the concept of plan in a post-positivist psychology of action, where possible, and I look forward to a greater integration in future.

My consideration of slips and errors in Chapter 5 was based upon the well-established approaches in cognitive psychology. I considered Reason's work on human error because of its direct relevance to the psychology of action. Relating this work to the critical psychology paradigms was something of a challenge but I feel that a number of interesting points of contact were established, especially through the concepts of rule and role, the use of accounts and the use of rhetoric and narrative.

In Chapter 6, I dealt with weakness of will and in so doing returned to a number of philosophical issues. I felt that the psychological research (relating to willpower, for example) provided a useful balance to the purely philosophical arguments. Baumeister, in drawing on the notion of the TOTE unit, gave me a link back to my treatment of plan in Chapter 4, and some of the conceptual arguments about akrasia could be related to the TRA/TPB (Chapter 2). Gosling's philosophical treatment of last-ditch akrasia, in particular, seemed to fit well with my idea that the TRA equation be regarded as the formal expression of a rule of intelligibility.

Sabini and Silver introduced several facets of procrastination and their analysis provided a convenient range of hypothetical examples drawn largely from the realm of undergraduate study. The positivist questionnaire research showed that procrastination has a negative relation to academic performance. Sabini and Silver's approach differed markedly from the questionnaire research but I argued that the two perspectives might be brought closer together to provide some degree of paradigmatic triangulation on the topic. The questionnaires could be used to identify procrastinators and non-procrastinators for a series of case studies focusing on problems in the execution of plans. Ironically, the consideration of the positivist idea of trait procrastination took me back into the philosophical debate about last-ditch akrasia. Once again, a topic ripe for fusion psychology (see later in this chapter).

In Chapter 7, I turned my attention to agentic improvement and started by considering DIY self-help. Rather than attempt to cover the breadth of material within this category (which might legitimately include books on physical fitness and diet, for example), I decided to focus attention on one 'reputable' manual for time management. Despite the fact that I had not expressed much enthusiasm for deconstructionism and discursive psychology in Chapter 3, I found myself engaged in a largely rhetorical analysis of Fontana's (1993) book. I also saw some parallels between his use of storytelling and that of Reason's (1990) or Merttens' (1998). Many of Fontana's (1993) techniques could be construed as correctives or antidotes to various problems in the execution of plans (and thus linked to Chapters 4, 5, and 6).

I felt that it made sense to draw what may well be an arbitrary line between DIY agentic improvement and what happens when the professionals are called in. My treatment of counselling had to be very selective, owing to constraints of space. Given the fact that I had articulated the tensions that exist between behaviourism and the post-positivist psychology of action in Chapter 1, I decided to take the bull by the horns and go for behaviour modification from a rhetorical standpoint. This enabled me to draw on material presented in Chapter 2 for the foundation of my critique. Having established the link between the concept of reinforcement and expectancy-value models, I was able to deploy my interpretation of the TRA/TPB as a rule of intelligibility in my arguments against behaviour modification (and the token economy). Once again, I found Abelson's molecular model for the representation of plan (discussed in Chapter 2) to be of use in developing my analysis of the conditioning situation. In my conclusion, I was quite clear that behaviour modification could not be construed as a medical technique and that the use of punishment in behaviour modification could not be justified on medical grounds. I left as an open question the matter as to whether it might ever be justified on other grounds, and pointed to self-injurious behaviour in children as an area likely to throw up difficult moral dilemmas in this regard.

I then turned my attention to rational emotive behavioural counselling (REBC) on the grounds that it seemed to have one foot in the tradition of behaviour modification but also seemed to be close to the psychology of action. It is difficult to see how a therapy which rides on an alphabetical mnemonic such as the ABCDE of REBC could ever be taken seriously, but this I endeavoured to do. Given my treatment of behaviour modification, I found it interesting that in REBC a rhetorical stance was also adopted. In the case of REBC, it is done in order to provide the therapist with flexible strategies when approaching their clients. The importance placed on planning and goal setting in REBC provided a link to matters introduced in Chapter 4. REBC makes considerable demands on the client and I cannot see how it could succeed unless therapist and client manage to establish a good working relationship with one another based upon an agentic contract (I am not suggesting that this would be a written commercial contract) and this led me directly to matters considered in Chapters 8 and 9.

I considered four topics which presented difficulties for agency and the psychology of action: hypnosis, obedience, masochism and suicide. The topic of hypnosis is one surrounded by academic debate and there is a wealth of theoretical material to choose from. Of the dissociation theories, I felt that neodissociation theory was closest to my perspective on the psychology of action. I very much liked Wagstaff's (1998) proposal that, in postulating an altered state of consciousness, a category mistake might be made, although I found his solution a little too neat and tidy. Once again, I was drawn back to rhetorical psychology, this time to Billig's (1997) ideas on the dialogic unconscious and repression, in an attempt to make sense of the language of hypnosis and the norms of polite hypnotic conversation. Once hypnosis is underway, it seems not too much to expect that, if such norms were relaxed, access to repressed material might be possible. This is something which might happen in the context of both stage hypnosis and therapy.

I remain uneasy that in my discussion of hypnosis as ritual I have resorted to a conceptual legerdemain. The attractiveness of this step is that in ritual (or speech act) the subjective experience of the hypnotised subject fades from the spotlight as irrelevant. And what better way to extract oneself from the tangled arguments about altered states of consciousness? I love it. Still, I can afford to be a little blasé about this since my prime concern is not with hypnosis *per se* but with agency. Some of the problems about who (or what bit of consciousness) is in control vanish if hypnosis is construed as a speech act.

The question of control (and the related issue of responsibility) extends to obedience. I was very happy to spend some time discussing Milgram's (1974) classic experimental work on obedience. I very much liked his account of how individuals located within a social hierarchy might shift into an *agentic* state, passing control to a person occupying a superior position in the hierarchy. His terminology, in the context of the psychology of action, is a little confusing. In Chapter 1, for example, I introduced the concept of agency in order to make the distinction between agent and patient. In this sense, the obedient subject could be regarded as a patient, with the authority figure (the experimenter) acting as the agent within the Milgram experiment. What Milgram has in mind when he uses the term 'the agentic state' is closer to what is involved in a commercial contract between an agent and a principal.

The extent to which an individual agent has freedom to act as he or she chooses, in this situation, will be dependent on the level of abstraction at which the goals of the contract are specified. Higher order 'do best' goals will allow more degrees of freedom than will lower order specific goals. It is my view that as the degrees of freedom grow, so does the agent's responsibility. My consideration of this issue led me to the distinction between executive and robotic modes of agency. Returning to the topic of hypnosis, I thought that this might start from the robotic and move upwards to the executive level of agentic obedience. I found the argument that obedience might be accounted for by personality was most convincing when tied to the concept of trust (possibly seen as a character trait), since this allowed Mixon's creative interpretation of Milgram's work to be incorporated. This is, perhaps, not completely unrelated to the hypnotic situation.

As often happens when talking about the psychology of action, progress in one area throws up problems in another. Just as I began to feel that some progress was being made in the discussion of hypnosis as obedience between two people, the phenomenon of self-hypnosis began to assume more importance (as it does in the critique of dissociation control theory). I considered a number of analogies in order to keep this problem in perspective (for example tickling, flagellation). I felt that the chances of successful auto-hypnosis lay higher than those for successful self-tickling. One idea which I did not mention earlier because it seemed a trifle 'off-the-wall' was that ticklishness could turn out to be an indicator of hypnotic susceptibility. Maybe one day someone will check that out. In the end, I returned to some of Harré's (1983) ideas on personal being to help me pull the talk of dissociation across into my preferred language game (which I would describe as the post-positivist psychology of action).

In Chapter 9, I turned to the topic of masochism which presents a problem for theories of action with hedonistic underpinnings. The literature on masochism seemed to be split between sexual masochism and masochistic identity. I may be guilty of oversimplification when I describe the former as recreational in character, but its dramaturgical properties invite such a description. I found it interesting that both Warren's (1985) and Baumeister's (1997) accounts of masochism invoked the notion of identity. For Baumeister, the masochist uses sexual masochism as a device for forcing an escape from the individual's overburdened ordinary identity; for Warren, it is precisely this regular and essential identity that the masochist fears to leave. Just as the concept of dissociation has been invoked in explanations of hypnosis, so too in masochism. In the case of masochism, such explanations come laden fully with the conceptual baggage of psychoanalytic theory and for me that is too much to take on board. Once again, I travelled to Harré's (1983) theory of personal being to get me off the psychoanalytic hook with regard to dissociated identity. Phillips' (1998) treatment of masochism brings to the fore the sense of adopting a dramaturgical perspective, especially in relation to the more ritualistic aspects of the phenomenon. Dramaturgy was an integral part of the 1970s new paradigm social psychology but seems to have fallen away over the course of the 1980s and 90s (discursive psychologists tend to be hostile to the notion of social scripts acting as templates to generate social action). However, the recent interest in ritual shown by Rothenbuhler (1998), while coming primarily from communication studies and sociology, may herald a return of matters dramaturgical to social psychology.

I concluded Chapter 9 with a consideration of the topic of suicide. I was impressed by Werth's (1996) arguments that suicide could be a rational choice for some individuals, especially where terminal illness is concerned. Suicide as an act stands above all others, since it is the only act which reflexively destroys the agent. On this ground alone, it can be said to be the most potent act possible for an agent to execute. Because this most potent display of agency also annuls itself, suicide has a paradoxical edge to it.

Once again, Baumeister (1990) offers an interesting account of the topic by suggesting that cognitive deconstruction plays a central role in precipitating suicide. The escape from self in suicide is not dissimilar to the temporary escape from a burdensome identity that features in his explanation for sexual masochism. All the same, I am not happy to dismiss Werth's (1996) arguments regarding rational suicide on the basis of Baumeister's (1990) antithetical position. I am inclined to think that in some cases suicide may be rational while in others it may involve an escape from self facilitated by cognitive deconstruction. If this is so, there is no need to choose between the two.

I concluded Chapter 9 with a grim picture of the life-world, one rich with reasons for suicide. At this point I will briefly introduce a note of optimism by noting some connections between communitarianism (see Etzioni, 1998) and the social democratic politics of the third way (see Giddens, 1998) espoused by people like Tony Blair in the UK. Communitarianism starts by noting the fact that for many people civic society appears to have broken down in the industrialised west, especially in inner cities (see Siegel, 1998). Crime, drugs, mess and menace conjure up feelings of hopelessness and depression. I am reminded of Calhoun's (1962) work on overcrowding in animals (rats) where the social order was observed to break down in a startling fashion. Nests and litters were scattered and adults could even be seen to eat their young. Calhoun (1962) coined the term *behavioural sink* to describe the situation. In some post-industrial cities something like the behavioural sink may have evolved, although not necessarily as a result of overcrowding. The reason why I think the behavioural sink is such an interesting metaphor is because it suggests that human agency has atrophied. This is not the rational evil of meticulously planned genocide or persecution; this is humans reduced to unprincipled, irrational behaviour. I may be guilty of hyperbole but I see behavioural sinks as places where agency is in retreat, if not fully absent. What humans do is thus closer to something like animal behaviour, as opposed to civic action. Newman (1972) thought that part of the problem with crime, rape and mugging in inner-city environments could be attributed to the design of the buildings in which the people were obliged to live. He thought that the architects had given people urban territories which were impossible to defend; hence his concept of defensible space. Very often it would be the high-rise apartments that were the most indefensible. Buildings and estates or developments where the hierarchical organisation of space was preserved (from public to semi-public, through to the private apartment) using real and symbolic markers faired better. Things were also improved when good surveillance opportunities in the form of well-positioned windows were a feature of the dwellings. In terms of the psychology of action, good architecture built in accordance with the principles of defensible space swings the locus of control more firmly to the internal for the residents who are then better able to function as agents within their environment, as opposed to suffering as patients.

I think that communitarianism (see Etzioni, 1998) can be seen as a response to the proliferation of behavioural sinks across the globe, and especially in urban environments. 'Third way' politics attempts to chart a course which avoids both the failure of socialism and the excesses of free-market conservatism or neoliberalism (Giddens, 1998). This programme has apparently gained momentum from the emergence of post-materialism in the developed countries. Because it places more emphasis on the quality of life than on economic issues it reminds me of Maslow's ideas concerning the hierarchy of needs. It is not surprising that communitarianism highlights a range of green environmental issues as being of importance, given the emphasis placed upon quality of life. Giddens (1998) warns that the transition into a communitarian world will not be without its difficulties. For example, globalisation, left/right politics, individualism and a poorly developed sense of political agency may all present a challenge. It is beyond the scope of this book to discuss these issues in any detail, but most solutions put forward in third way politics would appear to involve a heightened sense of agency among individuals, resulting in a shift away from behavioural sinks towards civic societies.

Having concluded my recapitulation with a brief examination of broader societal issues, I now wish to stand back and look briefly at the range of theoretical perspectives, on offer from the various paradigms in psychology, which can be applied to agentic phenomena. I have to say that I find much in the way of swings and roundabouts when picking among the alternatives and this softens me to the notion of eclecticism.

Eclecticism and fusion psychology

Aristotle is an advocate of the middle path, the avoidance of the extremes. I endorse this position, even though such eclecticism brings with it the dangers of fudge, lack of clarity and feebleness of conviction. Still, I can live without the extreme views of J. B. Watson (see Chapter 1). It may be useful at this point to mention some of the more obvious difficulties that arise from taking up the extreme position with regard to some of the main schools of psychological thought, be they built upon behaviourist, existentialist, discursive, ethogenic, psychoanalytic, rationalist, cognitivist, or post-modernist foundations. I realise that I have not included all the possible perspectives in this list but limitations of space prevent me from casting my net any wider.

The behaviourists, by outlawing mental experience from the domain of psychology, placed themselves in an awkward position. In learning theory they had some success in explaining how regular patterns of behaviour may be law-governed through reinforcement schedules. Their theoretical framework, based on conditioning, led them into serious difficulties when it came to explaining creative activity. It really is unlikely that Shakespeare produced Hamlet on a chance basis or as a result of operant conditioning. The freedom from law-governed behaviour is the hallmark of creativity. Looked at another way, creativity and freedom constitute the Achilles heel of learning theory.

The pitfalls of adopting the platform of environmental determinism were avoided by existentialists such as Jean-Paul Sartre. For Sartre, the default human state involves freedom of choice.

The problem facing theories based on existentialism (and I would place the humanistic theories of Rogers and Maslow in that category), is how to account for all those instances where people are being boringly predictable as they go about their daily lives. Sartre (1969) saw this difficulty and he illustrated it using the example of a waiter who is consumed with being a waiter (as opposed to acting authentically and freely choosing what he will do from moment to moment). The way Sartre got round this difficulty was to invoke the notion of *bad faith* (see Sartre, 1969, Chapter 2).

The strengths of the behaviourist standpoint surface as difficulties for the existentialist perspective and vice versa. Behaviourism is optimally tuned to account for predictable, regular patterns of behaviour but is ill equipped to deal with novel and creative acts. Existentialism thrives on the notions of freedom and choice and thus takes in its stride the unpredictable. However, I think it is less successful when it comes to explaining the dull predictable facets of mundane human reality. Both behaviourism and existentialism are the sort of monolithic belief systems dismissed by relativists and postmodernists.

In Chapter 3 I argued against the extreme relativist position advocated by Potter (1996) and Edwards *et al.* (1995). I indicated that part of the difficulty for me in accepting the relativists' position was their reluctance to take language as a window onto a world of external reality. However, I readily admit that many other facets of discursive psychology provide the psychologist with an excellent set of analytic tools. The examination of talk as the performance of speech acts, as the management of impression and as a clue to issues of stake or facticity are things that can be addressed in a coherent fashion from the discursive platform. Behaviourists, attempting to make sense of this sort of thing, would be reduced to irrelevant and nonsensical comments about stimuli, responses and reinforcers; a complete waste of time and effort, in my view.

Just as I am warming up to discursive psychology, I begin to sense a limitation. If the discursive standpoint is adopted, it is very difficult to see how to break out of talk and get into the world of experience and action. For the discursive psychologist, the focus of the analysis is on the function of language. The researcher may sometimes compare different bits of talk (focus group transcripts versus newspaper cuttings, for example) but this is a bounded activity. It is very difficult to see how the discourse analysts can escape their own research game. There is no legitimate route out (via observation, for example) to an external reality, since that is taboo.

The ability to move beyond talk is not a problem for the 1970s ethogenic new paradigm. This can easily be achieved using observation and the negotiation of accounts. However, if the discursive psychologists have a problem in getting to grips with external reality, they point out with some justification that the ethogenic psychologists overstretch themselves when it comes to internal reality. There is a great temptation to reify the role–rule models and to see the dramaturgical scripts as mental templates churning out acts like cookies from a biscuit cutter. Reification might be said to be the Achilles heel of the 1970s ethogenic paradigm. Of course, a different challenge to the hegemony of the 1970s new paradigm comes from psychoanalytic theory, since the last thing a Freudian would accept would be an agent's account at face value.

Freud advanced a position which I would not describe as particularly clear cut. At the risk of oversimplification, he is often interpreted as advocating a form of psychic determinism. In a nutshell, human actions are determined by unconscious wishes and desires and, in the last resort, these will be sexual or aggressive in nature. I think that the psychoanalytic framework runs into difficulty when it comes to dealing with all those boringly rational bits of behaviour which can be accommodated so easily by the theory of reasoned action (see Chapter 2). I suppose the Freudians might say that what I mean by rational behaviour is covered by the ego. Although I am largely unsympathetic to Freudian theory, some contexts may strongly suggest that a surface account lacks credibility as a candidate for what Peters describes as the *real* reason (see Chapter 1). Repressed sexual desire, projected anger, displaced aggression may all compete, on occasion, for the status of being the preferred account. Setting aside the negotiation of accounts, psychoanalytic concepts may also be imported into the psychology of action through the back door via Billig's rhetorical approach to the dialogic unconscious.

I have tried to show that when it comes to the psychology of action there may be a case for fusing ideas from different paradigms and for rifling concepts from apparently incompatible language games. This is not quite the same as naively operating in an ill-suited paradigm. For example, I argued (in Chapter 2) that in many ways the positivist theories of action (TRA/TPB and SET) failed because of that. What I tried to do was to relocate the models in a more conducive theoretical framework. I did not reject the empirical evidence out of hand on the grounds that correlation coefficients belonged to the language game delineated by the doctrine of the objective experiment. Rather, I provided an alternative interpretation of them drawn from the post-positivist paradigm. It is in this sense that I regard what I did as eclectic fusion psychology.

I am not suggesting that the bizarre juxtaposition of ideas will always work and I do not believe that it should be done for its own sake. However, I do think that it can produce some surprises. For example, Reason (1990) is a respected applied cognitive psychologist. His work can certainly be tied in to the hard-nosed experimental side of the discipline and his writing is virtually devoid of post-modernist tendencies. This is what tempted me to explore parallels with Merttens' (1998) applied work in educational psychology. When notions of narrative, rhetoric and discourse were brought to bear on some aspects of Reason's (1990) work, they yielded novel constructions of the topic. Once started on the path to fusion in the domain of human error research, I felt strongly compelled to push for additional links with the 1970s new paradigm. The dramaturgical perspective makes a strange bedfellow for the applied cognitive stance when rule-based training is likened to tightly scripted dramatic performance, and training in knowledge-based problem solving is construed as semi-structured improvisation. I make no strong claim to originality in this regard, since the potential union between dramaturgy and applied cognitive psychology lies latently present in simulation techniques and these would appear to be used extensively in this area.

The discussion and illustration of eclectic fusion in agentic psychology could go on for ever, but limitations of space mean that I must draw matters to a close. One of the problems facing any enthusiast of eclectic fusion is that the number of concepts and ideas that need to be kept in mind for any given agentic analysis becomes large and unwieldy. In the excitement of conceptual cross-fertilisation, it is easy for the analytic edifice to topple, implode, self-destruct or whatever. I am going to finish this book by setting out a framework for agentic analysis which I find useful for coping with those times when fusion threatens to wobble out of control.

A pyramidic framework for agentic analysis

In Chapter 3, I examined some of the deconstructive tendencies in the texts of a number of critical social psychologists. Although I pointed out that I was not following their footsteps in using the dialogue of interpolated interlocutors or graphically boxed meta-commentary, I have to say that, in writing this section, I am sensitive to my own rhetorical strategy. I fully acknowledge that there is an arbitrariness about the way I have organised my conceptual framework into the shape of a two-dimensional pyramid, (see Figure 10.1). For ease of reference, I shall refer to this as my pyramidic framework (PF). The PF may be thought of as a conceptual toolkit for those seeking to carry out research into the psychology of action. I think it lends itself to the transparadigmatic perspective of fusion psychology but does not have to be used that way. The framework comprises ten blocks, each containing three items, arranged in four layers from apex to base.

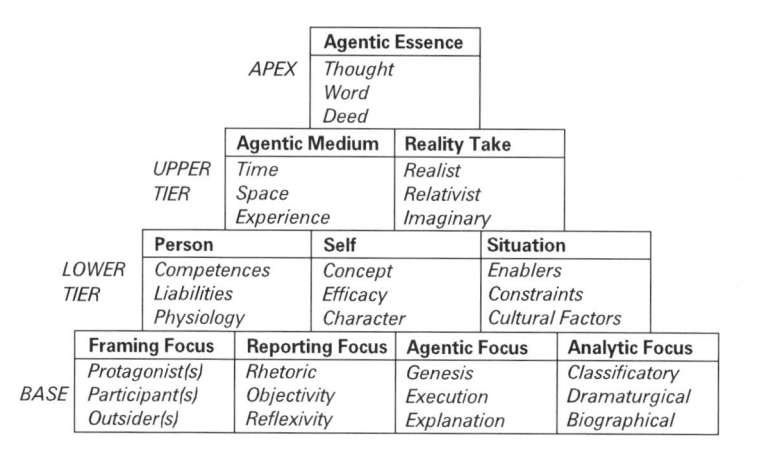

		Agentic Essence		
	APEX	Thought Word Deed		
		Agentic Medium	**Reality Take**	
	UPPER TIER	Time Space Experience	Realist Relativist Imaginary	
	Person	**Self**	**Situation**	
LOWER TIER	Competences Liabilities Physiology	Concept Efficacy Character	Enablers Constraints Cultural Factors	
Framing Focus	**Reporting Focus**	**Agentic Focus**	**Analytic Focus**
BASE	Protagonist(s) Participant(s) Outsider(s)	Rhetoric Objectivity Reflexivity	Genesis Execution Explanation	Classificatory Dramaturgical Biographical

Figure 10.1 Pyramidic framework for agentic analysis

Preliminary orientation

It is important to bear in mind that, despite my leanings towards fusion psychology, I come to the psychology of action with a post-positivist stance, broadly in tune with critical social psychology. Given this, it would be wrong to expect my framework to do the job of a predictive model from which hypotheses might be derived and experimentally tested. A better orientation to the framework is provided by the recipe: take such and such ingredients into your research project and you will end up with this sort of report or analysis.

I will not pretend that the task of choosing which items to include in the PF (or which to leave out) was easy, and the choice of appropriate terms with which to describe the concepts was, in some cases, fraught with difficulty (I would not go to the gallows on the distinction between agentic essence and agentic medium, for example). A framework such as this is not given up or discovered from an external reality, it is a construction developed in order to impose some structure on the world as perceived and, perhaps more importantly for the purposes of this book, as filtered through the research writings and analyses of academic psychologists.

The pyramidic framework as hermeneutic circle

I shall start my description at the apex of the pyramid, and from there work down through the upper and lower tiers to the base. Gauld and Shotter (1977) emphasise the fact that many concepts relating to action are tied together in a hermeneutic circle. They mean by this that it is often impossible to define or describe one term without reference to others within the circle (see also my discussion of key concepts in the psychology and philosophy of action in Chapter 2). I think that this applies to my PF. Although I shall start by talking about the items in the *agentic essence* box, I shall have to refer frequently to items which reside in other boxes lower down the pyramid in order to do this.

Comment on the levels

The PF is arranged in four tiers or levels and although the relation between them is a trifle fuzzy from a conceptual and functional point of view, there is some degree of coherence within each level. The apex deals with the **agentic essence** of action which manifests itself in *thought, word* or *deed*. The upper tier consists in the **agentic medium** in which the action occurs. This may be regarded as the open canvass or backdrop upon which the action unfolds. Because researchers' attitudes to this are so divided, I have included the **reality take** box which contains items relating directly to the split between *relativist* and *realist*. In the lower tier I have placed some of the major psychological categories of interest relating to the agent acting in his or her life space. The base of the PF deals mainly with the research orientation to the psychology of action. I shall provide further comment on these points as I move through my detailed description of the framework, level by level.

Apex

I have designated the **agentic essence** as *thought, word,* or *deed*. In the context of the debate about action and behaviour, which I outlined in Chapter 1, I align myself with the language of agency, as opposed to that of behaviourism. There are active connotations in the term 'deed' which are not present in the learning theorist's notion of 'response'. In terms of the 1970s new paradigm, deed maps to action, and word, whether written or spoken, covers accounts of action and sometimes features within it (again, see Chapter 1). The concept of plan (see Chapters 2 and 4), which also features in the ethogenic approach, would more typically reside in thought, as would the mental calculus involved in the TRA/TPB (see Chapter 2).

Plan may also be regarded as a concept that integrates thought, word and deed, and, as such, may exist in written or diagrammatic form. An Abelsonian plans molecule may thus be construed as making a contribution to the semiology of action, if only within a small segment of academia (see Chapters 2 and 4). More generally, writing is an act whose product may persist through time as a testimony to the interface of thought and word (this also applies to the spoken word when captured in any of the diverse techniques of audiovisual recording). My interpretation of the TRA/TPB (see Chapter 2) suggests that someone who bungles the interface between thought, word and deed risks insanity, unless linguistic incompetence can be convincingly demonstrated. Incidentally, psychoanalysts can be seen as specialists at generating weird mapping between these three domains (see Chapter 5).

I feel that action is not synonymous with deed (by refraining from the deed of drinking the glass of whisky, I carry out my intention to go on the wagon). Sometimes, it would appear that action is minimally dependent on thought. The importance of thought is downplayed both in ritual (see my discussion of Rothenbuhler, 1998, in the context of hypnosis, Chapter 8) and in behaviourism (see Chapter 1), for example. In the main, however, action permeates and is permeated by the triad of thought, word and deed.

I have already indicated that in the 1970s the emphasis tended to be placed on the deed by the ethogenic social psychologists. By the 1980s and 90s the focus of interest had moved to the *word*. In the discursive action model (DAM), deeds are manifest as speech acts (see Chapter 3). Although I think that the discursive psychologists try to guess the thoughts of agents (when explicating how what was said belies the management of a particular impression given off for strategic reasons of stake or interest, for example), thoughts can form no part of a discursive transcript, unless they are spoken. This is because the transcript is confined only to words (although it can handle some of the paralinguistic features of talk, such as pause length or change in pitch). I find it faintly ironic that, while the discursive psychologists turned their backs on *dramaturgical* analysis, the play script could be said to be the underlying model for their chosen form of data representation. A good transcript should enable actors to generate a replica of the original social episode (of course, it will not be an exact replica). A fusion between ethogenic and discursive data representation might be achieved were the comic strip to be taken as the underlying model. Here, the discursive transcript would appear in 'speech bubbles', the drawings would come from ethogenic observation (video stills?) and the thoughts of the *protagonists*, possibly revealed in collected accounts, would appear in 'think bubbles'. The ethogenic researcher's field notes would appear as prose commentary beneath the action frame. If data were to be represented in a web page medium, accounts (thoughts) and field notes could be accessed via clickable links (a trivially easy thing to sort out in HTML script).

Although I started by discussing the relative emphasis placed upon thought and word in ethogenic and discursive psychology, I seem to have ended by bringing up matters relating to the **reporting focus** (especially the *rhetorical* style in which data is recorded and reported), featured at the base of the PF. I now return to the top of the PF, to consider the next row down from the apex.

Upper tier

The upper tier provides the backdrop against which action takes place. The **agentic medium** can be related to Harré's (1983) spatio-temporal matrix for personal being and thus to Kant's (1781/1993) treatment of the transcendental aesthetic in the *Critique of Pure Reason* (see Chapter 3). The agent's experience in *time* and *space* may also be thought of in terms of Lewin's concept of the life space (see Chapter 4). The **reality take** box includes items that have featured strongly in this book. The debate on *realist* versus *relativist* perspectives on the agentic medium continues to rage (see Chapter 3). I have included the *imaginary* item, since I particularly liked Lewin's idea that representations of the life space might be stacked like pancakes moving from an objective *reality*, through degrees of irreality, into the realm of fantasy (see Chapter 4). Yet another way to construe psychoanalytic activity is to see it as teasing out deviously twisted threads between disparate levels of Lewinian pancakes arrayed across the dimension of irreality (see Chapter 5 for an example of Freudian association). Jung, with sense of balance and allegiance to matters of common-sense, merely pours on the maple syrup.

Some aspects of the psychology of action will be closely related to one particular item in the PF, while others will be more diffusely spread. In the upper tier, for example, the topic of time management (see Chapter 6) is closely tagged to the question of *time*, while the topic of defensible space (see discussion in previous section in this chapter) is, obviously, concerned with *space*.

Lower tier

The three categories in the lower tier are well represented in conventional approaches within psychology. For example, behaviour has long been seen as a function of **person** and **situation** (see my discussion of Blass, 1991, in Chapter 8). However, placing person and situation in a triadic relation with **self**, I pave the way for a more clearly post-positivist arrangement. For example, Harré (1983) uses the opposition of person and self to provide an alternative to the Cartesian dualism of mind/body. *Competences* and *liabilities*, in the person box, are closely bound to the concept of person as agent (as set out in Harré and Secord, 1972). Competences (for example knowledge of algebra) and liabilities (for example poor numeracy skills) are properties of the person which mirror, in terms of agency, the *enablers* (for example having enough money to do something) and *constraints* (for example being locked up in prison) in the external situation or environment. Enablers and constraints feature strongly in the representation of plans (see my discussion of Abelson in Chapters 2 and 4). Where actions go wrong there is plenty of scope for misattribution and confusion between personal liabilities and situational constraints. In counselling situations this may underpin feelings of helplessness or low self-efficacy (see Chapter 7); in accident research it may relate to issues of blame and negligence (see Chapter 5).

I have included two big items in this tier, one each in the person and situation boxes. These are *physiology* and *cultural factors*. These form the major points of departure to academic disciplines beyond psychology and highlight the limitations or boundaries of psychology. Within the person, I take physiology to represent the person as a physical object. Physiology leads out into science and the causal explanations of our behaviour and movements which only occasionally jump into the limelight in the explanation of action (see my discussion of Peters and Watson in Chapter 1). It is here that mainstream psychologists with reductionist tendencies wish to ground the whole of psychology. From the critical realist standpoint (see Chapter 3), things are not wholly symmetrical in my PF. The intransitive facets of personal being are covered by the physiology item whereas the intransitive facts of the physical environment would be covered by the enablers and constraints in the situation box.

Given that the meaning of action is established by convention, cultural factors are hugely important. However, it is here that psychology blends towards sociology (especially in the way that social institutions exist outside individual action and yet are reproduced in and by such action) and cultural studies (where the embodiment of particular categories of person, such as men or women, is traced as a manifestation of a particular culture, as are the categories themselves). I intend the cultural factors item to be interpreted very broadly as a grounding into the social sciences. In this way the economic reality of being born in a third world country or the social reality of being born into a particular ethnic group may be acknowledged as placing a particular lens on to the agentic medium and personal being.

The self box is the only one to be completely surrounded by others in my PF. This is not entirely inappropriate since it generates womb-like, tomb-like images of the homunculus in the sarcophagus buried deep in the inner psyche, to say nothing of the inner chamber of my pyramid!

Harré (1983) did a good job in arguing against this sort of nonsense; he proposed that the self was nothing but a *concept* and therefore there were no empirical discoveries to be made through introspective diggings beneath the surface, as it were. In this regard, both meditative and psychoanalytic excavations to lay bare or discover the 'true' self would be futile, in my view, but anyone signing up to the archaeology of knowledge may have a different take on this.

I have not included the self in my PF merely as a contrast to the *person*. The *efficacy* item is intimately bound up with the power of the agent and, transparadigmatically, provides a link to Bandura's SET (see Chapters 2 and 4). On the other hand, the *character* item leads attention away from agentic power to dramaturgical considerations. Character also provides links to the sociological and ethogenic concept of role (see Chapter 1). In terms of mainstream personality theory, the notion of trait may translate sometimes to the competences item in the person box (for example she is highly intelligent) and sometimes to the character item in the self box (for example he's pretty devious). I move on, now, to consider the base of my PF.

Base

I have included four boxes at the base of my PF, all of which lend a particular focus to research into the psychology of action. The first I call the **framing focus** and this is concerned with the point of view from which the action is considered.

The focus of attention may often be on the principal *protagonist* of the action episode. Only in some schools of psychology is this taken to extremes (phenomenological psychology or, perhaps, introspectionism, for example). Sometimes it is the participant's perspective which provides the primary data for an investigation, as would be the case for an ethogenic social psychologist using participant observation as his or her chosen method (I would not describe this as a method open to a discursive psychologist, although discursive psychologists may sometimes participate in the discussions they record). In Chapter 4, when discussing causal attribution, I suggested that attribution theory took the observer's perspective while locus of control was concerned with the protagonist's view. In mainstream psychology, observers are more likely to adopt the *outsider's* perspective as metaphorical flies on walls. Discursive psychology shares with experimental psychology the fact that there is no reason, in principle, why the researcher should be implicated in the target episode under consideration in any way, shape or form. Other approaches require a presence from the researcher either in the primary action episode or at secondary research episodes (such as the collection of accounts). New paradigm humanistic psychology is an approach requiring maximum collaboration between the researcher and the participants, with the researcher minimising his or her role as principal protagonist in the research episode.

I have already discussed some aspects of the **reporting focus**, when considering the use of rhetoric in critical psychology texts, in Chapter 3. One of the definitive guides on reporting within the doctrine of the objective experiment is the *Publication Manual of the American Psychological Association* (American Psychological Association, 1994). I suggested, in Chapter 3, that this style lends rhetorical force to a sense of authority and *objectivity* in the author, and this is what makes the post-modernists wary. The reason for this is that the objectivity in the discursive style supports the fiction that psychological science, monolithically, has a claim on the truth. I also provided illustrations as to how some critical psychologists introduced an element of *reflexive* deconstruction into their own texts in order to guard against the possibility that they be confused with the mainstream in this regard.

With regard to the **agentic focus**, I have singled out three facets of action (*genesis*, *execution* and *explanation*) which may be taken as the main thrust of an investigation, individually or in combination. The TRA/TPB might be said to have placed the emphasis on the *genesis* of action, with its primary concern being the formulation of intentions (see Chapter 2). Much of the work on plans is tied more closely to the execution of action (see my discussion of Miller *et al.*, 1960, in Chapter 4). Problems in the execution of action are very much to the fore in human error research (see Chapter 5). The explanation of action has been the prime concern for attribution theory, in mainstream psychology, and for accounting methodology, in ethogenic new paradigm social psychology (see Chapter 1).

Although there is a relationship between the items in the agentic focus box and the time element in the agentic medium box, it is not straightforward. As far as an investigation goes, research or otherwise, the deed may be in the past. However, the investigator, having put him or herself back in time, now looks to the future from the protagonist's point of view as it was then, prior to the execution of the deed. The investigator may then attempt to discover the thought which matches, makes sense of, and defines the deed, thus furnishing an *explanation*.

In one sense the *genesis* of action has to occur at the start and, once the deed has been *executed*, the moment of genesis will appear in the relative past. However, if the action is generated so that particular goals may be achieved, it could be said that the genesis involved a future orientation. Explanation may point to future or past, depending on whether it is teleological or not. It is for these reasons that time perspective does not map straightforwardly on to the three facets of action in the agentic focus box. Finally, I come to the *analytic focus*.

Classification refers to the way episodes may be named and, as in other classification schemes, such naming will often involve the placing of one category in an hierarchical relationship to others. For example, travelling may involve travelling on a bus, on a car or on a plane; celebrating may involve having a party, going for a meal or going for a drink). These are the types of thing that might be captured by the tail of one of Tolman's lassos (Chapter 4). Another way to classify episodes is to break them down into the sub-episodes that form them. Studying for a degree may involve taking a series of modules, sometimes in sequence, the modules may be broken down into attending lectures, writing papers, taking exams and so forth.

There is also a close relation between classification and *script*. One interpretation of a script is to see it as a way of imposing a descriptive classification of the action into a series of episodes organised thematically or temporally into the conventional hierarchy of acts and scenes. I have included dramaturgical as an item within the analytic focus box mainly to provide a point of contact with the analysis advocated by Goffman (1959) and incorporated in Harré and Secord's (1972) ethogenic approach. Of course, the concept of script may be found in other areas of psychology. For example, Schank and Abelson (1977) used it in their approach to natural language programming (see Chapter 4) and what is nice about that is that they rely heavily on the concepts of plan and role to provide structure for sequences of action (see, also, my discussion of these points in relation to human error research in Chapter 5).

The use of scripts in transactional analysis bears some relation to the notion of *biography* (or autobiography, depending on point of view). I have made some reference to the way scripts feature in transactional analysis (see Chapters 7 and 9) and these may be seen as a liturgical prescription for an individual's passage through a Lewinian life space (see Chapter 4). A biographical focus was at the heart of De Waele and Harré's (1979) research into the life histories of Belgian murderers. Narratological approaches may also be adapted for use in biographical research projects (see Chapter 5 for a somewhat broader consideration of narratology).

This concludes my description of the PF. It now remains for me to draw matters to a close.

Concluding remarks

I started this book by describing the rift that opened up within psychology, over the course of the twentieth century, attributable to the insistence that the discipline be defined as the science of behaviour. The opposition of the concept of behaviour against that of action brought with it a clash of methods: in a nutshell, the doctrine of the objective experiment versus the hermeneutic endeavour. There can be no doubt as to who won this battle in academia. The power of the mainstream psychological establishment is there for all to see: in the yards of positivist journals and books in the university library stacks; in the design of psychology departments, with their experimental cubicles, their wet physiology labs, and their animal facilities; and in the abundance of support given to positivist research and researchers. I present no evidence for this, I merely rant.

There has always been an opposition to behaviourism and positivist experimental psychology (psychoanalysis, Gestalt psychology, humanistic psychology, to name but three of the earlier movements). My background is closer to the opposition provided by the critical social psychology which emerged mainly in the 1970s and developed over the subsequent decades. The situation at the millennium is that there is a broader coalition now in opposition to the doctrine of the objective experiment and that this would include the critical psychology which has close ties to feminist and cultural theory, for example. At the risk of oversimplifying, I see psychology spread between two extremes. At one extreme lies physiological psychology and neuroscience and it seems to me a moot point as to whether researchers working at the physiological boundaries in this domain should be thought of as physiologists or psychologists. At the other extreme lies critical psychology. I have already said that critical psychology is an umbrella term catching a number of disparate approaches united only by their opposition to mainstream experimental psychology. However, I would single out researchers operating within the domain of cultural studies as occupying the furthest oppositional reaches from those of the physiological psychologists. And once again, I think it may be somewhat arbitrary as to whether such researchers be described as psychologists or cultural theorists.

My position is that while I am happy to see a contribution to psychology by physiologists or by academics working within cultural studies, I would not want to see psychology pulled exclusively in either direction. I think that over the course of the twentieth century, the hegemony of mainstream psychology resulted in a massive swing of the pendulum into the objective, experimental domain. I believe that the groundswell or backlash to this is now beginning to be felt with an ever stronger and growing presence of critical psychology. Again, oversimplifying, there are three possible outcomes as to how things may turn out. First, the mainstream may fail to yield (experimentalists maintain tight control over academic journals, the undergraduate curriculum, research funds and postgraduate research training). In this case, my prediction would be that those working within critical psychology will leave the discipline (to work in cultural or media studies, for example). It is easy to see how this might happen. For example, although critical social psychology emerged as a vibrant force in UK psychology in the 1970s, I was unable to trace a single article in the *British Journal of Social Psychology* that could be vaguely described as falling within the new ethogenic or discursive paradigms until well into the 1990s (this represents roughly 20 barren years). However, during that time at least two new journals were established to cater for such publications (the *Journal for the Theory of Social Behaviour* and *Discourse and Society*). In this way, critical psychology paved the way for its own independent language games, open to the readers of such journals but separate from that of the mainstream. To summarise the first outcome, therefore, the status quo could be maintained with critical psychology breaking off as, for all intents and purposes, a separate discipline. This will become a viable alternative as the critical mass of critical psychologists grows. At some point, the relevance of a basically positivist undergraduate degree in psychology will be called into question, in this scenario, as an appropriate foundation for research in critical psychology. It is also likely that teachers and academics without a formal undergraduate training in (positivist) psychology may begin to be numbered more strongly among critical psychologists.

The second possibility involves an outcome that I personally doubt will come about. This is that there will be a massive swing of the pendulum and all mainstream experimental work in psychology, as we currently know it, will atrophy. In this scenario, the concern will be that psychology will be assimilated into sociology, cultural studies, or some such discipline as yet to be invented. I would be very surprised to see things turn out this way.

The third possibility, and the one which I favour, is that the discipline as a whole becomes more relaxed about the existence of disparate approaches within its boundaries. I think that an agentic psychology will provide a vehicle for a modicum of methodological and theoretical fusion. I believe that eclecticism in the centre will not necessarily ensure that those working dedicatedly at the extremes (the physiologist, or the cultural theorist, for example) will come closer to one another, but it may ensure that tensions from the extremes do not rend the discipline of psychology asunder. Another way of expressing this is to say that the future mainstream in psychology should embrace more strongly an eclecticism; at present, the mainstream is too closely identified with the doctrine of the objective experiment.

In this book, I have tried to show how this might be done through the development of a psychology of action. Where possible, I have taken material from the mainstream in order to explore the potential for integration with post-positivist or critical psychological ideas (an example would be the way I provided an alternative reading of the TRA/TPB in Chapter 2). But the psychology of action does not *have* to take the burden of the coherence of the discipline upon its shoulders. In this chapter I offered up my pyramidic framework for agentic analysis as a heuristic tool for psychological research and I think that this could be deployed to kick-start a research investigation on any topic within the psychology of action with the researcher's interest being focused intrinsically upon the topic and not spread across the meta-disciplinary issues.

Still, I will end with a statement on the broad perspective. I started by saying that if psychology were to be defined as the study of action, then this book might simply be entitled *Psychology*. For the reasons I outlined in Chapter 1, I'm going to stay with my other title, *The Psychology of Action*. However, as a result of the arguments I have developed over the course of the book, I would now go as far as to say that psychology *ought* to be defined as the study of action. Of course, as a practical definition this lies heavy with implications for curriculum design, research funding and professional practice. As a conceptual definition it brims with contentious philosophical and scientific resonance. But as I said at the beginning, this is a large part of what makes psychology such a fascinating academic discipline.

Appendix

Formal statement of the theories of reasoned action and planned behaviour

Theory of reasoned action

The theoretical equation is as follows:

$$B \sim I = (A_B)w_1 + (SN)w_2$$

where

B = Behaviour in question
I = Intention to perform behaviour in question
A_B = Attitude towards performing behaviour in question
SN = Subjective norm regarding the performance of behaviour B

w_1 and w_2 are empirically determined weights

The attitude component A_B may be further defined as follows:

$$A_B = \sum_{i=1}^{N} b_i e_i$$

where

b = the belief that performing behaviour B leads to a particular consequence or outcome (i)
e = the person's evaluation of the outcome (i)
N = the number of beliefs concerning outcome(s) of behaviour B
i = a particular consequence or outcome

The subjective norm component SN may be further defined as follows:

$$SN = \sum_{j=1}^{N} nb_j mc_j$$

where

nb = the person's normative belief that a particular reference person or group (j) thinks that she or he should or should not perform behaviour B
mc = the person's motivation to conform or comply with referent (j)
N = the number of normative beliefs relevant to behaviour B
j = a particular normative belief

Theory of planned behaviour

The formal statement of the theory of planned behaviour is further presented below as a linear regression function of behavioural intentions, and perceived behavioural control (PBC).

$$B = w_1 I + w_2 PBC$$

where

B = Behaviour in question
I = Intention to perform behaviour in question
PBC = Perceived behavioural control
w_1 and w_2 are empirically determined weights

The perceived behavioural control component PBC may be further defined as follows:

$$PBC = \sum_{j=1}^{N} c_j p_j$$

where

c = the perceived frequency or likelihood of occurrence of factor (j)
p = the perceived facilitating or inhibiting power of the factor (j)
N = the number of control factors
j = a particular control factor

Based on Fishbein & Ajzen (1975), Ajzen & Fishbein (1980), and Conner and Sparks (1996).

References

Abelson, R.P. (1973) The structure of belief systems. In Shank, R.C. and Colby, K.M. (eds) *Computer Models of Thought and Language*. San Francisco: Freeman.

Abelson, R.P. (1975) Concepts for representing mundane reality in plans. In Borrow, D.G. and Collins, A. (eds) *Representation and Understanding: Studies in Cognitive Science*. London: Academic Press.

Ajzen, I. (1988) *Attitudes, Personality, and Behavior*. Milton Keynes: Open University Press.

Ajzen, I. (1991) The theory of planned behavior. *Organisational Behavior and Human Decision Processes*, 50: 1–33.

Ajzen, I. and Fishbein, M. (1980) *Understanding Attitudes and Predicting Social Behavior*. Englewood Cliffs, NJ: Prentice Hall.

American Psychiatric Association (1994) *Diagnostic and Statistical Manual of Mental Disorders: DSM-IV*, 4th edn. Washington, DC: APA.

American Psychological Association (1994) 4th edn. *Publication Manual of the American Psychological Association*. Washington, DC: American Psychological Association.

Anscombe, G.E.M. (1963) *Intention*, 2nd edn. Oxford: Blackwell.

Antaki, C. (ed.) (1988) *Analysing Everyday Explanation: A Casebook of Methods*. London: Sage.

Antaki, C. (1994) *Explaining and Arguing: The Social Organisation of Accounts*. London: Sage.

Aristotle (1926) *The Art of Rhetoric*. Tr. Freese, J.H. Cambridge, MA: Harvard University Press.

Armistead, N. (1974) *Reconstructing Social Psychology*. Harmondsworth: Penguin.

Atkinson, J.M. and Drew, P. (1979) *Order in Court: The Organisation of Verbal Interaction in Judicial Settings*. London: Macmillan.

Austin, J.L. (1962) *How to do Things with Words*. Oxford: Oxford University Press.

Austin, J.T. and Vancouver, J.B. (1996) Goal constructs in psychology: structure, process, and content. *Psychological Bulletin*, 120(3): 338–75.

Bandura, A. (1977) Self-efficacy: towards a unifying theory of behavioral change. *Psychological Review*, 84: 191–215.

Bandura, A. (1986) *Social Foundations of Thought and Action: A Social Cognitive Theory*. Englewood Cliffs, NJ: Prentice Hall.

Bandura, A. (1997) *Self-efficacy: The Exercise of Control*. New York: WH Freeman.

REFERENCES

Bandura, A. and Walters, R.H. (1963) *Social Learning and Personality Development*. London: Holt, Rinehart & Winston.

Bandura, A., Ross, D. and Ross, S.A. (1961) Transmission of aggression through imitation of aggressive models. *Journal of Abnormal and Social Psychology*. **63**(3): 575–82.

Bannister, D. and Fransella, F. (1971) *Inquiring Man: The Theory of Personal Constructs*. Harmondsworth: Penguin.

Barber, T.X. and Wilson, S.C. (1978) The Barber Suggestibility Scale and the Creative Imagination Scale: experimental and clinical applications. *American Journal of Clinical Hypnosis*, **21**: 84–108.

Barthes, R. (1972) *Mythologies*. London: Granada.

Baumeister, R.F. (1990) Suicide as escape from self. *Psychological Review*, **97**: 90–113.

Baumeister, R.F. (1997) The enigmatic appeal of sexual masochism: why people desire pain, bondage, and humiliation in sex. *Journal of Social and Clinical Psychology*, **16**: 133–50.

Baumeister, R.F., Heatherton, T.F. and Tice, D.M. (1994) *Losing Control: How and Why People Fail at Self-regulation*. London: Academic Press.

Bentler, P.M., and Speckart, G. (1979) Models of attitude-behavior relations. *Psychological Review*, **86**(5): 452–64.

Berger, P.L. and Luckman, T. (1966) *The Social Construction of Reality*. Harmondsworth: Penguin.

Berne, E. (1964) *Games People Play: The Psychology of Human Relationships*. Harmondsworth: Penguin.

Berne, E. (1972) *What Do You Say After You Say Hello?* London: Corgi.

Bhaskar, R. (1989) *Reclaiming Reality: A Critical Introduction to Contemporary Philosophy*. London: Verso.

Billig, M. (1997) The dialogic unconscious: psychoanalysis, discursive psychology and the nature of repression. *British Journal of Social Psychology*, **36**: 139–59.

Blass, T. (1991) Understanding behavior in the Milgram obedience experiment: the role of personality, situations, and their interactions. *Journal of Personality and Social Psychology*, **60**: 398–413.

Blue, C.L. (1995) The predictive capacity of the theory of reasoned action and the theory of planned behavior in exercise research: an integrated literature review. *Research in Nursing and Health*, **18**: 105–21.

Boring, E.G. (1963) *History, Psychology, and Science: Selected Papers*. New York: Wiley.

Brendl, C.M. and Higgins, E.T. (1996) Principles of judging valence: what makes events positive or negative? *Advances in Experimental Social Psychology*, **28**: 95–160.

Buchanan, T. and Smith, J.L. (in press) Research on the Internet: Validation of a World-Wide Web Mediated Personality Scale. Behavior Research Methods, Instruments & Computers.

Budd, M. (1989) *Wittgenstein's Philosophy of Psychology*. London: Routledge.

Buehler, R., Griffin, D., and Ross, M. (1994) Exploring the 'planning falacy': Why people underestimate their task completion times. *Journal of Personality and Social Psychology*, **67**(3): 366–81.

Button, G. and Casey, N. (1984) Generating topic: the use of topic initial elicitors. In Atkinson, J.M. and Heritage, J. (eds) *Structures of Social Action: Studies in Conversation Analysis*. Cambridge: Cambridge University Press.

Calhoun, J.B. (1962) A behavioral sink. In Bliss, E.L. (ed.) *Roots of Behavior*. New York: Harper & Brothers.

Carnegie, D. (1936/1998) *How to Win Friends and Influence People*. London: Vermilion.

Chaiken, S. and Stangor, C. (1987) Attitudes and attitude change. *Annual Review of Psychology*, **38**: 575–630.

Chomsky, N. (1996) *The Minimalist Program*. Cambridge, MA: MIT Press.

Cialdini, R.B., Petty, R.E. and Cacioppo, J.T. (1981) Attitude and attitude change. *Annual Review of Psychology*, **32**: 357–404.

Cockroft, R. and Cockroft, S.M. (1992) *Persuading People: An Introduction to Rhetoric*. London: Macmillan.

Colman, A.M. (1987) *Facts, Fallacies and Frauds in Psychology*. London: Hutchinson.

Conley, J.M. and O'Barr, W.M. (1990) Rules versus relationships in small claims disputes. In Grimshaw, A.D. (ed.) *Conflict Talk*. Cambridge: Cambridge University Press.

Conner, M. and Sparks, P. (1996) The theory of planned behaviour and health behaviours. In Conner, M. and Norman, P. (eds) *Predicting Health Behaviour: Research and Practice with Social Cognition Models*. Buckingham: Open University Press.

Cooper, J. and Croyle, R.T. (1984) Attitudes and attitude change. *Annual Review of Psychology*, **35**: 395–426.

De Waele, J.P. and Harré, R. (1979) Autobiography as a psychological method. In Ginsberg, G.P (ed.) *Emerging Strategies in Social Psychological Research*. Chichester: Wiley.

Dennett, D.C. (1996) *Kinds of Minds*. London: Phoenix.

Denzin, N.K. (1995) Symbolic interactionism. In Smith, J.A., Harré, R. and Van Langenhove, L. (eds) *Rethinking Psychology*. London: Sage.

DiGiuseppe, R. (1991) Comprehensive cognitive disputing in rational-emotive therapy. In Bernard, M. (ed.) *Using Rational-emotive Therapy Effectively*. New York: Plenum.

Drew, P. (1995) Conversation analysis. In Smith, J.A., Harré, R. and Van Langenhove, L. (eds) *Rethinking Methods in Psychology*. London: Sage.

Dryden, W. and Yankura, J. (1995) *Developing Rational Emotive Behavioural Counselling*. London: Sage.

Eagly, A.H. and Chaiken, S. (1993) *The Psychology of Attitudes*. New York: Harcourt Brace, Jovanovich.

Eagly, A.H. and Himmelfarb, S. (1978) Attitudes and opinions. *Annual Review of Psychology*, **29**: 517–54.

Edwards, D. and Potter, J. (1992) *Discursive Psychology*. London: Sage.

Edwards, D., Ashmore, M. and Potter, J. (1995) Death and furniture: the rhetoric, politics and theology of bottom line arguments against relativism. *History of the Human Sciences*, **8**: 25–49.

Etzioni, A. (ed.) (1998) *The Essential Communitarian Reader*. Oxford: Rowman & Littlefield.

Ferrari, J.R. (1991) Compulsive procrastination: some self-reported personality characteristics. *Psychological Reports*, **68**: 455–8.

Ferrari, J.R., Johnson, J.L., and McCown, W.G. (1995) *Procrastination and Task Avoidance: Theory, Research and Treatment*. London: Plenum.

Festinger, L. (1957) *A Theory of Cognitive Dissonance*. Stanford: Stanford University Press.

Fishbein, M. and Ajzen, I. (1975) *Belief, Attitude, Intention and Behavior*. Reading, MA: Addison-Wesley.

Fontana, D. (1993) *Managing Time: Personal and Professional Development*. Leicester: BPS Books (The British Psychological Society).

Ford, M.E. (1992) *Motivating Humans: Goals, Emotions, and Personal Agency Beliefs*. London: Sage.

Freud, S. (1901/1975) *The Psychopathology of Everyday Life*. Harmondsworth: Penguin.

Frye, N. (1957) *Anatomy of Criticism*. Princeton, NJ: Princeton University Press.

Fuller, S. (1994) Making agency count: a brief foray into the foundations of social theory. *American Behavioral Scientist*, **37**(6): 741–53.

Gauld, A. and Shotter, J. (1977) *Human Action and its Psychological Investigation*. London: Routledge & Kegan Paul.

Gergen, K.J. (1998) Constructionism and realism: how are we to go on? In Parker, I. (ed.) *Social Constructionism, Discourse and Realism*. London: Sage.

Giddens, A. (1979) *Central Problems in Social Theory: Action, Structure and Contradiction in Social Analysis*. London: Macmillan.

Giddens, A. (1984) *The Constitution of Society: Outline of the Theory of Structuration*. Cambridge: Polity Press.

Giddens, A. (1998) *The Third Way: The Renewal of Social Democracy*. Cambridge: Polity Press.

Gilbert, D.G., Krull, D.S., and Pelham, B.W. (1988) Of thoughts unspoken: social inference and the self-regulation of behavior. *Journal of Personality and Social Psychology*, **55**: 685–94.

Godin, G. and Kok, G. (1996) The theory of planned behavior: a review of its applications to health-related behaviors. *American Journal of Health Promotion*, **11**: 87–98.

Goffman, E (1959) *The Presentation of Self in Everyday Life*. New York: Allen Lane.

Gosling, J. (1990) *Weakness of the Will*. London: Routledge.

Grayling, A.C. (1996) *Wittgenstein*. Oxford: Oxford University Press.

Harré, R. (1971) Joynson's dilemma. *Bulletin of the British Psychological Society*. **24**: 115–19.

Harré, R. (1979) *Social Being: A Theory for Social Psychology*. Oxford: Blackwell.

Harré, R. (1983) *Personal Being: A Theory for Individual Psychology*. Oxford: Blackwell.

Harré, R. and Gillett, G. (1994) *The Discursive Mind*. London: Sage.

Harré, R. and Secord, P.F. (1972) *The Explanation of Social Behaviour*. Oxford: Blackwell.

Hausenblas, H.A., Carron, A.V. and Mack, D.E. (1997) Application of the theories of reasoned action and planned behavior to exercise behavior: a meta-analysis. *Journal of Sport & Exercise Psychology*, **19**: 36–51.

Hilgard, E.R. (1986) *Divided Consciousness: Multiple Controls in Human Thought and Action*. New York: Wiley.

Howell, E.F. (1996) Dissociation in masochism and psychopathic sadism. *Contemporary Psychoanalysis*, **32**: 427–53.

Hunt, S.M. (1979) Hypnosis as obedience behaviour. *British Journal of Social and Clinical Psychology*, **18**: 21–7.

James, W. (1892/1910) *Textbook of Psychology*. London: Macmillan.

Jones, E.E. and Davis, K.E. (1965) A theory of correspondent inferences: from acts to dispositions. In Berkowitz, L. (ed.) *Advances in Experimental Social Psychology*, 2. New York: Academic Press.

Joynson, R.B. (1970) The breakdown of modern psychology. *Bulletin of the British Psychological Society*, **23**: 261–9.

Kant, I. (1781/1993) ed. Politis, V., trans. Meiklejohn. *Critique of Pure Reason*. London: Dent.

Karniol, R. and Ross, M. (1996) The motivational impact of temporal focus: thinking about the future and the past. *Annual Review of Psychology*, **47**: 593–620.

Karoly, P. (1993) Mechanisms of self-regulation: a systems view. *Annual Review of Psychology*, **44**: 23–52.

Kazdin, A.E. (1977) *The Token Economy: A Review and Evaluation*. New York: Plenum Press.

Kazdin, A.E. (1981) The token economy. In Davey, G. (ed.) *Applications of Conditioning Theory*. London: Methuen.

Kelly, G.A. (1955) *The Psychology of Personal Constructs*, vols 1 and 2. New York: Norton.

Kelley, H.H. (1967) Attribution theory in social psychology. In Vine, D.L. (ed.) *Nebraska Symposium on Motivation*. Lincoln: University of Nebraska Press.

Kirsch, I. and Lynn, S.J. (1998) Dissociation theories of hypnosis. *Psychological Bulletin*, **123**: 100–15.

Kohlberg, L. (1969) Stage and sequence: the cognitive-developmental approach to socialization. In Goslin, D.A. (ed.) *Handbook of Socialization Theory and Research*. Chicago: Rand-McNally.

Latané, B. and Darley, J.M. (1970) *The Unresponsive Bystander: Why Doesn't he Help?* New York: Appleton-Century-Crofts.

Lay, C.H. (1986) At last, my research article on procrastination. *Journal of Research in Personality*, **20**: 474–95.

Lewin, K. (1936/1966) *Principles of Topological Psychology* trans. Heider, F. and Heider, G.M. New York: McGraw-Hill.

Locke, J. (1690/1964) *An Essay Concerning Human Understanding*. London: Fontana.

Locke, E.A. and Latham, G.P. (1990) *A Theory of Goal-setting and Task Performance*. Englewood Cliffs, NJ: Prentice Hall.

Lodge, D. (1992) *The Art of Fiction*. Harmondsworth: Penguin.

Luchins, A.S. (1942) Mechanization in problem solving – the effect of einstellung. *Psychological Monographs*, **54**: 1–95.

Marcuse, F.L. (1959) *Hypnosis: Fact and Fiction*. Harmondsworth: Penguin.
Marsh, P., Rosser, E. and Harré, R. (1978) *The Rules of Disorder*. London: Routledge & Kegan Paul.
Mele, A.R. (1992) Recent work on intentional action. *American Philosophical Quarterly*, 29(3): 199–217.
Merttens, R. (1998) What is to be done? (with apologies to Lenin!) In Parker, I. (ed.) *Social Constructionism, Discourse and Realism*. London: Sage.
Milgram, S. (1974) *Obedience to Authority: An Experimental View*. New York: HarperCollins.
Miller, G.A., Gallanter, E. and Pribram, K.H. (1960) *Plans and the Structure of Behaviour*. London: Holt, Rinehart & Winston.
Mixon, D. (1979) Understanding shocking and puzzling conduct. In Ginsburg, G.P. (ed.) *Emerging Strategies in Social Psychological Research*. Chichester: John Wiley.
Morrison, D.M., Simpson, E.E., Gillmore, M.R., Wells, E.A. and Hoppe, M.J. (1996) Children's decisions about substance use: an application and extension of the theory of reasoned action. *Journal of Applied Social Psychology*, 26: 1658–79.
Murray, K.D. (1995) Narratology. In Smith, J.A., Harré, R. and Van Langenhove, L. (eds) *Rethinking Psychology*. London: Sage.
Nemeroff, C.J. and Karoly, P. (1991) Operant methods. In Kanfer, F.H. and Goldstein, A.P. (eds) *Helping People Change: A Textbook of Methods*, 4th edn. New York: Pergamon Press.
Newman, O. (1972) *Defensible Space: People and Design in The Violent City*. London: Architectural Press.
Norris, C. (1996) *Reclaiming Truth: Contribution to a Critique of Cultural Relativism*. London: Lawrence & Wishart.
NUREG (1985) *Loss of Main and Auxiliary Feedwater Event at the Davis-Besse Plant on June 9, 1985*. NUREG-1154. Washington, DC: US Nuclear Regulatory Commission.
Olson, J.M. and Zanna, M.P. (1993) Attitudes and attitude change. *Annual Review of Psychology*, 44: 117–54.
Palatano, A.L. and Seifert, C.M. (1997) Opportunistic planning: being reminded of pending goals. *Cognitive Psychology*, 34: 1–36.
Parker, I. (ed.) (1998) *Social Constructionism, Discourse and Realism*. London: Sage.
Pearson, L. and Tweddle, D. (1984) The formulation and use of educational objectives. In Fontana, D. (ed.) *Behaviourism and Learning Theory in Education*. Edinburgh: Scottish Academic Press.
Peters, R.S. (1949) The nature of psychological enquiries. Unpublished doctoral dissertation. University of London.
Peters, R.S. (1960) *The Concept of Motivation*, 2nd edn. London: Routledge & Kegan Paul.
Petty, R.E. Wegner, D.T. and Fabrigar, L.R. (1997) Attitudes and attitude change. *Annual Review of Psychology*, 48: 609–47.
Phillips, A. (1998) *A Defence of Masochism*. London: Faber and Faber.
Potter, J. (1996) *Representing Reality: Discourse, Rhetoric and Social Construction*. London: Sage.

Potter, J. and Wetherell, M. (1987) *Discourse and Social Psychology: Beyond Attitudes and Behaviour*. London: Sage.
Pritchard, C. (1995) *Suicide – The Ultimate Rejection: A Psycho-Social Study*. Buckingham: Open University Press.
Pugmire, D. (1982) Motivated irrationality. *Proceedings of the Aristotelian Society*, **56**: 179–96.
Reason, J.T. (1990) *Human Error*. Cambridge: Cambridge University Press.
Reason, J. and Rowan, P. (1981) *Human Inquiry: A Sourcebook of New Paradigm Research*. New York: John Wiley.
Rorty, R (1991) *Objectivity, Relativism, and Truth*. Philosophical papers, vol. 1. Cambridge: Cambridge University Press.
Rossi, E.L. (1996) *The Symptom Path to Enlightenment*. Pacific Palisades: Palisades Gateway.
Rothenbuhler, E.W. (1998) *Ritual Communication: From Everyday Conversation to Mediated Ceremony*. London: Sage.
Rotter, J.B. (1942) Level of aspiration as a method of studying personality: I. A critical review of methodology. *Psychological Review*, **49**: 463–74.
Rotter, J.B. (1954/1973) *Social Learning and Clinical Psychology*. Englewood Cliffs, NJ: Prentice Hall.
Rotter, J.B. (1966) Generalised expectancies for internal versus external control of reinforcement. *Psychological Monographs*, **80**(1): 1–28.
Rotter, J.B. (1982) Social learning theory. In Feather, N.T. (ed.) *Expectations and Actions: Expectancy-value Models in Psychology*. Hillsdale, NJ: Lawrence Erlbaum.
Ryle, G. (1949/1963) *The Concept of Mind*. Harmondsworth: Penguin.
Sabini, J. and Silver, M. (1982) *Moralities of Everyday Life*. Oxford: Oxford University Press.
Sandler, J. and Steele, H.V. (1991) Aversion methods. In Kanfer, F.H. and Goldstein, A.P. (eds) *Helping People Change: A Textbook of Methods*, 4th edn. New York: Pergamon Press.
Sarbin, T.R. (1950) Contributions to role-taking theory: 1. Hypnotic behavior. *Psychological Review*, **57**: 255–70.
Sartre, J.-P. (1969) Trans. Barnes, H.E. *Being and Nothingness: An Essay on Phenomenological Ontology*. London: Methuen.
Saussure, F. de (1959/1966) Trans. Baskin, W. *Course in General Linguistics*. London: McGraw-Hill.
Schank, R. and Abelson, R.P. (1977) *Scripts, Plans, Goals and Understanding*. Hillsdale, NJ: Lawrence Erlbaum.
Schlenker, B.R., Weigold, M.F., and Doherty, K. (1991) Coping with accountability: self-identification and evaluative reckonings. In Snyder, C.R. and Forsyth, D.R. (eds) *Handbook of Social and Clinical Psychology: The Health Perspective*. New York: Permagon.
Scott, M.B. and Lyman, S. (1968) Accounts. *American Sociological Review*, **33**: 46–62.
Scott, M.J., Stradling, S.G. and Dryden, W. (1995) *Developing Cognitive-behavioural Counselling*. London: Sage.
Searle, J.R. (1969) *Speech Acts: An Essay in the Philosophy of Language*. Cambridge: Cambridge University Press.

Sellen, A.J. (1994) Detection of everyday errors. *Applied Psychology: An International Review.* **43**: 475–98.
Semin, G.R. and Manstead, A.S.R. (1983) *The Accountability of Conduct: A Social Psychological Analysis.* London: Academic Press.
Sheppard, B., Hartwick, J. and Warshaw, P.R. (1988) The theory of reasoned action: a meta-analysis of past research with recommendations for modifications and future research. *Journal of Consumer Research*, **15**: 325–43.
Shotter, J. (1975) *Images of Man in Psychological Research.* London: Methuen.
Shotter, J. and Gergen, K.J. (eds) (1989) *Texts of Identity.* London: Sage.
Siegel, K. (1986) Psychosocial aspects of rational suicide. *American Journal of Psychotherapy*, **40**: 405–18.
Siegel, F. (1998) The Loss of Public Space. In Etzioni, A. (ed.) *The Essential Communitarian Reader.* Oxford: Rowman & Littlefield.
Skinner, B.F. (1988) *Beyond Freedom and Dignity.* Harmondsworth: Penguin.
Smiles, S. (1859/1969) *Self-help: The Art of Achievement Illustrated by Accounts of the Lives of Great Men.* London: John Murray.
Smith, J.L. (1982) A structuralist interpretation of the Fishbeinian model of intention. *Journal for the Theory of Social Behaviour*, **12**: 29–46.
Smith, J.L. (1987) Making people offers they can't refuse: a social psychological analysis of attitude change. In Hawthorn, J. (ed.) *Propoganda, Persuasion and Polemic.* London: Edward Arnold.
Smith, J.L. (1996) Expectancy, value, and attitudinal semantics. *European Journal of Social Psychology*, **26**: 501–6.
Smith, J.L. (1999) An agentic psychology model based on the paradigmatic repositioning of the theory of planned behaviour. *Theory and Psychology*, **9**(5).
Smith, M.J. (1975) *When I Say No, I Feel Guilty.* New York: Bantam.
Smith, P.B. (1980) *Group Processes and Personal Change.* London: Harper & Row.
Snyder, M. (1987) *Public Appearances, Private Realities: The Psychology of Self-monitoring.* New York: WH Freeman.
Spears, R. (1997) Introduction. In Ibáñez, T. and Iñiguez, L. *Critical Social Psychology.* London: Sage.
Stainton Rogers, R., Stenner, P., Gleeson, K. and Stainton Rogers, W. (1995) *Social Psychology: A Critical Agenda.* Cambridge: Polity.
Stout, G.F. (1898/1938) *A Manual of Psychology*, 5th edn. London: London University Press.
Stringer, P. (1990) Prefacing social psychology: a textbook example. In Parker, I. and Shotter, J. (eds) *Deconstructing Social Psychology.* London: Routledge.
Szalai, A. (ed.) (1972) *The Use of Time: Daily Activities of Urban and Suburban Populations in Twelve Countries.* The Hague: Mouton.
Szasz, T. (1986) The case against suicide prevention. *American Psychologist*, **41**: 806–12.
Taylor, F.W. (1911/1967) *Principles of Scientific Management.* New York: Norton.

Taylor, R. (1979) Procrastination: the personality and situational correlates of procrastination behavior for achievement tasks. *Dissertation Abstracts International*, **40**: 4, 1967b.

Tesser, A. and Shaffer, D.R. (1990) Attitudes and attitude change. *Annual Review of Psychology*, **41**: 479–523.

Thomson, R. (1968) *The Pelican History of Psychology*. Harmondsworth: Penguin.

Tice, D.M. and Baumeister, R.F. (1997) Longitudinal study of procrastination, performance, stress, and health: the costs and benefits of dawdling. *Psychological Science*. **8**(6): 454–8.

Tolman, E.C. (1951) A psychological model. In Parsons, T. and Shils, E.A. (eds) *Towards a General Theory of Action*. Cambridge, MA: Harvard University Press.

Trainer, F.E. (1977) A critical analysis of Kohlberg's contributions to the study of moral thought. *Journal for the Theory of Social Behaviour*, **7**: 41–63.

Wagstaff, G. (1998) The semantics and physiology of hypnosis as an altered state: towards a definitiion of hypnosis. *Contemporary Hypnosis*, **15**: 149–65.

Walker, A.F. (1989) The problem of weakness of will. *Noûs*, **23**: 653–76.

Warren, V.L (1985) Explaining masochism. *Journal for the Theory of Social Behaviour*, **15**: 103–29.

Waugh, P. (1984) *Metafiction: The Theory and Practice of Self-Conscious Fiction*. London: Methuen.

Werth, J.L. (1996) *Rational Suicide: Implications for Mental Health Professionals*. Washington, DC: Taylor & Francis.

Wesolowski, M.D. and Zawlocki, R.J. (1982) The differential effects of procedures to eliminate an injurious self-stimulatory behavior (digito-ocular sign) in blind retarded twins. *Behavior Therapy*, **13**: 334–45.

Wetherell, M. and Potter, J. (1988) Discourse analysis and the identification of interpretative repertoires. In Antaki, C. (ed.) *Analysing Everyday Explanation: A Casebook of Methods*. London: Sage.

Wittgenstein, L. (1921/1974) *Tractatus Logico-philosophicus* Trans. Pears, D.F. and McGuinness, B.F. Atlantic Highlands, NJ: Humanities Press International.

Wittgenstein, L. (1953) *Philosophical Investigations* Trans. Anscombe, G.E.M. Oxford: Blackwell.

Woody, E.Z. and Bowers, K.S. (1994) A frontal assault on dissociated control. In Lynn, S.J. and Rhue, J.W. (eds) *Dissociation: Clinical, Theoretical and Research Perspectives*. New York: Guilford Press.

Woody, E. and Sadler, P. (1998) The rhetoric and science of 'nothing but'. *Contemporary Hypnosis*, **15**: 178–81.

Zapf, D. and Reason, J.T. (1994) Introduction: human errors and error handling. *Applied Psychology: An International Review*, **43**: 427–32.

Name Index

A
Abelson, R.P. 9, 38–9, 75, 84–5, 87, 100, 134–5, 194, 209, 216
Ajzen, I. 10, 14–15, 19–20, 30–1, 34, 66, 75
Anscombe, G.E.M. 20–1, 30
Antaki, C. 21, 89, 103
Aristotle 4, 133, 143
Armistead, N. 51, 195
Ashmore, M. 52–6, 63–5, 204
Atkinson, J.M. 103
Austin, J.L. 43
Austin, J.T. 88–9

B
Bandura, A. 10, 14–16, 23, 65–70, 71–2, 89, 130, 195, 213
Bannister, D. 71
Barber, T.X. 156
Barthes, R. 44, 104
Baumeister, R.F. 152, 110–14, 119, 122–4, 169–71, 177–9, 181, 184–9, 192, 200–1
Bentler, P.M. 72
Berger, P.L. 162
Berne, E. 8, 142, 172–5, 177
Bhaskar, R. 64–5
Billig, M. 8, 152–4, 157, 159–60, 198
Blass, T. 163, 164
Blue, C.L. 31
Boring, E.G. 4
Bowers, K.S. 149
Brendl, C.M. 87
Buchanan, T. 181
Budd, M. 59
Buehler, R. 88
Button, G. 61

C
Cacioppo, J.T. 31
Calhoun, J.B. 201
Carnegie, D. 127
Carron, A.V. 31
Casey, N. 61
Chaiken, S. 31, 39
Chomsky, N. 36, 60–3
Cialdini, R.B. 31
Cockroft, R. 132, 144
Cockroft, S.M. 132, 144
Colman, A.M. 158
Conley, J.M. 103
Cooper, J. 31
Croyle, R.T. 31

D
Darley, J.M. 94
De Waele, J.P. 23, 73, 216
Dennett, D.C. 56–8, 60
Denzin, N.K. 79
DiGiuseppe, R. 143
Doherty, K. 89
Drew, P. 103, 152
Dryden, W. 141–4

E
Eagly, A.H. 31, 39
Edwards, D. 34, 42–3, 49–50, 52–6, 58–9, 63–5, 103, 194, 204
Etzioni, A. 193, 201–2

F
Fabrigar, L.R. 31
Ferrari, J.R. 121–3
Festinger, L. 110
Fishbein, M. 10, 14, 20, 30–1, 34, 75

Fontana, D. 127–31, 145, 197
Ford, M.E. 89
Fransella, F. 71
Freud, S. 88, 90–3, 107, 205, 211
Frye, N. 82
Fuller, S. 68

G

Gallanter, E. 11, 39, 75, 83–8, 111–12, 115, 149–50, 152, 157, 167, 185, 195, 215
Gauld, A. 17, 73, 208
Gergen, K.J. 82, 102
Giddens, A. 68, 193–4, 201–2
Gilbert, D.G. 112
Gillett, G. 9, 42, 64
Gillmore, M.R. 30
Gleeson, K. 49–51, 128, 162
Godin, G. 31
Goffman, E. 8, 45, 85, 120, 126, 161, 171, 181, 216
Gosling, J. 115–18
Grayling, A.C. 59–60
Griffin, D. 88

H

Harré, R. 5, 7, 9, 21, 23, 24, 26–7, 42–3, 45–7, 52, 63–4, 68, 72–3, 85, 99–101, 116, 142, 150, 155, 167–8, 180–2, 193, 200, 211–13, 216
Hartwick, J. 31
Hausenblas, H.A. 31
Heatherton, T.F. 110–14, 119
Higgins, E.T. 87
Hilgard, E.R. 149
Himmelfarb, S. 31
Holmes, S. 66
Hoppe, M.J. 30
Howell, E.F. 176–7, 181
Hunt, S.M. 154, 156

J

Jagger, M. 50–1
James, W. 17–18, 21–6, 43, 88, 126, 150

Johnson, J.L. 121–3
Jones, E.E. and Davis, K.E. 74
Joynson, R.B. 7

K

Kant, I. 64, 211
Karniol, R. 39, 88
Karoly, P. 39, 88–9
Kazdin, A.E. 136, 140
Kelley, H.H. 75
Kelly, G.A. 71
Kirsch, I. 148, 149
Kohlberg, L. 163
Kok, G. 31
Krull, D.S. 112

L

Lasnik, H. 162
Latané, B. 94
Latham, G.P. 86–7, 144
Lay, C.H. 124
Lewin, K. 11, 66–8, 73–6, 81–3, 88, 195, 211
Locke, E.A. 86–7, 144
Locke, J. 4, 26–7
Lodge, D. 49
Luchins, A.S. 70
Luckman, T. 162
Lyman, S. 103
Lynn, S.J. 148, 149

M

McCown, W.G. 121–3
Mack, D.E. 31
Manstead, A.S.R. 103
Marcuse, F.L. 147
Marsh, P. 46–7, 52, 64
Mele, A.R. 108
Merttens, R. 104–6, 145, 206
Milgram, S. 158–64, 166, 199
Miller, G.A. 11, 39, 75, 83–8, 111–12, 115, 149–50, 152, 157, 167, 185, 195, 215
Mixon, D. 163–4, 199
Morrison, D.M. 30
Murray, K.D. 81–2, 177

N

Nemeroff, C.J. and Karoly, P. 134–5, 137
Newman, O. 201
Norris, C. 56–8, 64–5
NUREG 96, 106, 129

O

O'Barr, W.M. 103
Olson, J.M. 31

P

Palatano, A.L. 39, 88
Parker, I. 104
Pearson, L. 131
Pelham, B.W. 112
Peters, R.S. 5–6, 8, 193, 205
Petty, R.E. 31
Phillips, A. 167, 170–1, 178, 181, 200
Potter, J. 34, 42–4, 46, 49–50, 52–6, 58–65, 72, 82, 103, 194, 204
Pribram, K.H. 11, 39, 75, 83–8, 111–12, 115, 149–50, 152, 157, 167, 185, 195, 215
Pritchard, C. 190–1
Pugmire, D. 112

R

Reason, J. 7
Reason, J.T. 11, 90, 93–5, 97–9, 101, 103–7, 129, 131, 145, 206
Rorty, R. 52–3, 60, 63, 65, 72, 82
Ross, D. 69
Ross, M. 39, 88
Ross, S.A. 69
Rosser, E. 46–7, 52, 64
Rossi, E.L. 152
Rothenbuhler, E.W. 9, 100, 155, 200
Rotter, J.B. 16, 66–7, 70–5, 81, 88, 133–4, 163, 195
Rowan, P. 7
Ryle, G. 24–5, 28–9, 150

S

Sabini, J. 117–24, 126, 196
Sadler, P. 150, 157
Sandler, J. 137–8
Sarbin, T.R. 155
Sartre, J.-P. 203–4
Saussure, F. de 3, 34, 44, 56–7
Schank, R. 9, 75, 84–5, 87, 100, 216
Schlenker, B.R. 89
Scott, M.B. 103
Scott, M.J. 144
Searle, J.R. 34, 43
Secord, P.F. 5, 7, 9, 21, 26–7, 43, 45, 63, 72–3, 85, 99–101, 155, 193, 216
Seifert, C.M. 39, 88
Sellen, A.J. 90, 92–3, 107
Semin, G.R. 103
Shaffer, D.R. 31
Sheppard, B. 31
Shotter, J. 17, 73, 82, 106, 208
Siegel, F. 201
Siegel, K. 184
Silver, M. 117–24, 126, 196
Simpson, E.E. 30
Skinner, B.F. 5
Smiles, S. 127
Smith, J.L. 30, 32, 35–7, 40, 135, 181
Smith, M.J. 127
Smith, P.B. 144
Snyder, M. 143
Spears, R. 7, 11
Speckart, G. 72
Stainton Rogers, R. 49–51, 128, 162
Stainton Rogers, W. 49–51, 128, 162
Stangor, C. 31
Steele, H.V. 137–8
Stenner, P. 49–51, 128, 162
Stout, G.F. 22–3, 148
Stradling, S.G. 144
Stringer, P. 49
Szalai, A. 131
Szasz, T. 187–9

T

Taylor, F.W. 86
Taylor, R. 123
Tesser, A. 31
Thomson, R. 4
Tice, D.M. 110–14, 119, 122–4
Tolman, E.C. 66, 74–81, 83, 134, 195
Trainer, F.E. 163
Tweddle, D. 131

V

Vancouver, J.B. 88–9

W

Wagstaff, G. 149–50, 157, 198
Walker, A.F. 109–13
Walters, R.H. 69–70
Warren, V.L. 171–5, 181, 200
Warshaw, P.R. 31

Waugh, P. 49, 105
Wegner, D.T. 31
Weigold, M.F. 89
Wells, E.A. 30
Werth, J.L. 184, 186–8, 201
Wesolowski, M.D. 137
Wetherell, M. 42, 44, 46, 58–64
Wilson, S.C. 156
Wittgenstein, L. 18, 28, 58–60, 89
Woody, E. 149, 150, 157

Y

Yankura, J. 141–4

Z

Zanna, M.P. 31
Zapf, D. 93–4, 97
Zawlocki, R.J. 137

Subject Index

A

abuse 175
accountability 140
accounts 21, 89, 193, 196, 210, 215
  cluster of 33, 35
  collection of 8, 9, 44, 194
  negotiation of 8, 9, 44, 72, 194, 205
action 1–3, 7, 10, 22, 193, 209, 210, 215
  discursive model of 42–6, 194
  execution 39, 85, 97, 111, 215
  intentional 2, 19, 94
  slips 11, 90–3, 97
  theory of reasoned 10, 14–17, 30–41, 72, 116, 134–5, 141, 194
  see also TRA/TPB
actor network theory 68
acts
  illocutionary 43
  propositional 43
adjacency pair 155
aesthetic, transcendental 64, 211
affect 20
agency 1–4, 5, 10, 16, 23, 26–7, 68, 199
  collective 68
  executive 132, 165, 166, 199
  robotic 166, 199
agent 1, 2, 5, 7, 12, 27, 116, 165, 166, 193, 199, 202
agentic essence 209
agentic improvement 12, 125, 127–46, 197
agentic medium 211, 215

agentic modification 138–40
agentic state 159–64, 199
akrasia 108–17, 196
  backward connection argument 109
  enslavement argument 109
  last ditch 109, 113, 115–17, 196–7
amnesic barrier 149
analysis, transactional 8, 172, 175, 177, 142, 216
analytic focus 216
array of persons 167–8, 180–1
artificial intelligence 9, 75, 85, 195
assertiveness training 127
association, free 91
attitude 14, 81
attribution theory 74, 172, 214–15
autobiography 23, 73, 195, 216
automaton, self-regulating 159
awfulising 141–2

B

bad faith 204
behaviour 2, 3, 4, 193
  modification 12, 132, 133–40, 197–8
  self-injurious 137–8, 197
  theory of planned 10, 14–17, 134–5, 194
  see also TRA/TPB
behaviour space, immediate 75–81, 83
behavioural sink 201–3
behaviourism 4–6, 7, 9, 12, 203, 217
belief lasso 77–81

belief systems, monolithic 204
belief–value matrix 75, 77–81
biography 216
biology 1
bondage 13, 170, 179
bubbles,
   speech 210
   thinks 210
bystander apathy 94

C

category mistake 150–1, 157, 198
causal law 5, 9
causation, triadic reciprocal 67
causes 8, 9
character 213
chemistry 1
circle, hermeneutical 17, 208
   see also hermeneutics
classification 89, 215
cognitive deconstruction 186–7, 189–90, 201
cognitive dissonance, theory of 110
comic strip 210
command 22
communitarianism 201–2
communities
   socio-linguistic 35
   virtual linguistic 36
competences 212–13
conation 20
consciousness, altered state of 147, 157, 198
constatives 43
constraints 212
construct 71
control 113
conversational test-frame 36–7
correlation, multiple 33
counselling 132–46, 197
counselling, rational emotive behavioural 132, 140–4, 198
cultural factors 212–13
cultural theory 217
cupboard, broom 110
cybernetics 84

D

death 55–6, 195
decision 24–6
deconstruction 195, 197
deconstruction reflexive 49, 195
deed 209, 215
definition, psychology 1, 219
deliberation 24–6
desire 17, 18–20
diary record 130–1
discourse 43, 206
discourse analysis 144, 197
discursive action model 42–6, 210
displacement activity 119–20
dissociated control, theory of 148–51
dissociation 175–8
dissociation theory 148–51, 198
dissociative capacity 176
dissociative identity disorder 175
doll, bobo 69
doublemindedness 174, 175
dramatisation 120
dramaturgy 8, 9, 85, 200, 206
drive arousal 75
DSM-IV 169, 170, 175, 192

E

eclecticism 10, 13, 219
ego 205
ego, executive 149
enablers 212–13
enabling conditions, frustrated 38–40, 119
episodes 8, 9, 72, 215
error 93–9, 196
error, human 215
escapologist, failed 60
ethogenic paradigm 6, 8, 16, 21, 27, 46–8, 85
existentialism 203–4
expectancy 11
expectancy-value matrix, modal 79, 80–1

SUBJECT INDEX

explanation
 causal 5–6, 19, 27, 166, 212
 sufficient 6
 teleological 5, 27, 166

F

feminist theory 217
focus groups 80
forgetting 90–2
frame, breaking 48–52
framing focus 214
frittering 119–20
frontal lobe disorder 149, 189
furniture 54–5, 195

G

garlic 177
generic error modelling system (GEMS) 97–9
Gestalt 23, 68, 217
globalisation 202
goal 198–9
goal-setting, theory of 86–7, 195
goals, pending 88

H

habit 24
hedonism 133, 200
hedonism, psychological 13, 173
hermeneutics 73, 217
 see also circle, hermeneutical
humiliation 13, 170, 172, 178–9
humour, self-deprecating 172
hypnosis 12, 147–56, 198
 hetero- 149
 induction 147, 152, 154, 167
 self- 149, 167, 199–200
 simulators 155–6
 trance state 147, 149, 151

I

image 83
indexicals 180
insanity 210
intelligibility, rule for 10, 33, 116, 126, 133–5, 194, 196–7

intention 14, 17, 20–1, 30–1, 94, 215
 behavioural 20, 27
 model of 14
 see also TRA/TPB
 intention–behaviour relation 21–4
interlocutor
 imaginary 195
 interpolated 50–1
internet 'handles' 181
interpretive repertoire 44
introspection 7, 148, 214

K

kettles, black 131

L

language game 48–50, 218
lapse-activated causal patterns 113
lapses 97
laws, causal 9
liabilities 212
life space 11, 67
linguistic community, virtual 36
linguistics, structural 36, 56
locomotion 75–6
locus of control 73, 163, 202, 214

M

masochism 13, 169–82, 198, 200–1
masochism, as central identity 171–82
meta-fiction 11, 49
mistake 92–3, 97
mistake, category 150–1
model
 expectancy-value 15, 195, 197
 role–rule 72, 205
modelling 69–70
molecules, plans 85, 93, 113, 194, 197
moral development 163

moral principles, superordinate 39
movement 4, 5, 6, 7

N

narrative 82, 103, 196, 206
narratology 82, 177, 216
natural language programming 9, 85, 216
needs, hierarchy of 202
negative gating 38
neodissociation theory 152–5, 198
neurochemistry 3
norm, subjective 14–15

O

obedience 12, 23, 158–68, 198–9
 binding factors 162
 role-play 199
 situational buffers 162–3
objective experiment, doctrine of 7, 214, 217, 219
observation 9, 194, 205

P

pain 13, 179
pancakes, stacked 82
paradigmatic relocation 32–41, 194
participant observation 214
patient 1, 2, 27, 166, 193, 199, 202
 see also agent
perceived behavioural control 15, 17, 18, 19–20
performatives 43
person 5, 212–13
personal construct theory 71
phobias, snake 69
physiology 3, 212
plan 2, 9, 11, 18, 39, 83–9, 94, 115–16, 144, 151–2, 194–5, 197–8, 209, 215
planned behaviour, theory of 15, 30–41, 125
 see also TRA/TPB

planning failures 115
planning fallacy 88
politeness 153
positivism 217
power 26–7
pragmatists 52–3
principles and parameters, theory of 62
probability, subjective 14, 20
procrastination 12, 117–26, 196
 fear of failure 112
 lack of motivation 112
 questionnaires 121–6, 196
programming, artificial intelligence 9, 75, 85, 195
protagonist 214
psychoanalysis 8, 90–2, 217
psychology
 agentic 13, 194, 219
 critical 48, 104, 196, 217–18
 critical social 7, 21, 81, 88, 99, 217
 discursive 8, 9, 42–65, 194, 195, 200, 204, 214
 ethogenic new paradigm 6, 8, 9, 46–8, 100, 194–5, 200, 205, 214–15
 experimental 214, 217
 fusion 13, 219
 humanistic 7, 214, 217
 mainstream 9, 14, 195, 212, 214, 217–18
 narrative 82
 phenomenological 214
 rhetorical 198
 social 6, 9, 200
 stimulus-response 7, 83
 topological 75, 81–2
punishment 137
pyramidic framework 207–16, 219

R

rational emotive behavioural counselling 132, 140–4, 198
realism 52–65, 211
realist, critical 65, 97, 100, 102, 212
reality 211

S

reality, degrees of 82
reason 2, 5–6, 8
 the 8
 the *real* 8, 205
reflexivity 49, 215
reification 23, 205
reinforcement 18, 134–5, 197
reinforcement, schedule of 135
relativism 11, 47, 52–65, 211
reporting focus 211, 214
repression 91, 152–5, 198
response 5–7, 209
response-contingent aversive stimulation *see* punishment
responsibility 5–6
revolution
 first cognitive 9
 second cognitive 9
rhetoric 44, 48–52, 104, 132–3, 143, 196, 198, 206
 deliberative 132, 143
 epideictic 143
 forensic 143
ritual 9, 99, 100, 155–6, 167, 198, 200
role 9, 85, 99, 196, 213
role–rule 9
routine 99
rudeness 153–4
rule 7, 9, 97, 99, 196

S

sadism, psychopathic 176
sadist 176
sado-masochism 170–1
schema 24
script 9, 85, 97, 100, 205, 216
script, HTML 211
self 212–13
self, concept of 22, 116, 213
self-efficacy theory 10, 15–17, 69–71, 194
self-handicapping 172
self-regulation 88, 111, 113
self-regulation failure 110, 114–15
self-stopping 111–12, 119, 152
semantics, attitudinal 34–5, 194
semiology 56–8

side effect 93
simulation 93
situation 212
slip 92–3, 97
 Freudian 90–2
snowballing 114, 119, 126, 162
social cognitive theory 67–9
social learning theory 69
sociology 68
sociology, critical 194
space, defensible 202, 211
speech acts, theory of 43, 155, 198, 204, 210
spell 177
stake 44, 48
statements, clusters of 35
stimulus 7
story 103–7
story-telling 197
structural descriptions 63
submission 179
suicide 13, 182–92, 198, 201
 assisted 189
 coercive prevention of 188
 paradoxical edge 200
 rational 184, 187, 200
superego 159
symbiosis, psychological 168
symbolic interactionism 79
syrup, maple 211

T

tables, thumping of 54–5
talk 44
template 9
third way politics 201–2
thought 209
time 211, 215
time-management 127–32, 211
token economy 197
TOTE unit 84, 88, 111, 114, 120, 125, 185, 196
TRA/TPB 14–15, 17–22, 24–5, 27–40, 66, 75, 81, 109–10, 116, 125–6, 133–5, 146, 182, 184, 188–9, 191, 194–6, 206, 209, 215, 219
trait 22, 45, 213

transactional analysis *see* analysis, transactional
transcendental aesthetic 64, 211
transcript 61
translation, problems in 57–8
treacle tart, walnut 11
triangulation, paradigmatic 196

U

unconscious, dialogic 152–5, 198, 205
utterance 43, 153

V

vacillation 24
valence 87

value 11, 14
victims 172, 176
voice, authorial 49
volition 19, 28–9

W

will, weakness of 12, 108–26, 196
willing 17–19
willpower 196
wish 17
wishes, unconscious 6

Z

zero tolerance 114